Black

Culture

and the

Harlem

Renaissance

BLACK CULTURE AND THE HARLEM RENAIS/ SANCE

Cary D. Wintz

Rice University Press / Houston, Texas

Requests for permission
to reproduce material from
this work should be addressed
to Rice University Press
Post Office Box 1892
Rice University, Houston, TX 77251.

Library of Congress Cataloging-in-Publication Data

Wintz, Cary D., 1943–
    Black Culture and the Harlem Renaissance.

    Bibliography: p.
    Includes index.
    1. American literature—Afro-American authors—
History and criticism.   2. American literature—New York
(N.Y.)—History and criticism.   3. American literature—
20th century—History and criticism.   4. Harlem
Renaissance.   5. Afro-Americans in literature.
6. Afro-Americans—Intellectual life—20th century.
7. Afro-American arts—New York (N.Y.)   I. Title.
PS153.N5W57   1988   810'.9'896073   88-42620
ISBN 0-89263-267-4

To Celia

Contents

Figures and Tables

Figures

Tables

Acknowledgments

Many persons deserve thanks for their contributions to this book. A. Michael McMahon first introduced me to the Harlem Renaissance, many years ago, while Stephen E. Ambrose worked with me on the earliest version of this study. My friends and colleagues at Texas Southern University provided both encouragement and inspiration. Claude Levy and Merline Pitre, through the example of their own scholarship, inspired me to complete this project, while W.M. Akalou and Howard Beeth read sections of my work and served as a valuable sounding board, forcing me to hone my ideas and theories. The staff at the libraries and research centers that I visited were always helpful. The staff at the Beinecke Library at Yale University, at the Amistad Research Center at Tulane University, and at the Fisk University Library provided considerable assistance in helping me locate the manuscript materials in their collections that were essential to this study. Cathy Henderson and the staff at the Harry Ransom Humanities Research Center at the University of Texas at Austin were especially helpful in identifying the materials in the Knopf collection and other literary collections that proved so important to this book.

It is my family, though, that deserves my greatest thanks. My son Jason saved me both time and labor when he was drafted into service as a research assistant during one of my trips to the Humanities Research Center at the University of Texas. He also generously surrendered time on our PC to me during the months of writing and revising. My wife Celia also was a valuable research assistant and a treasured companion during my initial research trip to New Haven and Nashville. I truly appreciate her love, her support, and, most importantly, her patience during the months that this book occupied my time and my energies.

Introduction

In 1926 a white novelist, Carl Van Vechten, published the sensational bestseller *Nigger Heaven* and hundreds of white thrill-seekers ventured uptown from Manhattan to witness and experience firsthand the exotic and lusty life that, according to the novel, characterized Harlem. A year earlier black scholar Alain Locke had edited the March issue of *The Survey Graphic*, which portrayed the "New Negro," a term Locke coined to denote a new breed of blacks both inside and outside the arts that had emerged following the First World War. Also in 1926 a group of young writers, poets, and artists banded together to publish *Fire!!*, an extremely intense journal of black literary expression. Although *Fire!!* failed after a single issue, it mirrored the passion and the unrest of the young black writers. Each of these events reflected a significant aspect of the literary movement known variously as the New Negro movement, the Negro Renaissance, and the Harlem Renaissance; taken together, they provide a succinct and remarkably accurate glimpse of the diverse and diffuse currents that surfaced in the mid-1920s and gave rise to a surge of black literary creativity.

The Harlem Renaissance was primarily a literary and intellectual movement, the precise chronological limits of which are somewhat difficult to define. Generally the consensus among scholars has been that the Harlem Renaissance was an event of the 1920s, bounded on one side by the war and the race riots of 1919 and on the other side by the 1929 stock market crash. Some, however, have greatly extended or sharply limited the movement's lifespan. Abraham Chapman, for example, saw elements of the Renaissance in Claude McKay's poetry of 1917 and even in W.E.B. Du Bois's poem "Song of Smoke," which appeared in 1899. Nathan Huggins dated the beginning of the Renaissance to the period between World War I and 1920, when the locus of black leadership shifted from Tuskegee to New York, and he saw the Harlem Riots of 1935 as the final factor in its demise. John Hope Franklin argued that the Renaissance continued into the 1960s after suffering only slight and generally negligible interruptions during the Depression and the Second World War. Benjamin Brawley, on the other hand, gave only lip service to the "so-called Negro literary renaissance," which he felt was centered around the publication of *Nigger Heaven* and which he asserted had no significant

positive influence on black literature. Sterling Brown, one of the participants in the Renaissance, denied that Harlem was ever the center of the
New Negro literary movement.[1]

The Harlem Renaissance was basically a psychology—a state of mind
or an attitude—shared by a number of black writers and intellectuals who
centered their activities around Harlem in the late 1920s and early
1930s. These men and women shared little but a consciousness that they
were participants in a new awakening of black culture in the United
States. Those directly involved in the movement were all black, although
Carl Van Vechten to a major degree and other white writers, patrons, and
publishers to a lesser degree participated in and influenced the movement. There was no common bond of political or racial ideology, personal
experience, background, or literary philosophy that united the various
elements in the Renaissance. What they held in common was a sense of
community, a feeling that they were all part of the same endeavor.

Given this interpretation, it is difficult to see the Renaissance beginning before the early twenties, when Jean Toomer published *Cane* and
black writers and scholars began to realize that something new was
happening in black literature. The movement extended well into the
1930s and included the later works of Zora Neale Hurston, Claude
McKay, and Langston Hughes. As long as they and other writers consciously identified with the Renaissance, the movement continued. It did
not, however, encompass the younger writers like James Baldwin and
Richard Wright who emerged in the late thirties and the forties. This
group of writers never really identified with or felt themselves to be part of
the Harlem Renaissance.

The Harlem Renaissance may best be conceptualized as a group of
young writers orbiting somewhat erratically around several older black
intellectuals who were established in the NAACP, in the Urban League,
or with black journals and universities. These older men and women,
while sometimes participating directly in the creative aspects of the
Renaissance, served chiefly as critics, advisers, and liaisons between the
younger black writers and the white literary establishment. This group,
consisting of people such as James Weldon Johnson, Alain Locke, and
W.E.B. Du Bois, generally helped lesser-known black writers make
contacts with white publishers and potential patrons. As such, they
exerted considerable influence and a certain amount of control over
aspiring black writers.

The focal point of the Renaissance was Harlem. Next to the feeling that they belonged to a common literary movement, Harlem was the experience that bound the otherwise diverse participants to one another. Although not every writer made Harlem his or her home, everyone associated with the Renaissance spent at least some time there, and, more important, all of them viewed Harlem as the hub of black literary activity. Even those who were critical of the Renaissance recognized the strong pull of the city on black writers. Benjamin Brawley, for example, blasted those who saw Harlem as the center of the Negro's literary ambition. [2] James Weldon Johnson, on the other hand, encouraged black writers to come to Harlem. In 1928 he urged Claude McKay to cease his wanderings and return to New York, where he could benefit from the literary opportunities offered by the Renaissance, then at the height of its popularity, and at the same time provide strength to the movement. As Johnson later observed, during the 1920s Harlem had become the "black metropolis" in the heart of the white city, the acknowledged capital of black America. [3] For the New Negro, Harlem was the Mecca of the black world.

Harlem was significant to the Renaissance for another reason. Besides serving as the spiritual home of the movement, it also provided the material and the setting for many literary creations of the Renaissance. The poetry, short stories, and novels of the period abound with scenes and characters lifted from Harlem's streets and cabarets. Most of the Renaissance writers produced at least some work of Harlem local color. Rudolph Fisher, Claude McKay, and Langston Hughes were especially adept at portraying New York's ghetto life. Works about Harlem also found a ready market among some blacks who wanted to read about life in *the* black metropolis, but particularly among whites who were attracted to the exotic, strange, and colorful rhythms of "nigger heaven." Harlem, though, was more than a playground for white Manhattan. It was a teeming, overcrowded ghetto, and much of its laughter and gaiety only thinly veiled the misery and poverty that was becoming the standard of life for the new black urban masses. This, too, was reflected by the Harlem Renaissance.

Harlem played an important role in the Renaissance because Harlem itself symbolized the central experience of American blacks in the early twentieth century—the urbanization of black America. Harlem housed the first major concentration of blacks who settled outside the South, and it reflected on a larger and more concentrated scale the patterns of change that were occurring in Philadelphia, Chicago, Detroit, and dozens of other northern industrial cities in the first half of the twentieth century.

The black writers of the Harlem Renaissance were in the vanguard of the attempt to come to terms with black urbanization. They lived it, reflected on it, and through their art endeavored to resolve some of the problems arising from it.

As a final word of introduction to the Harlem Renaissance, it is necessary to say something about the relationship between black literary creativity of the twenties and the similarly intense creativity among white writers of the same period. Like their black counterparts, the white writers of the 1920s engaged in experimentation in form, revolted against what they considered the restrictions imposed by an obsolete morality, and sought to identify truth and meaning in a world of violence, oppression, and absurdity. However, except for a brief examination of those few whites who focused on race in the 1920s and a more detailed discussion of the relationship between black literature and the publishers and promoters of the white literary establishment, this book will not attempt to weave the work of the Harlem Renaissance into the larger pattern of post-World War I American literature. There are several reasons for this decision. First, in spite of the similarities between white and black literature of the period, black writers faced unique problems that were related to the racial situation in America. These problems included the crucial issue within the black literary world concerning the very validity of and then the appropriate nature of black writing as a distinctive body of literature, as well as the difficulties faced by black writers who had to contend with a literary establishment in America that was entirely white. Second, white writers during the twenties and white critics during that period and generally since have perpetuated the segregation of black and white literature, usually to the exclusion of the former. Finally, in spite of similarities, the experience of blacks in this country is substantially different from that of whites, and this difference is reflected in literature. Race and race-consciousness were constant themes in the literature of the Harlem Renaissance; this was not true of white literature during the period. Instead, during the twenties white writers ignored the race question more than at any other time in American literary history.[4]

Thus, the Harlem Renaissance will be considered as a movement distinct from the white literature of the twenties. This does not mean, however, that the role whites played in the movement will be ignored. Indeed, a great deal of attention will be focused on the role of white writers, and especially white publishers, promoters, and patrons. However, it is important to remember that the Harlem Renaissance was part of the black experience and that even the relation between black writers and the white literary establishment reflected the black experience. More than miles separated the writers in Harlem from those in Greenwich Village or the cafes of Paris. The Harlem Renaissance was the product of a history and a way of life about which most white writers knew very little. This, of course, was a natural outcome of life in racially segregated America.

This book also will not focus on the lives and careers of individual writers of the Renaissance, nor will it attempt to analyze or critique the literature of the period. This task has been done already and does not need to be repeated here.[5] Instead, I will examine the Harlem Renaissance as a social and intellectual movement within the framework of black social and intellectual history in early twentieth-century America. In particular I examine the relationship of the Renaissance to earlier black literature and its relationship to its new urban setting. I relate the Renaissance to the ongoing debate within the black community about the appropriate response of blacks to the racial situation in the United States and the role of art and literature in that response. I also explore the relationship of the Renaissance to Garveyism and to the other political alternatives that blacks faced in the 1920s and 1930s. Finally, I investigate the relationship between black writers and the larger literary and intellectual communities of black critics and promoters and of white publishers and patrons. The primary task is to place the Harlem Renaissance within its historical setting and to determine how it emerged out of black America and how it related to the white literary establishment.

1   The
Social and
Political
Background

Two of the most significant elements in the black experience around the turn of the century were the steady deterioration of the race's social and political position in America, and especially in the South, and the steadily growing exodus of blacks from their homes in the rural South to the industrial cities of the South and North. The effect of these developments on black history must not be underestimated. Besides the obvious changes evidenced by the growth of black ghettos in northern cities and the resurgence of black militancy in the face of an apparently unremitting chain of racism, violence, and injustice, there was also a more subtle shift of attitude among blacks. By the 1920s few black intellectuals still believed that the future of their race lay in the South. As they turned their attention northward and focused their hope on the emerging black communities in northern cities, however, they also were turning their backs on their southern heritage.

The basic political experience of blacks at the turn of the century was that during the two decades following the end of Reconstruction they had witnessed the systematic erosion of the rights they had achieved under the Fourteenth and Fifteenth Amendments and through the various acts of Congress and the Reconstruction governments in the South. Although in the half century following emancipation a number of blacks successfully accumulated property and acquired an education, most remained poorly educated and mired in rural poverty. Even those who had achieved some material success saw these accomplishments threatened by the growth of segregation and racial violence. Supreme Court reinterpretations of the Fourteenth and Fifteenth Amendments left blacks defenseless against the segregationist enactments of southern legislatures. In *Williams* v. *Mis-*

sissippi (1898), *Giles* v. *Harris* (1903), and *Giles* v. *Teasley* (1904) the Court endorsed various strategies that southern states devised to disenfranchise blacks, while *Plessy* v. *Ferguson* (1896) was the most dramatic of a series of decisions that legitimized laws segregating public facilities—from schools, railroad cars, and restrooms to public parks and residential neighborhoods.[1]

Northern blacks fared hardly better than their southern counterparts. Throughout the North, theaters, restaurants, and hotels discriminated against blacks, often in violation of northern civil rights laws. Many communities also established segregated school systems in spite of state law. Blacks who attempted to challenge this growing segregation were so often unsuccessful that most chose simply to try to live with the situation. Even more serious was the discrimination blacks faced in the workplace. For example, in Philadelphia in the late nineteenth century employers were reluctant to hire blacks for any but the worst jobs because to do so would precipitate trouble with white workers and their unions. As a result of the refusal of most unions to admit blacks to membership, blacks were excluded from entire industries and generally found employment in "the two worst categories in the occupational lexicon: 'domestic and personal service' and 'unskilled labor.'"[2]

Black participation in northern politics also declined in the early twentieth century. Although blacks never constituted a powerful force in local or state politics, they were a visibly present minority in public office throughout the North as late as the early 1890s. By the turn of the century blacks in elected office had become quite rare. Nowhere was the declining political status of blacks more apparent than in Washington during Theodore Roosevelt's administration. During his first term Roosevelt won black approval by praising the valor of black troops during the Battle of San Juan Hill, by dining with Booker T. Washington at the White House, and by standing by his controversial black political appointments in the South. Before the end of his second term, however, Roosevelt had done a complete about-face. The troops he had earlier praised he now branded as cowards, and more and more he linked his political machine to the conservative, lily-white faction in the southern Republican party. In 1905 he toured the South and publicly praised former Confederate leaders and the Confederacy; in 1906 he infuriated blacks with his harsh treatment of the black troops who were involved in the Brownsville riots and by his statements to Congress falsely asserting that lynchings were caused by black sexual assaults on white women. Conditions deteriorated further under Roosevelt's successors. William Howard Taft publicly endorsed restrictions on black suffrage and refused to appoint blacks to office when whites objected. Taft also began the practice of segregating federal offices in Washington, a policy that was expanded under President Wilson. By the time that World War I began, blacks had seen their political rights and political influence almost totally evaporate in the North as well as in the South. Conditions did not improve in the early 1920s. President Harding, while promising to enforce civil rights, denounced racial amalgamation and social equality.[3]

More alarming even than this decline in political and civil rights was the upsurge in racial violence and terrorism. Lynchings, while declining in number from approximately 150 per year in the early 1890s to about half that number after 1905, continued to outrage as well as terrorize the black community. Far more ominous was the marked increase in the number of race riots around the turn of the century. In 1898, for example, a highly emotional campaign to eliminate black suffrage triggered a riot in Wilmington, North Carolina, which resulted in thirty-six black casualties. In 1904 racial violence swept through the small town of Statesboro, Georgia. Following the conviction of two blacks for the murder of a white family, a white mob took action against the growing "insolence" of local blacks. After capturing and burning the two murderers, the mob turned its wrath on the entire black community. They attacked blacks indiscriminately, burned their houses, and drove a number from the town. Two years later an even more serious riot erupted in Atlanta. Like the Wilmington riot, trouble began in Atlanta during a campaign to disenfranchise blacks. For several months before the election on the suffrage provision, local newspapers inflamed the public with racial hatred. Finally, on September 22, 1906, a white mob gathered and began attacking every black in sight. In the four days of violence that followed four blacks died, many others were injured, and there was wholesale destruction of black property.[4]

The racial violence of this period was not confined to the South. There were large-scale race riots in New York (1900), Springfield, Illinois (1904), and Greensburg, Indiana (1906). In addition, white gangs frequently assaulted blacks in large northern cities, while several small towns in Ohio and Indiana sought to avoid racial disorder by simply preventing blacks from settling there.[5]

The most serious northern riot before World War I took place in

Springfield, Illinois, in 1908. Trouble began when a black man, George Richardson, was accused of raping a white woman. By the time that a grand jury cleared Richardson of the charges, whites in Springfield were determined to seek vengeance on their own. Unable to get their hands on Richardson, they vented their anger on the entire black community. It took 5,000 state militia to restore order, but not before two blacks were lynched, four whites were dead, and more than seventy persons were injured. As usual, there was widespread destruction of black property. The Springfield riot also struck a symbolic blow to the hopes of black Americans, coming so close to the centennial of Lincoln's birth and occurring just two miles from the great emancipator's burial place.[6]

In many ways these riots sounded an ominous warning about the state of race relations in the country. Even more than lynchings, they expressed an intense and highly advanced form of racial prejudice. Lynching, as barbaric as it was, constituted violence committed against an individual in response to a specific transgression, real or imagined. Lynching targeted "bad" blacks to serve as an example for all blacks. On the other hand, the race riots that occurred at the turn of the century were characterized by indiscriminate, wholesale violence directed against all blacks regardless of their actions. A law-abiding, accommodating black could reasonably expect to be safe from lynching, but there was no protection from the random violence unleashed by these riots.

More depressing, and ultimately more threatening to blacks, was the almost complete acceptance of scientific and pseudo-scientific theories of racism in America at the turn of the century. Racist ideology, in fact, was a dominant theme in both America and Europe at this time. The anti-Negro literature of the period was only one aspect of a generally racist outlook in western thought in the late nineteenth century. Other examples included concepts such as the "white man's burden" and the poetry of Rudyard Kipling, both of which were use to justify a racially based imperialism, and the emergence of a racially based anti-semitism that was fueled by monographs such as Houston Stewart Chamberlain's *Foundations of the Nineteenth Century* (1900), and that was reflected in outbursts of anti-semitic prejudice such as that which surfaced dramatically in France during the Dreyfus affair. In the United States men like Josiah Strong and Henry Cabot Lodge used theories of Anglo-Saxon racial superiority to justify acquisition of the Philippines; these same theories were manifested in the Chinese Exclusion Act of 1882, the anti-Japanese hysteria that swept California in 1905, and the growing demand for immigration restriction voiced by nativists.

Anti-black propagandists at the turn of the century often took extreme positions. Thomas Dixon popularized concepts of black inferiority in his widely read novels, *The Leopard's Spots* (1902) and *The Clansman* (1905). Dixon's open racism, however, was surpassed by the fanatical and often fantastic arguments advanced in pseudo-scientific studies such as Charles Carroll's *The Negro, Beast or in the Image of God* (1900), which was one of three books that Carroll wrote that combined scientific and biblical evidence to argue that blacks (indeed all nonwhite races) were subhuman hybrid species that lacked souls but had been granted the power of speech so that they might better serve (white) mankind; or in the work of Frederick L. Hoffman, whose *Race Traits and Tendencies of the American Negro* (1896) used demographic data to postulate that the high death rate among blacks, caused primarily by their innately inferior physical structure, their moral decline, and their high rate of illegitimacy, ultimately would lead the race to extinction.[7]

The predominant racial theory in the South at the turn of the century depicted blacks as an inferior and immoral race that would never achieve parity with whites. Slavery, it was argued, had Christianized blacks and restrained their baser tendencies, but freedom had resulted in a rapid reversion toward barbarism. Some southern writers even justified lynching as the only effective check against the black man's increasing tendency to rape, and argued that the only solution to the race problem was either colonization or extermination. Even the most tolerant southerners generally accepted the basic superiority of the white race, and dreamed of the old South—magnolia trees and contented slaves serenading "ole Marsa" and his family in the warm southern sunset—a South kept alive in the romantic novels of writers such as Thomas Nelson Page.[8]

Northern social scientists were hardly more tolerant than their southern counterparts. Armed with theories of eugenics and with IQ data gathered from recruits during World War I, they expressed concern about the intellectual and physical inferiority of blacks and alarm over miscegenation and a mongrelized America. They supported racist doctrines and interpreted history in a manner that justified white supremacy and the disenfranchisement of blacks. Even anthropologist Franz Boas, who generally advocated a cultural relativism which rejected the view of Western or European cultural superiority and who reacted against claims that the black race as a whole was anatomically or psychologically inferior to whites, believed that black Americans were genetically inferior to whites and that only through intermarriage and the subsequent modification of the black genetic inheritance would America solve its racial problems.[9]

The outbreak of World War I only intensified racial conflict in America. Traditionally blacks have supported America's war efforts in hopes that a display of loyalty and battlefield gallantry would win them popular support in their quest for equality. And, in their efforts to participate fully in their country's battles, blacks have traditionally confronted a government reluctant to accept their services. During World War I the already existing racial strife intensified these problems.

Most black leaders responded to the onset of the war by urging blacks to support their country wholeheartedly. Even W.E.B. Du Bois set aside his struggle for integration and asked his people to "close ranks" with white America and to "forget our present grievances" for the duration of the war, even though this meant accommodation with the segregationist policies of America's military forces. For some blacks, though, this was asking too much. Socialist and labor leader A. Philip Randolph was sentenced to thirty months in prison for publishing antiwar articles, while Francis Grimké argued bitterly that the atrocities which allied propagandists attributed to German troops could not equal the very real atrocities committed by white Americans against their black neighbors. Most blacks, however, made every effort to comply with Du Bois's request in spite of the openly discriminatory policies of their government. At the outset of the war, for example, Colonel Charles Young, the ranking black regular Army officer, was forced to resign. The Navy allowed blacks to serve only as mess boys, while the Marines would not accept blacks in any capacity. The Army eventually accepted blacks in all branches except for the pilot section of the Air Corps, and, after considerable agitation by the NAACP, established a segregated officer training camp for blacks. Of course the entire military was segregated.[10]

As serious as segregation was, the majority of wartime racial problems did not result so much from the problems of the military as from the unrealized expectations and frustrations of black soldiers. Blacks hoped that the uniform they wore and the sacrifices they were willing to make for their country would win them some measure of respect and equal treatment. They were proud of their military accomplishments and more reluctant than ever to accept a second-class position in society. From the beginning of the war, however, whites responded to black soldiers with hostility and fear. They did not view the black soldier as a friendly ally;

instead, they saw him as a potentially dangerous element which in the future would have to be even more carefully kept under control. These worries seemed quite realistic when racial strife erupted in towns surrounding several training bases before the first black troops even left for Europe. These base towns, especially those in the South, strongly resented the presence of black troops, usually refused to admit them to restaurants and theaters, and provided few, if any, recreational facilities for them. In addition the YMCA recreational units attached to Army camps restricted their services to whites and made no provisions for black soldiers.[11]

The most serious incident during the war occurred in 1917 in Houston. Trouble began when northern black soldiers stationed in the city confronted the overt segregation of the South. The riot began when rumors circulated that a popular black soldier had been arrested or killed by Houston police. Although the rumor was false, previous confrontations with the city's police made it believable. That night approximately a hundred black soldiers, with rifles and fixed bayonets, marched into the city seeking vengeance against the police and whites in general. Before the Army restored order, sixteen whites and four blacks were dead; eleven more whites were seriously wounded. In the series of court martials that followed, nineteen black soldiers were executed, sixty-three received life sentences, twenty-eight received lesser prison terms, and seven were acquitted. At Spartanburg, South Carolina, Fort Riley, Kansas, and other bases around the country similar incidents were narrowly averted. The Army did nothing to improve facilities or protect black troops from discrimination; instead, whenever trouble threatened they either disarmed the soldiers or quickly dispatched them to Europe.[12]

The Atlantic Ocean did not dilute the Army's discriminatory policies. In Europe black troops experienced the same sort of inequity and prejudice at the hands of the military that they had encountered in the United States. White entertainment groups almost always bypassed their units, and they did not receive the same benefits from service organizations like the YMCA and the Federal Council of Churches. But what really underscored this discrimination was the contrast between the way black troops were treated by their own countrymen and by the French. With few exceptions the French received American blacks warmly and with no visible prejudice. In fact French women associated so freely with blacks that white officers attempted to intervene. The most extreme examples of this were an order issued by General James Erwin forbidding blacks to associate with French women and a document, *Secret Information Concerning Black Troops*, which was circulated among the French in 1918 warning that racial separation was necessary to prevent blacks from assaulting and raping white women.[13]

The equality black soldiers enjoyed in their association with the French contrasted sharply with developments on the home front. During the war lynchings rose from thirty-eight in 1917 to fifty-eight in 1918. In Tennessee three thousand spectators responded to the invitation of a local newspaper to come out and watch a "live Negro" being burned, while in East St. Louis the employment of blacks in a factory holding government contracts sparked a race riot that left at least forty blacks dead, including a two-year-old who was shot and thrown into a burning building.[14]

These incidents were only a prelude to the racial violence that greeted the troops on their return from war. During the long hot summer of 1919 race riots erupted in more than twenty cities, in both the North and the South. In most cases these riots, like the earlier ones at the turn of the century, were characterized by white mobs indiscriminately attacking blacks with little or no interference from local police. However, there was a new element in the 1919 riots, as blacks, no longer willing to rely on ineffective police protection and no longer believing that the government would provide justice for them, armed themselves and fought back against white mobs. In Washington, Chicago, and even in southern towns like Elaine, Arkansas and Longview, Texas, blacks shot back when fired upon or even shot first to protect themselves and their property. The pride engendered by their wartime service and the self-confidence resulting from their military training combined with frustration over apparently unending racial injustice to give birth to a new militancy among American blacks.[15]

The second major social development that dominated the black experience during the first quarter of the twentieth century was the vast migration which brought tens of thousands of blacks from the rural South into northern industrial cities. Although the early signs of this population shift can be detected in the 1890s, as late as 1910 census figures show that 75 percent of American blacks lived in rural areas and that 90 percent lived in the South. Before 1910 most of the black migration was within the South, and generally in a westward direction from one agricultural region to another more prosperous one, or from a rural area to a small town or city. Although several northern cities did substantially increase their black population before 1910, with New York growing from 60,666 in

Table 1
Black Population Growth, 1890–1930

	New York City	Manhattan
1890	33,888	20,312
1900	60,666	36,246
1910	91,709	60,534
1920	152,467	109,153
1930	327,706	224,670

Source: U.S. Department of Commerce, Bureau of the Census, *Negro Population, 1790–1915* (Washington, D.C.: Government Printing Office, 1918), 101. 156; U.S. Department of Commerce, Bureau of the Census, *Fourteenth Census of the United States, Taken in the Year 1920*, vol. 3 *Population* (Washington, D.C.: Government Printing Office, 1922), 679; U.S. Department of Commerce, Bureau of the Census, *Negroes in the United States, 1920–1932* (Washington, D.C.: Government Printing Office, 1935), 62; Osofsky, 205–206.

1900 to 91,709 in 1910, most of this new black population came from the border states. The real mass migration of blacks northward began about 1915 and continued through the 1920s. During this period New York's black population grew over 250 percent, from 91,709 in 1910 to 327,706 in 1930. Although New York would attract more blacks than any other city, other industrial centers such as Chicago, Detroit, and Cleveland saw their black population grow at an even faster rate.[16]

Like most major population relocations in American history, the black migration was influenced by both "push" and "pull" factors and affected most by economic developments. The push factors included an economic depression which spread across the South in 1914 and 1915 and which undermined the economic position of black farmers and farm workers; the ravages of the cotton boll weevil in the summers of 1915 and 1916 and the devastating flooding of the lower South during the summer of 1915 added to the misery and aggravated the economic problems of rural blacks. Finally, the outbreak of the war caused food prices in the South to increase more rapidly than farm wages. These developments intensified the general dissatisfaction of blacks with their economic status in the rural South and provided the major motivation for the exodus. When these economic factors are combined with the deteriorating racial situation, it is no surprise that thousands of blacks chose to seek a better life elsewhere. It is important to note, however, that economic factors dominated the decision to migrate. Also, 1930 census figures indicate that three border

Figure 1

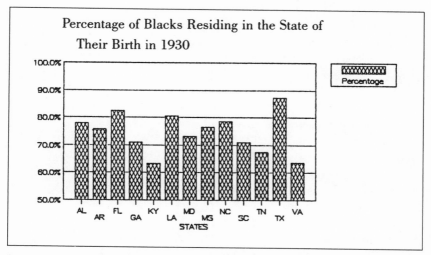

Percentage of Blacks Residing in the State of
Their Birth in 1930

Source: U.S. Department of Commerce, Bureau of the Census, *Negroes in the United States,
1920–1932* (Washington, D.C.: Government Printing Office, 1935), 40–43.

states of the upper South—Virginia, Kentucky, and Tennessee—continued to lose the largest percentage of their black population, suggesting that proximity to northern employment centers was the major factor influencing migration patterns.[17]

From the days of slavery the North had held a special position in the mythology of southern blacks as a place of refuge where equality and racial justice abounded. However, the pull factors for the upsurge in black migration in 1915, like the push factors, were primarily economic. W.E.B. Du Bois and the Chicago *Defender* might urge blacks to come north to escape the oppression of the South, but the voice that called the loudest and attracted the attention of most southern blacks was the voice of the advertising pages of newspapers like the *Defender* which promised better jobs at higher pay. The *Defender* and other black newspapers that circulated widely in the South were filled with ads offering jobs at wages that were two or three times those paid in the South. Women domestics, for example, who received $2.50 per week in the South, could earn from $2.10 to $2.50 per day in the North, while their husbands could increase their earnings from $1.10 per day to $3.75 per day by taking a job in a northern factory. The reason for this sudden increase in the demand for labor was that northern industry, stimulated by war contracts, found that

Table 2

Destinations of Blacks Migrating out of Southern States

State of Origin	Primary Destinations					
	1st Choice	(%)	2nd Choice	(%)	3rd Choice	(%)
Alabama	Ohio	(3.0)	Mississippi	(2.2)	Illinois	(2.2)
Arkansas	Missouri	(4.8)	Illinois	(3.7)		
Florida	Georgia	(3.2)	New York	(3.1)		
Georgia	Florida	(6.7)	Ohio	(3.5)		
Kentucky	Ohio	(9.3)	Indiana	(8.7)	Illinois	(5.9)
Louisiana	Texas	(6.6)	Arkansas	(3.3)		
Maryland	Pennsylvania	(9.3)	D. C.	(5.9)		
Mississippi	Arkansas	(4.7)	Illinois	(4.1)		
N. Carolina	Virginia	(4.3)	New York	(3.8)		
S. Carolina	N. Carolina	(7.2)	New York	(3.8)		
Tennessee	Illinois	(6.5)	Ohio	(3.6)		
Texas	Oklahoma	(4.7)	California	(1.7)		
Virginia	Pennsylvania	(8.4)	New York	(6.5)		

Source: *Negroes in the U.S.*, 44–46.

the war also cut off its traditional source of industrial labor, the European immigrant. Many companies responded to this labor shortage by actively recruiting southern blacks for the low-paying, unskilled jobs that newly arrived immigrants had previously filled.[18]

It is important to remember that as significant as the black migration was, its major impact, particularly in terms of how it affected the racial or ethnic mix of a community, was on northern cities and not on the South. Even after 1910 most of the movement of blacks was within the South, to southern cities or to other southern or southwestern states that were experiencing economic growth. For example, the 1930 census figures indicate that more blacks had moved into Florida and Arkansas than had moved out of those states, and Texas had gained almost as many as it had lost. Table 2 indicates by percentage the most likely residence of blacks outside their home state in 1930. The overall pattern is that blacks who did leave their home state, especially in the deep South or Southwest,

Table 3

Source of Black Population in Manhattan, 1930

	Total Number of Migrants	Percentage of Population
Virginia	30,490	16.50%
S. Carolina	23,850	12.90%
N. Carolina	15,658	8.47%
Georgia	14,483	7.84%
Florida	6,831	3.70%
Maryland	5,034	2.72%
Total	96,346	52.13%

Source: *Negroes in the U.S.*, 34–36.

tended to migrate to another southern state rather than to a northern one. For example, 6.6 percent of the blacks born in Louisiana were living in Texas in 1930 and 3.3 percent of them were living in Arkansas, while a greater percentage of blacks from Mississippi moved to Arkansas than to Ohio. In addition, more than 50 percent of the blacks who migrated to New York before 1930 came from the six states of the South Atlantic region—Virginia, Maryland, North Carolina, South Carolina, Georgia, and Florida.[19]

One effect of the black migration was the emergence of Harlem as the black metropolis and the social and cultural center of black America. Before 1900 Harlem had been an extremely desirable upper-middle-class neighborhood of finé homes and apartment houses. It also housed a significant number of the city's more prosperous Jewish residents. Confidence in the future of this area of the city led to extensive development and speculation there in the 1890s. When the speculative building boom collapsed in the early twentieth century, a number of investors discovered that many of the homes and apartments they had constructed were standing empty. The depressed housing market and the initiative of a number of black realtors brought a steadily increasing flow of black residents into West Harlem, beginning in 1903.[20]

In the late nineteenth century New York's sixty thousand blacks were

Figure 2

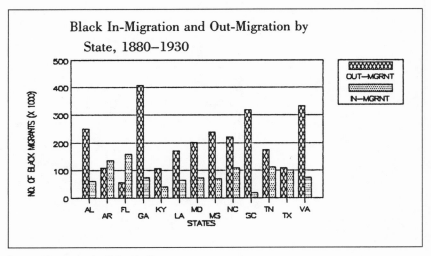

Black In-Migration and Out-Migration by State, 1880–1930

Source: *Negroes in the U.S.*, 40–43.

scattered through the five boroughs, with the largest concentration living in the Tenderloin and San Juan Hill sections of the west side of Manhattan. While some romanticized the west side area between Twenty-seventh and Fifty-third streets as "black bohemia," there was nothing glamorous about life in these segregated slums. Most inhabitants paid exorbitant rent for the privilege of space in one of the tiny apartments, rooming houses, and boarding houses that lined narrow, congested streets. In the Tenderloin district they had to contend with the fact that their neighborhood was the center of prostitution and gambling in the city, as well as home to most of its underworld elements. San Juan Hill was as bad or worse. It enjoyed the distinction of being perhaps the most densely populated area in the city, with 3,580 people living on just one of its streets.[21]

As newcomers from the South swelled the city's black population, pressure for additional and hopefully better housing pushed blacks northward up the west side toward Harlem. Ambitious blacks, who had achieved some economic success, were eager to move their families out of the congested, vice-ridden slums. The racial violence that swept through the Tenderloin during the 1900 riots intensified their determination to escape, while Harlem, with its abundance of good housing, seemed to be the logical place to move.

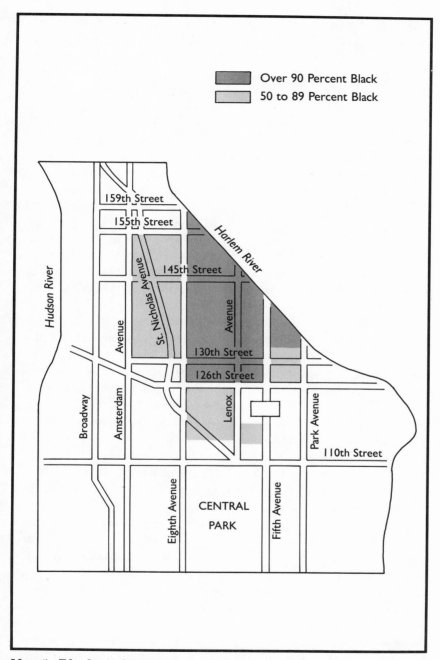

Map 1. Blacks in Manhattan, 1900-1930

Harlem's transition, once it began, followed fairly traditional patterns. As soon as blacks started moving onto a block, it became more and more difficult to maintain property values, and whites began to move out. Both black and white realtors took advantage of declining property values in Harlem, the panic selling that resulted when blacks moved in, and the pressure to provide housing for the city's rapidly growing black population, to acquire, subdivide, and lease Harlem property to black tenants. Some white residents of Harlem attempted to block the black invasion. They established organizations like the Harlem Property Owners' Improvement Association and the West Side Improvement Association to protect their neighborhood. The latter organization tried to evict blacks from the area between West 90th and 110th Streets, claiming that they were not racially prejudiced but worried about the declining value of their property. In spite of these efforts, year by year the line between white and black Harlem moved steadily north, as blacks, desperate for decent housing, streamed into Harlem as quickly as housing was made available to them. By 1910 they had established themselves as the majority group on the west side of Harlem north of 130th Street.[22]

During the next two decades black Harlem continued to grow as tens of thousands of migrants from the South were joined by thousands of black immigrants from the West Indies. All seemed to find their way to Harlem's streets and tenements. In 1920 black Harlem extended from 130th Street to 145th Street and from Fifth to Eighth Avenue, and it contained approximately 73,000 blacks (66.9 percent of the total number of blacks in the borough of Manhattan); by 1930 black Harlem had expanded north ten blocks to 155th, spread from the Harlem River to Amsterdam Avenue, and housed approximately 164,000 blacks (73.0 percent of Manhattan's blacks). In 1930 the heart of black Harlem, bounded roughly by 126th Street on the south, 159th Street on the north, the Harlem River and Park Avenue on the east, and Eighth Avenue on the west, had a population of more than 106,000 that was 95.1 percent black. By 1920 Harlem, by virtue of the sheer size of its black population, had emerged as the capital of black America; its name evoked a magic that lured all classes of blacks from all sections of the country to its streets. Impoverished southern farmers and sharecroppers poured northward, where they were joined in Harlem by black intellectuals such as W.E.B. Du Bois and James Weldon Johnson. Although the old black social elites of Washington, D.C., were disdainful of Harlem's vulgar splendor, and while it housed no great black university as did Washington, Atlanta, and Nashville, Harlem still be-

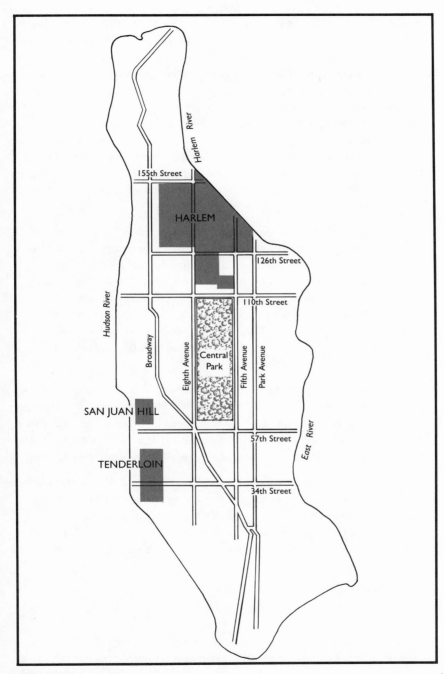

Map 2. Harlem in 1930

came the race's cultural center and a Mecca for its aspiring young. It was the headquarters for the NAACP and the Urban League, Marcus Garvey launched his ill-fated brand of black nationalism among its masses, and it became the geographical focal point of the black literary movement of the 1920s. Harlem, in short, was where the action was in black America during the decade following World War I.[23]

More important, perhaps, than the reality of Harlem as a city within a city—as an emerging ghetto in the nation's greatest city—were the various images associated with this community of more than 100,000 blacks. Rudolph Fisher, for example, captured one aspect of Harlem when he described it as seen through the eyes of a recently arrived southern black in his short story "City of Refuge":

> Gillis set down his tan-cardboard extension case and wiped his black, shining brow. Then slowly, spreadingly, he grinned at what he saw: Negroes at every turn; up and down Lenox Avenue, up and down One Hundred and Thirty-fifth Street; big, lanky ones; men standing idle on the curb, women, bundle-laden, trudging reluctantly homeward, children rattle-trapping about the sidewalks; here and there a white face drifting along, but Negroes predominately, overwhelmingly everywhere. There was assuredly no doubt of his where-abouts. This was Negro Harlem.[24]

This passage illustrates the awe and excitement that Harlem's sheer magnitude generated in most newcomers. "Harlem must be a better world," reasoned most blacks. The reason was clearly visible as Fisher's Gillis turned and noticed to his astonishment that a *black* policeman was directing traffic, and white drivers obediently followed his commands:

> Yet most of the vehicles that leaped or crouched at his bidding carried white passengers. One of these overdrove bounds a few feet and Gillis heard the officer's shrill whistle and gruff reproof, and saw the driver's face turn red and his car draw back like a threatened pup. It was beyond belief—impossible. Black might be white, but it couldn't be that white![25]

For thousands of blacks Harlem was just that—a city of refuge where, at least it was thought, one could escape from the white control that was omnipresent in the South.

Another young poet saw Harlem only slightly differently. Like many would-be black writers, Langston Hughes was strongly drawn to the black metropolis. When his father offered to send him to college in Europe, Hughes balked and then suggested Columbia University as a compromise "mainly because I wanted to see Harlem. . . . More than Paris, or the Shakespeare country, or Berlin, or the Alps, I wanted to see Harlem, the greatest Negro city in the world."[26] Like Fisher's Gillis, Langston Hughes was transfixed as he ascended from the subway into the heart of Harlem:

> I went up the steps and out into the bright September sunlight. Harlem! I stood there, dropped my bags, took a deep breath and felt happy again. I registered at the Y.
>
> When college opened, I did not want to move into the dormitory at Columbia. I really did not want to go the college at all. I didn't want to do anything but live in Harlem, get a job and work there.[27]

After his first year at college Hughes did exactly that. He dropped out of school and moved into Harlem. Hughes was enraptured of the place because of the masses who lived, toiled, and played there. Many of his early poems captured the life of the ghetto's streets and cabarets. Hughes always recognized that Harlem was a slum where one did not really escape racial oppression, but he nevertheless loved the vitality and life of the blacks who resided there.

James Weldon Johnson saw a still different Harlem. In 1930 he published *Black Manhattan*, in which he described the black metropolis as the race's great hope and its grand social experiment: "So here we have Harlem—not merely a colony or a community or a settlement—not at all a 'quarter' or a slum or a fringe—but a black city located in the heart of white Manhattan, and containing more Negroes to the square mile than any other spot on earth. It strikes the uninformed observer as a phenomenon, a miracle straight out of the skies." Johnson was so blinded by the image he held of the Harlem that could be that he saw the ghetto in only the most glowing terms, and described that area of Manhattan as "one of the most beautiful and healthful in the whole city. It is not a fringe, it is not a slum, nor is it a 'quarter' consisting of dilapidated tenements. It is a section of new-law apartment houses and handsome dwellings, with streets as well paved, as well lighted, and as well kept as in any other part of the city."[28]

Johnson concluded his study with the claim that Harlem would prove to be the great laboratory in which all of the racial misconceptions of white America would be laid to rest. He argued that Harlem proved that large numbers of blacks could live together in the North without creating racial disorder, and that it demonstrated the ability of blacks to create a viable community which offered its inhabitants opportunity and decent living conditions. He further maintained that Harlem and the literary movement associated with it would obliterate the stereotype that the Negro was a "beggar at the gates of the nation waiting to be thrown the crumbs of civilization," and would instead place blacks in an entirely new light that would ultimately eliminate the discrimination and disadvantages which had oppressed the race for centuries.[29]

Unfortunately, Johnson's idealism and optimism masked reality and prevented him from recognizing that in the 1920s Harlem was rapidly deteriorating. Granted, Harlem was a rapidly growing black metropolis, but, as Gilbert Osofsky documented, "the most profound change that Harlem experienced in the 1920s was its emergence as a slum. Largely within the space of a single decade Harlem was transformed from a potentially ideal community to a neighborhood with manifold social and economic problems called 'deplorable, unspeakable, incredible.'" Exorbitant rents in Harlem led to subdividing apartments and extreme overcrowding, making it the most congested area in the nation. This, in turn, resulted in serious health problems, which gave Harlem the highest infant mortality and general mortality rates in New York City. In addition the rapid influx of blacks made it difficult for many Harlem residents to find decent jobs. Job discrimination, which ironically was practiced in the heart of the black ghetto, exacerbated these employment problems. During the 1920s the vast majority of Harlem's retail establishments would only hire blacks for menial jobs such as porter, maid, or elevator operator. As a result of this and similar job discrimination most of Harlem's residents lived, at best, on the verge of poverty, a situation which contributed to the emergence of this area as the city's leader in vice, crime, juvenile delinquency, and drug addiction.[30]

Many of the pathologies of ghetto life are those linked to the breakup of the black family in American slums. While Herbert Gutman's study of the black family effectively refutes Osofsky's claim that slavery had undermined the black family prior to the great migration, the vitality of the black family in Harlem in the 1920s is not so clear. Gutman's argument that large numbers of lower-class southern blacks had effectively adapted familial and kinship ties to life in the ghetto may be accurate, but there is still evidence that indicates that the black family was a victim of ghetto life and that the ghetto, in turn, was adversely affected by the weakening of family ties. One problem confronting the black family in Harlem in the

1920s was the growing number of families or subfamilies that were headed by a female. While the percentage of female-headed households and subfamilies among blacks in New York City declined slightly from 17 percent in 1905 to 15 percent in 1925, it may be more significant that in the samples studied by Gutman the total number of male-absent families and subfamiles had grown from 587 in 1905 to 2,089 in 1925. In a congested urban area the absolute number of male-absent families (and the number of children raised in families where the father is absent) can have as great an impact on the community as the percentage of male-absent families does. The growing congestion of Harlem also impacted on family structure. Between 1905 and 1925 nuclear families became less prevalent, declining from 49 percent to 39 percent, while the number of households containing subfamilies increased from 12.7 percent to slightly over 30 percent; in addition, by 1925 nearly half of the black households contained a boarder or lodger.[31]

The most significant problem that confronted Harlem was the failure to establish a viable black middle class there. While Harlem attracted a substantial number of black intellectuals, writers, and poets in the 1920s, and it became the home of a large number of black churches, newspapers, and civil rights organizations, it housed relatively few black businesses. In 1930, for example, Manhattan, with a population of 224,670 blacks, contained only 258 black-owned retail stores, one fewer than Houston, with only 63,337 blacks, and significantly fewer than existed in either Atlanta, New Orleans, or even Detroit. Black-owned retail stores in Manhattan also had significantly lower sales per capita (of the black population) than did those in the other cities surveyed. As the table below indicates, black-owned retail businesses were involved primarily in food-related activities (groceries, restaurants, lunch counters), although these businesses were somewhat more diversified in Manhattan than in other cities. A survey of economic activity in Harlem in the mid-1930s found that blacks owned less than 19 percent of the 10,300 enterprises operating in Harlem, and the ones that blacks did operate were usually personal service businesses or businesses in fields that required little capital and little labor; in 1930 the average black-owned retail store in Manhattan employed only 1.49 full-time workers, including the proprietor. In 1925 less than 2 percent of Manhattan blacks were classified entrepreneurial, while 89 percent were employed as skilled, unskilled, or service workers.[32]

Undermining the emergence of a black middle class in Harlem was

Table 4

Number of Black-Owned Businesses, 1930

Type of Business	Manhattan	Atlanta	Houston	New Orleans
Food	81	110	73	376
General Merchandise	3	0	0	2
Automotive	5	13	22	13
Apparel	14	4	12	10
Furniture/Home	8	0	1	5
Restaurant	61	241	113	260
Lumber/Building Supply	3	0	0	1
Other	83	23	38	104
Total Black Businesses	258	391	259	771
Black Population	224,670	90,075	63,337	129,632

Source: *Negroes in the U.S.*, 520–26, 578.

widespread discrimination in employment and education. Even corporations that made their money from black patronage often refused to hire blacks. For example, in 1935 the Metropolitan Life Insurance Company, which insured more than 100,000 blacks in Harlem alone, did not employ a single black. Utility companies in the New York City area employed almost 135,000 persons, but only 1 percent were black (and most of these held janitorial positions), while discrimination was perpetuated even by the New York State Employment Service, which required racial identification on all applications and listed only menial jobs at its Harlem office, and both the city and state civil service systems. The New York educational system completed the pattern of discrimination that held blacks out of the middle class. Vocational schools in the city consistently refused to offer training to blacks in fields that were reserved for whites, while the practice of zoning school districts was manipulated effectively to segregate the public schools. As a result, most Harlem blacks attended high schools where the curriculum assumed (and assured) that they would occupy a marginal economic status in life.[33]

The available housing in Harlem, which had initially seemed so attractive, soon deteriorated. Existing brownstones and roomy apartments were

Table 5

Business Activity in Black-Owned Retail Establishments, 1930

	Manhattan	Atlanta	Houston	New Orleans	U.S. Average
Black per Capita Sales	$10.00	$13.00	$21.00	$18.00	$14.00
Full-Time Employees per Store	1.49	1.11	2.05	1.48	1.66
Sales per Store (Black-Owned)	$8,766.00	$2,946.00	$5,188.00	$2,984.00	$4,853.00

Source: *Negroes in the U.S.*, 578.

quickly subdivided, and then developers threw up cheap tenements to cash in on the area's burgeoning growth. Rents and demand for housing remained so high that many black families were forced to take in boarders or hold rent parties in order to afford even low-quality housing. Overcrowding and segregation combined to undermine the neighborhood. Faulty maintenance, violation of municipal codes, and outright vandalism accelerated the process. By the late 1930s, 30 percent of the area's dwellings lacked bathing facilities. The inevitable consequence of overcrowding and inadequate sanitation was the deterioration of public health. For example, in 1930 the death rate of blacks from tuberculosis in New York City was almost five times greater than it was for whites, and substantially higher than it was for blacks in large southern cities like Atlanta, Houston, and New Orleans; the average infant mortality rate for blacks in New York City between 1926 and 1931 was more than twice as high as it was for whites, and substantially higher than it was for blacks in other large northern industrial cities, while the gap between white and black rates for infant mortality was greater in New York than in other major cities in the North or the South. In short, the day-to-day realities that most Harlemites faced differed dramatically from the image of Harlem life presented by James Weldon Johnson. Perhaps Johnson finally became aware of how far reality had diverged from his dream, or perhaps he did not, but in 1931 Harlem's greatest booster abandoned black Manhattan for a position in Nashville at Fisk University.[34]

Harlem, then, was not so much a black metropolis as a black ghetto. If,

Table 6

Health Status of Blacks, 1930–31
Mortality Rates for Tuberculosis and Infant Mortality

	Tuberculosis 1930	Infant Mortality, 1931 (Deaths per 1000 Births)	
		Blacks	Whites
New York	2.63	106	52
Chicago	—	75	56
Detroit	3.25	85	56
Atlanta	1.53	121	84
Houston	1.51	—	—
New Orleans	2.31	104	75

Source: *Negroes in the U.S.*, 374–75, 454–55.

as Johnson observed, racial tension had declined in New York during the twenties, it was because whites had succeeded in confining most blacks to a separate, self-contained section of New York with institutions and services inferior to those in other parts of the city, had limited them to the more menial jobs, and had isolated them from the mainstream of the city's social and political life. As one character in Carl Van Vechten's novel *Nigger Heaven* bitterly remarked:

> Nigger Heaven! Byron moaned. Nigger Heaven! That's what Harlem is. We sit in our places in the gallery in this New York theater and watch the white world sitting down below in the good seats in the orchestra. Occasionally they turn their faces up towards us, their hard, cruel faces, to laugh or sneer, but they never beckon. It never seems to occur to them that Nigger Heaven is crowded, that there isn't another seat, that something has to be done. It doesn't seem to occur to them either, he went on fiercely, that we sit above them, that we can drop things on them and crush them, that we can swoop down from Nigger Heaven and take their seats. No, they have no fear of that! Harlem! The Mecca of the New Negro! My God![35]

Harlem, then, symbolized different things to different blacks. It was both their hope and their despair. More important, Harlem reflected the confusing and contradictory position of blacks in the early twentieth century. It was a symbol of the black migrant who left the South and went north with dreams of freedom and opportunity. It also symbolized the shattered pieces of those dreams which lay half-buried beneath the filth and garbage of the city slum. Harlem reflected the self-confidence, militancy, and pride of the New Negro in his or her demand for equality; it reflected the aspirations and genius of the writers and poets of the Harlem Renaissance; but Harlem, like the black migrant, like the New Negro, and like the Renaissance writers, did not resolve its problems or fulfill its dreams. Everything, it seemed, fell short of its goal.

2 Booker T. Washington, W.E.B. Du Bois, and the "New Negro" in Black America

During the period that Harlem was emerging as a black ghetto, a transformation was also underway in black social and political thought. It was the consensus of most black intellectuals that a "New Negro" emerged among black youth in the years immediately following World War I. As Alain Locke observed in 1926, "the younger generation is vibrant with a new psychology" which was manifested in a shift from "social disillusionment to race pride." Locke went on to note that this new psychology rejected the old stereotypes of black "aunties, uncles, and mammies" and substituted instead self-respect, self-dependence, and racial unity. Locke's New Negroes centered their hopes on a new vision of opportunity, social and economic freedom, and a chance to organize and fight for improved racial conditions. The New Negroes were unwilling to place their future in the hands of white America; they were no longer content to turn the other cheek when confronted with discrimination and prejudice. They were not really radical—in fact, their values and objectives were basically middle class; all they demanded was an end to American racial prejudice and the institution of equal opportunity and social justice. However, they often assumed a posture of militancy when they voiced these demands, such as when one cried, "the next time white folks pick on black folks, something's going to drop—dead white folks."[1]

Actually the term "New Negro" and the ideas associated with it did not originate in the 1920s. The first use of the term seems to have been on

June 28, 1895, when the Cleveland *Gazette* editorialized about a new class of blacks with education, class, and money that had arisen since the Civil War. From the moment that this concept originated around the turn of the century there were conflicting interpretations about precisely what the term meant. Some maintained that the essence of the New Negro was his commitment to the idea of self-help, while others argued that the New Negro was ready to protest against discrimination or any abridgment of his civil rights. Still others insisted that the New Negro was Pan-African in outlook and determined to link the future of black Americans with the other colored peoples of the world. What all agreed on was the belief that large numbers of black Americans had become proud of their race, self-reliant, and assimilated to American middle-class values, and that they were demanding their rights as American citizens. The term can be understood best as the culmination of extensive social and intellectual developments within the black community in the years following Reconstruction, and as the synthesis of a number of divergent strains that had dominated black thought prior to the First World War. This synthesis would then find literary expression in the Harlem Renaissance.[2]

The fundamental political reality that influenced the development of black thought during the last quarter of the nineteenth century was the steady deterioration of the position of blacks in American society. The black community responded to the increased racial tension in part by turning inward and developing attitudes of self-help and racial pride. Blacks reacted in a quite reasonable fashion to the political and social realities as white society defined them. Faced with growing hostility, characterized by the emergence of segregation and an increase in racial violence, blacks focused their energies on developing their own community and their own institutions. Faced with declining support from even liberal whites, blacks banded together in separate organizations to advance their cause. As political avenues of advancement were eliminated by disenfranchisement, blacks sought equality through economic and moral growth; when whites argued black inferiority, blacks attempted to demonstrate their equality by publicizing their past achievements, by cultivating racial pride and a sense of their own worth, and by competing successfully with whites in the economic arena. Most of all, in times of white hostility, blacks had to turn to each other and rely on themselves.

The most prominent early advocate of black self-help was Alexander Crumwell, the rector of St. Luke's Episcopal Church in Washington, D.C. For twenty years, beginning in 1853, Crumwell lived in Liberia, where he

was a militant advocate of black nationalism and a back-to-Africa movement. Following his return to America, Crumwell turned his attention to
black social and economic development within the United States. He
retained his militant black nationalism, but his goal of colonizing blacks
in Africa gave way to a philosophy of racial pride, solidarity, and self-help
within America. What Crumwell stressed was that blacks must recognize
that until prejudice disappeared they constituted a distinct nation within
the country. Therefore, rather than seeking a common heritage or destiny
with white America, blacks must strive for advancement along racial
lines. Crumwell hoped that this strategy would be a temporary one, lasting
only until racial justice prevailed, but until that day arrived blacks must
help themselves, not by political agitation, but through carefully coordinated economic effort aimed at establishing a strong black economic force
in America. A corollary to black economic development was mental and
moral improvement; taken together, accomplishments in these areas ultimately would bring power and social justice for blacks in America.[3]

Crumwell's self-help ideology reverberated through the black community in the 1870s and 1880s. Conventions of black business and fraternal
groups as well as most black newspapers endorsed self-help as the only
realistic strategy for blacks to improve their status in America. The
National Conference of Colored Men that met in Nashville in 1879, while
concerned about the erosion of civil rights, focused most of its attention
on self-help and argued:

> We are to a great extent the architects of our own fortune, and must
> rely mainly on our own exertions for success. We, therefore, recom-
> mended to the youth of our race the observation of strict morality,
> temperate habits, and the practice of the acquisition of land, the
> acquiring of agriculture, of advancing to mercantile positions, and
> forcing their way into the various productive channels of literature,
> art, science and mechanics.[4]

The black press echoed this theme. Leading magazines such as the
African Methodist Episcopal (A.M.E.) Church *Review* and the A.M.E.
Christian Recorder printed numerous articles stressing economic development, self-help, and racial solidarity. Among black newspapers, the
Washington *Bee* took the lead in developing this argument. Although
blacks did not unanimously endorse this point of view, generally Crumwell's ideas dominated black thought during the last two decades of the
nineteenth century.[5]

It is essential to remember that during the last quarter of the nineteenth century blacks were on the defensive in America, and their ideologies reflected this defensiveness. While arguments for self-help and racial pride are not inherently defensive in nature, they took this form in the two decades following Reconstruction. The tone of black speeches and pronouncements and of black editorials and articles reflected this. So did the black history that was written at the turn of the century.

Black history emerged concurrently with the self-help movement, and, like the latter, was part of the expression of racial pride. Early black historians used historical evidence to counter the racial stereotypes that characterized mainstream history and provided a basis for discrimination, and they presented historical arguments to support their claims of racial equality. These efforts took two forms: some attempted to establish a basis for racial equality through scriptural interpretation (and by refuting through logical argument scripturally based justifications for black inferiority) or by depicting the past greatness of black civilizations; others apologized for the backwardness of black culture by linking culture with environment.[6]

The first targets for black historians were the theological arguments that many whites used to justify discrimination. Edward A. Johnson developed the standard counter-argument in *A Short History of the Negro Race in America* (1890). Johnson refuted the interpretation that Ham, afflicted with Noah's curse, ceased to be the brother of Shem and Japeth, thus separating the races and providing a justification for prejudice. Johnson reasoned that since Noah was drunk when he cursed Ham, the curse could not have been an expression of God's will. Furthermore, since the Bible later identified the Babylonians and Canaanites as descendants of Ham, the curse was obviously invalid. Like most other black historians of the late nineteenth century, Johnson used his scriptural analysis as merely a prelude to his work and gave added emphasis to more scientific historical arguments. The most noted black historian of the period, George Washington Williams, in his *History of the Negro Race in America, from 1619 to 1880* (1883), sought to establish a basis for Negro greatness by demonstrating how the civilizations of Egypt, Greece, and Rome borrowed their culture from ancient black civilizations; the tragedy of Africa and the black race was that following their early greatness they had turned their backs on God, experienced moral decline, and lost their civilization. Perhaps the most interesting (and bizarre) claim of black greatness came from William T. Alexander, who advanced the theory that mythical Atlantis, the home of an advanced civilization which at one time had controlled the world, was inhabited and controlled by blacks.[7]

After establishing the past greatness of their race, black historians attempted to account for the racial disparity that characterized the world in the late nineteenth century. Most maintained, first, that in America, despite the handicap of slavery, blacks had made tremendous advancements, and, second, that Africa had declined from greatness into savagery because of environment or because they had incurred the wrath of God. Implicit in these arguments was the assumption that Africa had fallen far behind Western civilization in morality and social organization as well as in technology; that, in short, African history was a story of degeneration and devolution that ran counter to the Western story of evolution and progress. For Africa and the black race to rise again, they must re-acquire civilization from white society. This diagnosis fit well into the philosophy of self-help and economic advancement outlined by Crumwell.[8]

Similar attitudes were emerging in the field of black education. By the early 1890s Crumwell's self-help ideology, embodied in the concept of industrial education, had largely supplanted classical or liberal arts education as the principal focus of America's black colleges. The American Missionary Association and most other religious and secular bodies that supported black education in the post-Reconstruction South committed themselves to industrial education in the early 1880s. Their arguments for doing so were: first, industrial education more effectively addressed the needs of a majority of the students, who came to colleges from underdeveloped agricultural or industrial backgrounds; second, since few students arrived with adequate academic preparation, there was little demand for liberal arts courses; and, third, industrial and vocational classes provided immediate economic return to financially strapped institutions by raising crops and livestock, constructing buildings and furniture, and in other ways contributing directly to the survival of the institution. By the early 1890s the trend toward industrial education had become so pervasive that even prominent liberal arts colleges such as Fisk and Atlanta felt compelled to add courses in agriculture and the industrial arts.[9]

Industrial education enjoyed widespread popularity not only because it addressed the real needs of many black colleges and their students, but also because it met the needs of dominant elements in both the black and the white communities. Among blacks it was compatible with the concepts of self-help and racial solidarity. Industrial education had as its goal the creation of a race of thrifty, hard-working, industrious men and women focusing their energies on economic advancement rather than on political equality. In addition industrial education appeased whites who had criticized classical or liberal arts curricula at black colleges as either not addressing the educational needs of blacks or, even worse, creating black college graduates who refused to work as manual laborers. [10]

Conservative black clergymen also contributed to the development of the self-help ideology in the late nineteenth century. They developed an image of blacks which incorporated the patience, humility, and easygoing nature that had been one of the survival strategies during slavery and that was a defense mechanism against the racial hostility that was so widespread at the turn of the century. As S.P. Fullinwider explained:

> The "Christ-like" image (stereotype) of the Negro was born out of the formation of ego-defense mechanisms contrived in the slave's unconscious to maintain self-respect during a time when the choice in handling aggression was either to repress it or be destroyed. The slave's patience, humility, and good nature were necessary for his survival. Now, these were the very traits that the Christian religion set before the slave and the post-Emancipation generation as the ideal for which all men should strive—they were the traits of Christ, himself. It was not difficult, therefore, for the oppressed Negro to interpret his subservient behavior as being Christ-like. In fact it was necessary for his self-esteem (ego-defenses) that he see himself as not servile; that he see himself, rather, as the realization of the Christian ideal. [11]

With this image blacks could maintain their self-respect while avoiding a direct confrontation with racism. They could glorify their meekness, patience, and humility, while still condemning the inhumanity of white racism. Furthermore this image gave blacks a special mission—to carry the values of Christianity to a hostile and un-Christian world, to save Africa, America, or both. [12]

Although these arguments for self-help and racial pride were rapidly becoming dominant in black thought in the 1880s, as long as Frederick Douglass lived, he served as a strong counterbalance to these views. In the three decades that followed the Civil War Douglass stood at the very apex of black leadership in America. His credentials were impeccable; he was the undisputed leader of his race from the time of his emergence during the abolitionist movement until his death in 1895. Throughout his career Douglass symbolized protest and political agitation, although until the early 1880s he had combined protest for political rights with a call for racial pride, economic independence, and self-help. But, as most of the black community responded to the deteriorating racial situation by moving away from protest and toward self-help, Douglass moved in the opposite direction. During the last years of his life he increasingly expressed doubts about the effectiveness of self-help and concentrated instead on the struggle against segregation and disenfranchisement. For Douglass the racial problem was not merely a black problem but an American one; the fundamental issue was whether American justice applied equally to all citizens or only to some. In addition Douglass pointed out that black racial pride differed little from the arguments of white racists; instead of racial solidarity he stressed assimilation. [13]

When Douglass' dominating presence was removed by his death, his ideas quickly faded into the background, and the self-help ideology of men like Crumwell became dominant. This process was accelerated by the emergence of a successor to Douglass who embraced this ideology. By the mid-1890s Booker T. Washington had taken over the position recently vacated by Douglass as the most powerful man in black America.

Booker T. Washington had been born in slavery in 1856. Following emancipation he received an education at Hampton Institute in Virginia, where he became a disciple of Samuel Chapman Armstrong's brand of industrial education. In 1881 he established Tuskegee Institute and made it his power base as well as a major center of agricultural and industrial education. Washington was an educator, a spokesman, and an organizer, but not an originator of ideas. His biographer, Louis R. Harlan, saw him as "not an intellectual, but a man of action. Ideas he cared little for. Power was his game."[14] The concepts usually associated with his name, self-help and industrial education, had become dominant ideologies in the black community some time before he rose to prominence. Washington himself had been thoroughly indoctrinated in those views while a student at Hampton Institute, which had pioneered the program of industrial education for blacks in the late 1860s under the leadership of Samuel Chapman Armstrong.

Booker T. Washington's philosophy, as it was publicly expressed, was fairly simple and remarkably consistent over the course of his career. Essentially he argued that thrift, industry, and Christian morality would eventually earn blacks their Constitutional rights. The first essential step toward equality must be for blacks to learn trades so that they might compete effectively with whites in the economic arena. Therefore, blacks must make, as their educational objectives, the acquisition of those practical skills that would promote their economic development. Thus far Washington merely echoed the call for industrial education that was already widely accepted in the black community. Far more controversial was the corollary to his thesis for racial advancement that urged accommodation with segregation. The best-known public expression of this was his 1895 Atlanta speech in which he followed his call for economic self-help with the proclamation: "In all things that are purely social we can be as separate as the five fingers, yet one as the hand in all things essential to mutual progress. . . . The wisest among my race understand that the agitation of questions of social equality is the extremist folly."[15] Washington in Atlanta proposed that blacks put aside, for the time being, their quest for desegregation and the vote; in return they would be permitted to develop their own separate but equal economic, social, and educational institutions within the framework of the expanding southern economy. Although a few blacks criticized this approach as accommodationist, it was embraced by most of the black intellectual elite at the turn of the century and almost universally praised by white Americans.[16]

Washington would continue to stress the principles he outlined in his Atlanta speech. He consistently counseled patience in matters of racial injustice; he pronounced protest and racial agitation ineffective tactics and advised instead that living respectable lives and acquiring wealth was a much surer route to equality. In addition, in spite of the steadily deteriorating racial situation and the upsurge in racial violence, he continually expressed faith in the good will of southern whites. Late in his career Washington went so far as to argue that, notwithstanding the obvious racial problems, southern blacks enjoyed greater opportunity than blacks anywhere else and that American blacks were better off than the European poor.[17] Throughout his life Washington gave little public attention to racial injustice. Instead he directed his energies toward winning the good will of southern whites, whose support he believed was vital for racial advancement.

Although on the basis of most of his public statements and activities Washington earned the reputation of an extreme accommodationist, there was another, less public side to the man. While he was sincere in his commitment to self-help and industrial education and while he truly believed that racial progress depended on the support of southern whites, he often involved himself clandestinely in behind-the-scenes activities to combat racial injustice. While publicly denouncing protest and preaching patience, Washington secretly diverted funds to help finance court battles against segregation. In 1895, for example, he lobbied against black disenfranchisement in Georgia, and in the years that followed he supported the legal fight against discriminatory laws in several southern states, by both soliciting funds and contributing from his own pocket. Before the Atlanta speech he had been even more outspoken, condemning racial segregation of public transportation and as late as 1894 urging blacks to boycott segregated streetcars. Even after he donned his accommodationist cloak, his public statements, if examined very carefully, reveal a subtle protest against racial inequality. In the Atlanta speech itself, beneath the call for patience and ambiguous references to justice, progress, and uplift, Washington indicated that ultimately he expected blacks, through moderate means, to gain their full and unrestricted political and social rights. This theme was never dominant in Washington's rhetoric; most whites, distracted and seduced by his moderate tone and conciliatory phrases, remained blind to it, but the Tuskegeean's supporters stressed this side of his philosophy.[18]

Within a few months of his Atlanta speech Washington had become politically the most powerful black in America. There were several reasons for his rapid accumulation of power. First, Washington emerged as nationally prominent before anyone else had moved to fill the power vacuum left by the death of Frederick Douglass. Even more important, Washington's philosophy, and especially his association with industrial education, fitted well with the prevailing attitudes of both whites and blacks. The Tuskegeean reflected Crumwell's self-help ideology and the educational policies of his mentor at Hampton, Samuel Chapman Armstrong. His conciliatory tone and stress on an economic approach to racial problems placated whites and gained their enthusiastic support. President Grover Cleveland saw in the Atlanta speech a "new hope" for black Americans, while the Atlanta *Constitution* called Washington a "wise counselor and a safe leader."[19] Finally, Washington's position of leadership among blacks was secured by the fact that whites, in both the North and the South, elevated him to the position of spokesman for his race. Washington discovered soon after the Atlanta speech that politicians consulted him before they dispensed patronage to blacks, and more importantly, philanthropists sought his advice before they funded black institutions.

Washington's power increased rapidly after the turn of the century.

During Theodore Roosevelt's administration few blacks received political appointments without clearance from Tuskegee; black colleges, churches, and other institutions found it almost impossible to obtain contributions without his endorsement. Washington's power was also manifested in the control that he exerted over the editorial policy of the black press, especially the influential New York *Age*, and his influence over appointments in the black church and in black colleges. By 1905 Washington had become the virtual dictator of black America.

To complicate matters, as he grew in eminence, Washington became increasingly sensitive to criticism, especially by blacks, and used his influence to suppress those who opposed his policies or who threatened his personal position or prestige. He employed every means at his disposal against his critics. He placed spies in their organizations, used his influence with the press to discredit them and their policies, deprived them of their political, church, or college positions, and made it difficult for them to obtain financial support for their programs. If it had been within his power, Washington undoubtedly would have excommunicated his antagonists from the black race.

Initially Washington's tactics for dealing with his critics were relatively mild. In the late 1890s he used his control over patronage to lure more radical blacks into his camp. For example, in 1901 in an effort to muzzle one of his more outspoken critics, civil rights activist Mary Church Terrell, he arranged for her husband to become the first black federal judge in Washington, D.C.; he also headed off a move by James Weldon Johnson in late 1905 to affiliate a group of black writers and poets with the Niagara Movement, and in the process bought Johnson's loyalty by arranging for him to be appointed United States Consul to Venezuela and Nicaragua. As opposition coalesced against the "Tuskegee Machine," Washington's tactics became more aggressive. He used Melvin Chisum to spy on William Monroe Trotter and on the Niagara Movement in 1905–1906; he used his influence in the White House to block the appointment of W.E.B. Du Bois as assistant superintendent of Washington, D.C., schools in 1906, and to arrange the removal of Judson W. Lyons from his position as register of the U.S. Treasury. Lyons had made the mistake of voicing moderate support for Trotter.[20]

As Washington became more and more dictatorial, opposition to both his policies and his style of leadership grew within the black community. It is essential to remember that the ideas that Washington championed in the years following his Atlanta speech, although accepted by a majority of blacks, never enjoyed unanimous support. There were always those who remained within the more militant tradition of Frederick Douglass and who were unwilling to accept the accommodation that the Tuskegeean preached. Although as late as 1900 Washington was almost free of criticism, within three years opposition surfaced which ultimately split the black intellectual community into warring factions of Bookerites and anti-Bookerites. Men like Francis J. Grimké, while embracing many of the tenets of self-help and racial pride, carried these principles to militant rather than accommodationist conclusions. Grimké, for example, accepted self-help largely because he distrusted whites, whom he characterized as savage barbarians dedicated to re-enslaving blacks.[21] Thus, he could not accept Booker T. Washington's confidence that through self-help and industry blacks could win the admiration of whites. Grimké and other critics of Washington had only to point to the fact that during the Tuskegeean's ascendancy, while he preached moderation and patience, blacks were being disenfranchised and lynched without letup.

Francis Grimké and his brother Archibold formed the nucleus of a growing circle of black intellectuals who were dissatisfied with Washington. The split first surfaced because of the continuing question of whether black political strategy should be based on accommodation or agitation, but it soon spread to encompass a criticism of Washington's educational philosophy and his style of leadership—especially the heavyhanded tactics which he used to silence his opponents within the black community. In many respects Washington's critics returned to Douglass' emphasis on political action rather than on economic or moral improvement as the most effective way to achieve racial justice in America; in some ways, however, they accepted the Tuskegeean's emphasis on economic improvement, but combined self-help with a call for political action. Actually, it is difficult to define precisely the political and social ideology of Washington's opponents (whom some labeled the anti-Bookerites), because the group consisted of numerous elements with divergent views who often were united only in their antagonism toward Washington and his dominance of black America. August Meier presented the best description of these divisions in the black community when he characterized the Bookerite versus anti-Bookerite conflict as resulting in numerous groups "roughly correlated with each other, so that gradualism, conciliation, the middle-class virtues, racial solidarity, self-help, and sympathy for Washington tended to cluster together to form a 'conservative' outlook, while agitation for civil and political rights, advocacy of immediate and complete integration, interest in the labor movement, and opposition to the Tuskegeean also tended to cluster together to form a 'radical' outlook."[22] It is important to add that the conservative faction did not have a monopoly on racial pride and self-help; both factions endorsed those values.

Organized opposition to Washington first became significant during 1903. Several events that year underscored that deep divisions had developed in the black community. The first occurred during the annual meeting of the Afro-American Council. The Afro-American Council, which had originally been founded as the Afro-American League by T. Thomas Fortune in 1890 as a militant organization committed both to racial solidarity and agitation for equal rights, had, by the turn of the century, fallen under the control of the Tuskegeean. At the 1903 meeting militants attempted, unsuccessfully, to regain control of the organization. The blatant manner in which Washington retaliated to suppress his critics (who were not really all that militant) alienated a number of blacks.

This opposition strengthened in the aftermath of the so-called Boston riot. On July 30, 1903, as Washington addressed two thousand listeners in Boston, a small group of dissidents led by William Monroe Trotter disrupted the speech, and police were called in to restore order. Several of the anti-Washington hecklers were arrested, including Trotter, who spent a month in jail. This incident had a major impact on the politics of black America by driving a wedge between Booker T. Washington and W.E.B. Du Bois. Although Du Bois had no involvement in the disturbance, he spent time as a guest in the Trotter home later that summer, and he criticized his host's jail term; this convinced Washington that the young Atlanta professor was behind the riot and prompted the Tuskegeean to launch a campaign to discredit his opponent and punish him by denying him access to funding and by threatening his employer with a loss of funds.[23] This, plus the publication earlier in the year of *The Souls of Black Folk* with its chapter "Of Mr. Booker T. Washington and Others," intensified the philosophical differences between Washington and Du Bois, crystallized the growing split in the black intellectual community, and propelled Du Bois to the forefront of the anti-Bookerite faction.

Washington's opponents coalesced, first in the Niagara movement and then in the National Association for the Advancement of Colored People. In July 1905 Du Bois and twenty-eight other black leaders, impatient with accommodation, met in Fort Erie, Ontario, to organize a more militant civil rights organization. The resulting Niagara movement selected Du

Bois as its general secretary and dedicated itself to universal manhood suffrage and the elimination of "all caste distinctions based simply on race or color."[24] The major target of the movement was Booker T. Washington's domination of black America; in turn the Tuskegeean used his control of the black press to discredit the organization and his political influence and prestige to sabotage the careers of the Niagaraites. Faced with Washington's relentless opposition, the Niagara movement never gained sufficient funds or enough influence to achieve much success, and it disbanded in 1909.[25] Most of the blacks associated with it shifted their affiliation to the NAACP following its establishment in 1910 under the leadership of Du Bois and a number of white progressives. This bi-racial group was strong enough and well enough funded to withstand Washington's attacks and, after the Tuskegeean's death in 1915, succeeded in reconciling and uniting most of the factions in the black community.

During the first two decades of the twentieth century W.E.B. Du Bois was the man who symbolized an alternative to the philosophy and leadership of Booker T. Washington. The contrasting educational backgrounds of these two men reflect clearly their ideological differences. While Washington was immersed in industrial education at Hampton and Tuskegee, Du Bois graduated from Fisk and then pursued graduate study in history, philosophy, and psychology at Harvard and the University of Berlin. At Harvard, Du Bois studied with the best minds of late nineteenth-century America—William James, Josiah Royce, George Santayana, and Albert Bushnell Hart—and emerged with a deep commitment to scholarship and convinced that intellectual and scientific study were essential in countering racial prejudice and dispelling racial myths. After completing his Ph.D. he published his dissertation, *The Suppression of the African Slave Trade* (1896), and *The Philadelphia Negro: A Social Study* (1899), works which established his reputation as both a historian and a sociologist. He also became a professor of sociology at Atlanta University, where he attempted to instill a scientific approach to the study of black America.

In spite of their very different backgrounds, Du Bois initially supported Washington and his positions. He congratulated the Tuskegeean for the 1895 Atlanta speech, and he defended the Atlanta Compromise as offering the basis for a real settlement between whites and blacks in the South. As late as 1903 the Bookerites still hoped to recruit Du Bois for the faculty at Tuskegee and wed him to their faction. By that time, however, Du Bois had begun to express reservations about Washington's educational and political philosophies. In his assessment of Washington in *The Souls of Black Folk* he acknowledged that the Tuskegeean was the "most distinguished Southerner since Jefferson Davis, and the one with the largest personal following"; furthermore, Du Bois insisted that he sincerely valued his achievements and recognized the political realities in the South that forced moderation. However, he sharply criticized Washington for actually perpetuating the alleged inferiority of blacks through his educational system and for counseling blacks to give up temporarily their claims for political power, civil rights, and higher education for their youth. The most damning indictment of the Washington program, Du Bois maintained, was that during the ten years that it had dominated black thought, blacks indeed had been disenfranchised, had been legally segregated in a distinct and inferior civil status, and had witnessed the steady withdrawal of funds from liberal arts programs at black colleges.[26]

Du Bois responded to the shortcomings in Washington's program with his own agenda for American blacks. He based his approach on the conviction that blacks needed well-educated leadership to direct the uplifting of the race. To accomplish this, black colleges and universities should not focus their efforts exclusively on industrial education but should continue to offer a strong liberal arts program to produce the class of teachers and professionals necessary to carry out this task. Du Bois had no objections to practical education in the industrial arts (so long as it did not perpetuate skills that were becoming obsolete in industrial America), but he warned that it would be dangerous to ignore classical education because ultimately it would be the educated elite, the "talented tenth," that would bring culture and progress to the race. As Du Bois put it, "if we make money the object of man-training, we shall develop moneymakers but not necessarily men; if we make technical skill the object of education, we may possess artisans but not, in nature, men. Men we shall have only as we make manhood the object of the work of the schools— intelligence, broad sympathy, knowledge of the world that was and is, and of the relation of men to it—this is the curriculum of that Higher Education which must underlie true life."[27]

In addition to challenging Washington's ideas about education, Du Bois also rejected the Tuskegeean's political tactics. Du Bois insisted that protest, not accommodation, was the only viable way for blacks to secure their civil and political rights. He argued that blacks could never gain self-respect until they fought for their rights; they could never secure and defend their position as property owners until they achieved and exercised the right to vote. Du Bois never accepted segregation on even a temporary basis during this period of his life. Instead, he argued that "separate but equal" was never equal, but a system designed to foster inequality and perpetuate the subordination of blacks. Although he urged blacks to develop their own businesses and to patronize the businesses of other blacks, and while he recognized that integration might undermine the economic development of the black community, he insisted that the evils of segregation more than offset its short-term economic advantages. [28] Du Bois believed in racial solidarity, but not as an end in itself; rather, racial solidarity should be used as a weapon to protest disenfranchisement and segregation and to win the struggle for civil rights.

Thus far the differences between Du Bois and Washington, though substantial, were differences in degree rather than substance, differences in means rather than ends. Both men were committed to uplifting their race, instilling racial pride, and securing political and civil rights. However, Du Bois, the greatest black intellect of the prewar period, constantly explored concepts that were alien to the more conservative Washington. In 1910, for example, Du Bois shocked many moderates of both races when he condemned the prohibition of interracial marriage (although he qualified his stand with the observation that current conditions did not encourage widespread marriage between the races). He also flirted with the belief that there were inherent differences between the races and that strong ties existed between American blacks and other colored peoples. [29] Du Bois also examined socialism and attempted to explain racial discrimination in terms of class conflict. In 1911 he joined the Socialist party, and by the end of the decade he had become convinced that the ultimate solution of racial problems would be found through the elimination of class antagonisms and a union of black and white workers.

While Du Bois was challenging Washington's leadership, black historians also distanced themselves from the Tuskeegean, related to the more militant stance of black intellectuals in the early twentieth century, and helped popularize another concept that would characterize the New Negro. Whereas their colleagues in the late nineteenth century had been preoccupied with defending blacks against the attack of racially biased historians and anthropologists and had generally accepted the interpretation that their race lagged behind the West in terms of culture, after 1910 black historians became more aggressive and chauvinistic. They remained committed to the concepts of self-help and racial pride, but they were far less defensive in their interpretation of black history than their predecessors had been. One of their principal concerns was making sure that black history was included in the curricula of black schools. Organizations such as the Negro Society for Historical Research, founded in 1912, reflected this growing interest in black history. In addition to their interest in the history of black Americans, members of this organization also reinterpreted African history and placed new emphasis on the African roots of black culture. For example, A. A. Schomburg, the West Indian book collector and librarian at the Harlem branch of the New York Public Library, stressed the ties between American blacks and African and Arabic cultures and suggested that black history should be used to stimulate black patriotism; another member, John Edward Bruce, argued that whites feared black history because they knew that it would prove that African civilization predated European civilization and that the white man stole his alphabet and other tools of culture from blacks.[30]

This belief that their African heritage should be a source of pride and the basis of a racial solidarity that linked all colored people was another ingredient in the emerging black consciousness that would be known as the New Negro. Unlike an earlier generation that had addressed the decline and corruption of African culture, and in doing so apologized for their African roots, the New Negro embraced Africanism.

We can see elements of pan-Africanism as early as the 1890s in the thought of several prominent blacks, including both Du Bois and Washington. Alexander Crumwell, along with several other black leaders, participated in the Chicago Congress on Africa in 1893, where the idea of black emigration to Africa was a major topic of discussion, and four years later he promoted efforts of a group of African and Caribbean students to establish an African Association in London. Even Booker T. Washington endorsed pan-Africanism. Like a number of his contemporaries, he supported the idea of a pan-African conference during his 1899 visit to London. On a more concrete level Washington established an agricultural project in Togo, invited African dignitaries to speak at Tuskegee, and sent a number of graduates to jobs in several African countries. Ironically, W.E.B. Du Bois, who would become a major advocate of pan-Africanism, initially was suspicious of the idea. In 1897 he rejected as premature a plan calling for the migration of American blacks to the Congo Free State and proposed instead a more conservative effort to establish contacts between black Americans and Africa. Within a few years, however, he had embraced pan-Africanism. He served as a delegate to an international pan-African conference in London in 1900 and was selected to direct the American branch of the Pan-African Association. Du Bois's other obligations and interests would keep his commitment to pan-Africanism in the background until after the First World War. Nevertheless, the relationship between black Americans and the colonial peoples of Africa and the Caribbean would become an increasingly important concern during the first quarter of the twentieth century, especially following the war, when Marcus Garvey would base a mass movement on this issue.[31]

Marcus Garvey was born in a small town on the northern coast of Jamaica in 1887. As a young man, he worked as a printer and briefly operated a newspaper, *Garvey's Watchman*, in 1909. In 1910 he left Jamaica, traveling first to Central America and then to England, where he took courses at a college for working-class youth and observed British politics, from the debates in Parliament to the speeches in Hyde Park, while he lived among the small but diverse groups that made up London's ethnic community in the early twentieth century. In these surroundings Garvey first encountered pan-Africanism.[32]

When Garvey returned to Jamaica in 1914, he founded his Universal Negro Improvement Association (UNIA), which in its early years combined the ideas of pan-Africanism with the self-help and industrial education program of Booker T. Washington. Garvey did not enjoy much success as an organizer in Jamaica. After two years the UNIA had only about a hundred members, while his efforts to establish an institution modeled after Tuskegee did not get off the ground. In 1916 he left for the United States, primarily in an effort to raise funds for his school.

By 1917 Garvey had settled in Harlem, where he reestablished his UNIA and made contacts among other black political leaders, especially those who shared his commitment to pan-Africanism, but also black socialists and labor leaders like A. Philip Randolph. Garvey's goal was to unite (under his leadership) the four hundred million black people of the world; he preached a message that drew on the self-help doctrines of Washington and called for the creation of a black economy within the white capitalist world, that would both liberate the blacks of America from the oppression of discrimination and redeem the peoples of Africa from the oppression of colonialism.[33] Garvey's genius was his ability to capture the loyalty of the black masses in America. By August 1921 he reported a membership of over four million; even if these claims were inflated, before his organization began unraveling in 1923 Garvey had created and controlled the only large-scale organization among the black urban masses in America.

As the 1920s began, the various strains of prewar black thought each contributed to the new black consciousness that would be labeled the New Negro. The militancy symbolized by Du Bois become an integral part of this concept. While the accommodationist approach to racial problems associated with Washington was scorned by the new generation of black intellectuals, the New Negro accepted his doctrines of self-help and racial pride. Likewise, while most black intellectuals rejected the flamboyant and vulgar style of Garvey and his movement, they were attracted by the ideology of pan-Africanism. The New Negro was never a simple or comfortable blend of these ideologies; it was rather a dynamic ideology filled with internal conflicts and even contradictions whose fundamental questions remained unresolved. What was the true identity and nature of black Americans? Were they black, American, or African? Could they best achieve their destiny through integration and assimilation into American culture, or should they attempt to identify and preserve their own special traits—even through segregation? The New Negro emerged from the war years determined to be assertive and to stand up for his or her rights, but the New Negro also struggled with the diverse alternatives that blacks faced. These conflicts fueled black intellectual debates during the 1920s, and they fueled the artistic endeavors of black writers and poets. These conflicts, and the quest for their resolution, are the underlying themes of the Harlem Renaissance.

3   Literary

Roots

The literary roots of the Harlem Renaissance can be traced to the 1890s and the work of two Ohio writers. These two men are generally acknowledged by both black and white critics as being the most successful black writers before the twentieth century. In addition to this distinction, the career and the work of Dunbar and Chesnutt shed interesting illumination on the Harlem Renaissance. Both writers developed themes that later emerged in the Renaissance; both faced problems similar to those faced by their counterparts in the twenties. While neither Dunbar nor Chesnutt produced work of the quality or experienced the success of later black writers, both exerted influence on black literature which transcended their artistic limitations.

Of the two men, Paul Laurence Dunbar is the best known and had the most controversial reputation in the eyes of later black writers. Dunbar was born in 1872 in Dayton, Ohio. Early in life Dunbar hoped to be an attorney, but abandoned this dream, as he informed a friend in 1895, because he had found a higher calling—to "interpret my own people through song and story, and to prove to the many that after all we are more human than African."[1] He gained national recognition in 1896 when the foremost American literary critic, William Dean Howells, praised Dunbar's second book of poetry, *Majors and Minors*, in *Harper's Weekly*. In his review Howells described Dunbar as the first black writer "to study his race objectively, to analyze it to himself, and then to represent it in art as he felt it and found it to be; to represent it humorously, yet tenderly, and above all so faithfully that we know the portrayal to be undeniably true." Howells concluded these comments with extremely high praise for the young black poet, "I hope I have not praised too much, because he surprised me so very much, for his excellences were positive and not comparative."[2] This review catapulted the previously unknown poet into national prominence and opened previously closed literary doors. Later that year Dunbar arranged with Dodd, Mead, and Company to publish *Lyrics of the Lowly Life*, a collection of poems taken from his two earlier (and privately printed) books. Howells again aided the young poet by writing the introduction for this volume. During the next ten years, from 1896 until his death in 1906, Dunbar published sixteen additional books of poetry and fiction. His popular success was great enough so that for most of this ten-year period Dunbar supported himself solely on the income from his literary endeavors.

Dunbar owed much of his popular success to the assistance given him by Howells and other white patrons. As Darwin T. Turner observed, after he reached the age of twenty, every major job, every publication, and all national recognition resulted from the help of white benefactors. Although Dunbar obviously profited from this assistance, he also felt trapped by it. Howell's well-intentioned introduction to Dunbar's 1896 volume of poetry illustrated the problems that the black poet faced. Dunbar produced two types of poetry—dialect pieces and those written in standard English. Howells argued that it was the dialect poetry that was most praiseworthy, that these poems expressed in true artistic form what passed through the heart and mind of the black race, and he urged Dunbar to restrict his efforts to this literary form. Dunbar felt constrained by this advice, and the following year he wrote to a friend that "I see now very clearly that Mr. Howells has done me irrevocable harm in the dictum he laid down regarding my dialect verse."[3]

Dunbar focused his greatest literary efforts and his hope of becoming a great writer on his nondialect poetry but discovered that these verses were accepted only with reluctance, while editors and patrons urged him to submit more dialect material. But, as Dunbar complained, "I am tired of dialect, but the magazines aren't. Every time I send them something else, they write back asking for dialect. Nothing wrong with the poems—a Dunbar just has to be dialect, that's all." Dunbar expressed the intensity of these frustrations poetically:

> He sang of love when earth was
>   young,
> And Love, itself, was in his
>   lays,
> But ah, the world, it turned to
>   praise
> A jingle in a broken tongue.[4]

However, despite the strength of these sentiments, Dunbar continued to accept assistance from his white patrons, and he continued to produce dialect poetry.

The frustration that Dunbar felt reflected the fundamental problem that confronted most black writers at the turn of the century. The portrayal of blacks in literature at this time was dominated by the "plantation school" of writers, influenced chiefly by the work of Thomas Nelson Page. Basic to this approach was nostalgia for the good old days of antebellum plantation life by former slaves who remembered nothing of their former servitude except the good times, the carefree life, and the benevolent relationship between master and slave. The black writer confronting the plantation tradition in literature faced a real dilemma. He could conform to its vision of black life and, as Dunbar did with his dialect poetry, achieve considerable recognition and success; or he could realistically depict the black experience as he perceived it and risk alienating his patrons, his publisher, and his market.

Dunbar, for the most part, tried to avoid both horns of the dilemma. His goal was not to be a great black poet, but to be a great poet. He viewed himself as first of all a man, then as an American, and only lastly as a Negro. As admirable as this attitude was, it did not prepare Dunbar for the way the world viewed him, and it did not adequately prepare him to cope with reality. Because of his racial views and his refusal to use his poetry as a weapon in the struggle for equality, many later black writers were critical of both Dunbar and his work. As one argued, Dunbar's racial naiveté blinded him to social reality and hypnotized him into believing that he was simply a man, though the rest of the world saw him as a black. Furthermore, because of this contradiction, his poetry, which was written for a primarily white audience and studiously steered away from racial conflict, was "born of a divided will and a split personality."[5] While there is some truth in this assessment, Dunbar and his work are more complex and more subtle than many of his more outspoken critics assumed. In particular, Dunbar never succeeded completely in his efforts to divorce himself and his work from the reality of his racial experiences. Consequently his work reflected the complex and opposing pressures that society and his conscience placed on him.

Dunbar's dialect poetry, even that written in the plantation tradition, illustrates the difficulty in clearly assessing the quality and the racial impact of his work. Many critics argued that the dialect pieces merely reinforced negative racial stereotypes and hence did all blacks a disservice. In part this criticism was true. James Weldon Johnson was especially sensitive to the dangers of dialect poetry, which he maintained was a very limited artistic form that was typified by its "exaggerated geniality, childish optimism, forced comicality, and mawkish sentiment," and that was limited "as as instrument of expression to but two emotions, pathos and humor, thereby making every poem either only sad or only funny."[6] "Goin' Back" is an excellent example of the type of dialect poetry that Dunbar's critics dismissed because it reflected the plantation mentality. This poem tells the story of an old black man, who after spending thirty years in the North decided to return to his birthplace. He remembered none of the hardships of slavery or of southern life, only the good times and good people of the South. While this poem did not address the racial situation in the South at the turn of the century, it did, however, recognize a deeper truth—that a person's affection for his place of birth is an emotion that is irrational and not based on a logical assessment of the racial situation.

Not all critics condemned Dunbar's dialect verse. Some, both black and white, defended this genre as a viable medium through which to express a true representation of the black character and psychology. James Weldon Johnson, who clearly described the limits of dialect poetry, also recognized its potential power. While he worried about the naiveté and even the harm that could be done by some of Dunbar's dialect poetry, he also recognized the value of some of these pieces and argued that Dunbar was doing the same thing with the Negro dialect that Synge did with Irish and Burns did with the Scottish dialect.[7]

Johnson's apparently contradictory attitudes about the appropriateness and the value of dialect poetry reflect the difficulty in assessing such work. At their best Dunbar's dialect pieces capture a sense of vitality and energy; at their worst they mask the black experience with a comic superficiality. This selection from "The Party" illustrates well the appeal and the problems of Dunbar's dialect poetry:

> Dey had a gread big pahty
>   down to Tom's de othah
>   night;
> Was I dah? You bet! I nevah
>   in my lefe see sich a sight;
> .   .   .   .
> Evahbody dressed in deir fines'
>   Heish yo' mouf an' git
>   away,

> Ain't seen no sich fancy dressin'
>   sence las' quah'tly meetin'
>   day;
>
> .   .   .   .
>
> Well, we eat and drunk ouah
>   po'tion, 'twell dah wasn't
>   nothin' lef'
> An' we felt jes' like new sausage,
>   we was mos' nigh stuffed to
>   def!
> Tom, he knowed how we'd be
>   feelin', so he had de fiddlah
>   'roun',
> An' he made us cleah de cabin
>   fu' to dance dat suppah
>   down.[8]

This poem, obviously meant to be read aloud, possesses strength, vitality, and color, and its images of life are vivid. Clearly the use of black dialect here is appropriate and does not demean. Indeed, this poem could not have been written in standard English. However, it is also clear that this style would not be appropriate for other subject matter. As Johnson observed, for expressing joy or sadness it is fine, but other subject matter requires another type of poetry.

The vitality and color that characterized "The Party" is not evident in most of Dunbar's work written in standard English. Although he devoted most of his hopes and efforts to this latter area, the sad truth is that his accomplishments were meager. Dunbar does deserve some praise for emancipating black poetry from many of its earlier restraints. As Wallace Thurman wryly observed, Dunbar was the first black American poet who did not depend on the Methodist hymnbook for inspiration, style, and vocabulary, and the first to free his verses from the "puerile apotheosizing of the Almighty, and leaden allusions to scriptural passages."[9] Unfortunately Dunbar's model shifted from the hymnbook to the popular poetry of his day, and the result was not much of an improvement. Even the best of his work in this style, poems such as "Ships that Pass in the Night" or "Ere Sleep Comes Down to Soothe the Weary Eyes," are essentially sentimental relics of the Victorian period. While Dunbar should not be overly criticized for failing to transcend the popular standards of his day, neither should he be praised merely because in this case competent but mediocre verse was produced by a black man.

A notable feature of Dunbar's poetry written in standard English was that in most cases he made absolutely no reference to race. Indeed, he actually did write "as a man," not as a black. There were, however, several exceptions to this rule. In a few poems and several short stories Dunbar focused his attention on racial problems. In "Ode to Ethiopia," the "Haunted Oak," and several other poems he attempted to expose the suffering of blacks in America. These efforts, unfortunately, were notable only for their subject matter, not for a successful presentation of the material. Dunbar's social poetry was just too weak; he did not cry out forcefully against injustice, and the protests that he voiced were characterized more by restraint than militancy. Dunbar carefully tempered his discontent with patience, making him the perfect poet for the majority of his black contemporaries, who embraced the Booker T. Washington brand of accommodation. The result, as illustrated in this passage from "Ode to Ethiopia," was a rather weak plea for justice rather than a strong statement for civil rights:

> No other race, or white or black
> When bound as thou wert, to the
>   rack,
> So seldom stooped to grieving;
> No other race when free again,
> Forgot the past and proved them
>   men
> So noble in forgiving. [10]

In his short stories Dunbar occasionally was more aggressive and more successful. In this medium he addressed more complex themes than in his poetry, and directly discussed issues such as political and economic discrimination. "One Man's Fortune," for example, described the bitter realization on the part of a black college graduate that America's abundant opportunity was open only to his white classmates, while "Mr. Cornelius Johnson, Office-Seeker," chronicled the slow decline and humiliation of a political organizer attempting to collect a promised government job from a white politician. Most of Dunbar's short stories, however, were written in the plantation tradition and consisted of sentimental tales full of kindly masters and faithful, loyal slaves.

In addition to his many volumes of poetry and short stories, Dunbar wrote four novels, but only the last of them, *The Sport of the Gods*, focused on the black experience. This novel reflected most of Dunbar's failings as a writer. It was melodramatic, its plot relied heavily on coincidence and the sudden, unexpected turn of events, and it ended fairly happily with the main characters finding justice and returning to live out their days in the South. On the other hand, *The Sport of the Gods* was the first black novel to describe black life in the northern ghetto and the first to focus on the growing black community in New York. Dunbar wrote the novel in the naturalistic tradition and described the downfall and degradation of two young blacks following their move to New York. The city represented hope and the promise of greater freedom and greater opportunity for young blacks, but it also tempted them with vice and corruption. Dunbar's greatest accomplishment in this novel was his vivid description of life in the bars and cabarets of the city's emerging black slum and his exposure of the myth that the North offered blacks unlimited economic opportunity. Also, although the happy ending fitted well within the framework of the plantation tradition, Dunbar broke with this tradition by describing the decadence of southern society. Life in the plantation South was no utopia for blacks, but it still remained a welcome refuge from the urban ghetto.

Unfortunately *The Sport of the Gods* was Dunbar's last novel. It would have been interesting to see the direction that Dunbar's later work would have taken if he had not died in 1906, at only thirty-eight years of age. Clearly Dunbar would have been in a position to influence the direction of black literature in the early 1920s. Even though he died a decade before America entered the First World War, Dunbar in a number of ways anticipated and was an antecedent to the Harlem Renaissance. Although he resided in Washington during his adult life, he was keenly interested in the emerging black ghetto in New York. He not only used this as the setting of his last novel, but in the years around the turn of the century he also frequented the night spots and social affairs that characterized New York's black bohemia, and he was celebrated as the only black literary figure with New York connections. He was also one of the pioneers who helped establish the popularity of black musicals among white audiences in New York. In 1898 he teamed up with songwriter Will Marion Cook to produce *Clorindy, The Origin of the Cake-Walk*, one of the first black musicals to become a Broadway hit. If he had lived, he would have possessed literary credentials and a range of literary experiences matched only by James Weldon Johnson. [11]

As it stands, Dunbar is interesting more because he was one of the first to confront the problems of being a black writer in America than for his artistic accomplishments or for the answers that he found for the dilemma of his existence. At the time of his death Dunbar himself was far from satisfied with his accomplishments. Dunbar felt the need to defend his literary achievements, especially against the charge that he was either a literary freak or a phenomenon created by William Dean Howells. Dunbar answered these charges by asserting that he had begun writing when he was twelve and that he had supported himself by his literary efforts for three years before Howells intervened.[12] However, Dunbar remained his own harshest critic. As he reported to James Weldon Johnson during his last illness, "I've kept doing the same things, and doing them no better. I have never gotten to the things I really wanted to do."[13] This was an accurate assessment, for there is indeed a sense of incompleteness in Dunbar's work.

Dunbar's contemporary and major rival as the foremost early black writer was Charles W. Chesnutt. Chesnutt, like Dunbar, was born in Ohio, but then grew up in North Carolina before returning to Cleveland when he was twenty-four. Like Dunbar, he was one of the first black writers to publish in a major national magazine, and like Dunbar, he attracted the attention of William Dean Howells. This, however, is where the similarity between the two ends. Whereas Dunbar was principally a poet, Chesnutt earned a substantial salary as a court reporter, and, therefore, unlike Dunbar, never had to rely on his literary income for a living. This situation offered him greater literary freedom and enabled him to emphasize themes that Dunbar tended to avoid. This is seen most clearly by the fact that while Dunbar generally refrained from directly confronting the issues of race and racial injustice in his work, Chesnutt made these problems his major literary concern. Consequently, while Dunbar anticipated the Harlem Renaissance through his New York connections and the setting of his last novel, Chesnutt anticipated it by his uncompromising focus on racial themes.

Chesnutt achieved his first success as a short story writer. After several years of placing short pieces in a variety of magazines, in 1887 he placed his first piece in a major literary magazine when *Atlantic Monthly* accepted "The Goophered Grape Vine"; twelve years later he published two volumes of short stories, both collections differing greatly from anything published by Dunbar or any other black author around the turn of the century.

Chesnutt's first book, *The Conjure Woman*, is fairly complex, though somewhat deceptive in appearance. At first reading it seems to be a simple collection of dialect pieces about black life in the antebellum South written in the tradition of Joel Chandler Harris's "Uncle Remus" stories. Superficially Chesnutt's stories involve an elderly ex-slave narrator, Uncle Julius, who entertained his white employer with tales of the old plantation life. There was, however, no relationship between Chesnutt's vision of the slave South and that portrayed in the plantation tales of Thomas Nelson Page or even Paul Dunbar. Skillfully and subtly Chesnutt wove a delicate pattern of racism and the inhumanity of slavery through his stories. He accomplished this with such delicacy that the reader is often only half aware of it. Avoiding the spectacular but overly stereotyped clash between the cruel master and the rebellious slave, Chesnutt instead realistically captured the true injustice of slavery by illustrating the suffering experienced by good slaves at the hands of well-intentioned and humane masters.

In the story "Po' Sandy," Chesnutt developed this theme by chronicling the tragic fate of the best slave on "Mars Marrobo's" plantation. Sandy was a good worker, so good in fact that Mr. Marrobo's children frequently borrowed him to help out on their plantations. Once while Sandy was away from home, Marrobo sold his wife to a slave trader. Repentant for this, Marrobo gave Sandy a dollar and "'lowed he wuz monst'us sorry fer to break up de fambly, but de spekilater had gin 'im big boot, en times wuz hard en money skaese, en so he wuz bleedst to make de trade."[14] Sandy recovered from his loss and eventually remarried, but he lived in constant fear that he would return one day and find that his new wife had been traded away. His new wife, though, was a conjure woman who used her magic to turn Sandy into a tree so that he could remain on the plantation, but even this rather extreme attempt to find security in slavery ended in tragedy for both Sandy and his wife. Through tales like this one Chesnutt made his point that slavery was degrading and cruel—a point directly counter to his contemporaries' fond reminiscences of the antebellum slave's happy, carefree life.

In his second book of short stories, *The Wife of His Youth and Other Stories of the Color Line*, Chesnutt abandoned the subtlety of *The Conjure Woman* in favor of a more direct attack on prejudice. He also shifted the setting of several of his stories from the South to the urban North and redirected his focus from the relatively noncontroversial issue of slavery to the emotional and highly explosive subjects of racism, intermarriage and miscegenation, the problem of "passing," and color distinctions within the black community itself. While the stories in this collection tended toward melodrama and were not so skillfully written as those in his first volume, Chesnutt openly confronted many of the complex racial problems in America. Also in *The Wife of His Youth* Chesnutt shifted his attention to the rapidly growing number of middle- and upper-class blacks that had emerged in the North and the South after emancipation.

In the three novels that followed, Chesnutt continued to center his attention on the black bourgeoisie. Although these novels were defective in many respects, they are significant because they present the complete development of the author's racial themes. In each of his novels Chesnutt examined a different aspect of the social and psychological trauma that arose from America's racial prejudices. In the first novel, *The House Behind the Cedars* (1900), he focused on the stresses involved in passing and the complications that this act brought to personal relations among people of different races. The heroine of this work was a light-skinned mulatto who, seeking a better life by passing for white, became engaged to an upper-class white man. When her masquerade was exposed, she found herself isolated from both races, a victim of the prejudice of both black and white worlds.

In his second novel, *The Marrow of Tradition* (1901), Chesnutt turned his attention to the problems encountered by former slaves when they attempted to integrate themselves into the mainstream of American life following emancipation. Chesnutt was especially concerned with describing the stubborn and often violent resistance that blacks encountered when they tried to exercise their political rights in the late nineteenth century. The *Marrow of Tradition* was Chesnutt's most ambitious novel and the one for which he had the highest expectations. He hoped that it would be the *Uncle Tom's Cabin* of his day, focusing national attention on the deteriorating racial situation, triggering a moral revolution that would eradicate the evil of racial prejudice and discrimination, elevating its author to a status approaching that of Harriet Beecher Stowe, and, not incidentally, bringing appropriate financial rewards.[15] He based the novel on a bloody race riot that occurred in 1898 in Wilmington, North Carolina, as the culmination of a campaign by a white extremist faction to strip blacks of their political rights. Chesnutt examined both the social and political forces in the white community that culminated in the riot and the alternative approaches, accommodation and militancy, that were open to blacks confronting a hostile white-dominated society. The novel left the dilemma of choosing between these opposing tactics unresolved. Accommodation led to impotence and left blacks entirely at the mercy of whites; militancy, while honorable and courageous, was also suicidal.

The reality that Chesnutt depicted in his second novel did not offer southern blacks much hope. None of the characters succeeded in working out a viable relationship with white society. Those who sought safety in servitude to the white aristocracy found to their dismay that southern aristocracy was clearly dying, and, as that happened, the old paternalistic, protectoral relationship between servant and master was doomed. Even if blacks were willing to surrender their dignity and accept servitude, security still eluded them. On the other hand, those who rejected servitude and instead tried to gain acceptance through education and self-help were equally unsuccessful. One character, Dr. Miller, who espoused the political accommodation and practical education philosophy of Booker T. Washington, was also defenseless against the mob and found that those whites whom he thought were his friends could offer no protection. Although he refused to join the militants who wanted to defend black homes and lives by force, Miller still witnessed the destruction of his hospital and nursing school and had his only son killed by a stray bullet from the mob. Those who stood up to the mob fared even worse. The leader of the militants recognized the impotence and futility of servitude, accommodation, and patience and proclaimed to his followers, "I'd rather be a dead nigger any day than a live dog!"[16] Indeed, that was exactly what happened. Green and most of his followers were slaughtered by the mob.

Chesnutt continued this pessimistic tone in his third and last published novel, *The Colonel's Dream* (1905). Here he examined the ineffectiveness of the efforts of white liberals to upgrade social and economic conditions in the South. Colonel French, the main character in the novel, returned to his home in the South after spending a number of years in the North, where he had acquired a fortune and a number of liberal ideas. His efforts to revive the stagnant economy of his hometown were applauded by the local population until he began attacking racial injustice as well. In the ensuing power struggle, Colonel French saw his dreams shattered, and he retreated in defeat back to the North, leaving conditions in his hometown no better than when he arrived.

The tragedy that Chesnutt depicted in this novel was the inability of either northern liberals or southern aristocrats to stem the tide of racial prejudice that had become an integral part of southern life and politics. Even though, Chesnutt contended, many prominent southerners recognized that racial oppression was unjust, reactionary, and opposed to the best interests of the South, they lacked the courage and the strength to express these views publicly. Chesnutt unhappily concluded that the Civil War and Reconstruction had done nothing to alter the basic racial situation in the South.

In part Chesnutt's growing pessimism reflected his discouragement over his own literary career. Chesnutt, basically conservative in his personal behavior, always placed the financial security of his family ahead of his literary career. For example, even after he began to achieve some success as a short story writer in the late 1880s and early 1890s, he twice turned down offers of "literary" jobs because they did not promise the income that he was receiving from his profitable court reporting business and would jeopardize his family's comfortable middle-class standard of living. However, in 1899, on the basis of the critical success and moderately successful sales record of his two volumes of short stories, Chesnutt shut down his business activities to devote himself full-time to a career as a writer. Chesnutt would measure his literary achievement, not primarily by critical acclaim, but by the commercial success of his work. When the sales of *The Marrow of Tradition* did not approach his expectations, he reopened his court reporting business in early 1902 and returned to writing on a part-time basis. Because critics generally had responded favorably to his work, Chesnutt blamed the failure of his literary career on the refusal of the public to accept books in which the principal characters were black and which were written from a black point of view.[17]

Although Chesnutt lived until 1932, he sharply curtailed his literary activities after the publication of his third novel in 1905. Frustration over the critical and commercial failure of *The Colonel's Dream* and over his inability to find a producer for a four-act play he wrote in 1906 caused him to devote less and less energy to his literary efforts, at least until the Harlem Renaissance popularized black literature in the 1920s. Chesnutt also undoubtedly was frustrated that his efforts to propagandize for racial justice had fallen on deaf ears. But the principal reason that he withdrew from full-time writing was that his books simply did not sell well. Chesnutt was not a great writer; his novels were weak stylistically and his plots tended toward melodrama. Also his subject matter, especially his insistent exposure of racial prejudice, was offensive to the white book-buying public. Back in 1889 George Washington Cable had offered Chesnutt friendly advice. Never forget, he wrote, that your audience is white; remember that you must yield all the ground that you possibly can to the prejudices of your readers.[19] Chesnutt never really took this advice to heart. At the turn of the century, it was the nostalgia of a Thomas Nelson Page that sold books, not the realism of Chesnutt.

Of the two dominant black writers at the turn of the century, Chesnutt and Dunbar, it is clear that while Chesnutt devoted himself more completely to discussing racial issues in his work, Dunbar enjoyed vastly more popular success. Both writers approached their literary careers with different objectives, and neither was satisfied with the type of success that he achieved. Dunbar wanted to be a poet—not a black poet, but a poet judged on the basis of his craft with words, not by his race. He felt constrained by his race, especially the constant demands to produce dialect verse, and he never came to terms with this. His efforts to produce nonracial poetry were not successful, and his need to support himself financially forced him to produce what was in demand—dialect poetry. Chesnutt, on the other hand, never sought to free himself from the constraints of race. He never sought art for art's sake. Instead, from the moment he first contemplated a literary career, Chesnutt was determined to use literature primarily to address racial problems. In May 1880 Chesnutt outlined his literary objectives, stating that the purpose of his writing would be to effect a moral revolution in the attitudes of whites toward race and to change society by altering racial attitudes through literary works which subtly and gradually accustomed the public to the idea of racial equality.[19] Chesnutt's frustration came when his work did not attract sufficient readership to bring about the desired social revolution, and when he discovered that racially oriented books apparently were incompatible with financial success.

Chesnutt did portray realistically and honestly the racial situation as he saw it, and while he failed to achieve the objectives that he set for himself, he did touch on many of the themes that a quarter of a century later would characterize the literature of the Harlem Renaissance, and he confronted the issue of the political and social responsibility of black literature in a society where prejudice and racial discrimination prevailed. However, his work was never well known by whites or blacks. Dunbar, although sharply criticized by young black writers during the 1920s for avoiding racial themes and for reinforcing racial stereotypes with his dialect poetry, nevertheless addressed one issue of fundamental importance to many Renaissance writers—the freedom of black writers to choose their own subject matter and artistic style and not to be constrained by demands that they be racial poets. Dunbar, despite the criticism of the generation of black writers that followed, achieved considerable recognition and fame. By World War I his name, along with that of Booker T. Washington and Frederick Douglass, was one of the best known and most admired in the black community. Chesnutt had no imitators, but every black college contained aspiring young poets who wrote in the style of Dunbar. For at least a decade following his death Dunbar's ghost dominated black poetry. Even a figure as imposing as James Weldon Johnson, who would later reject dialect poetry as the best means of expressing the black experience, wrote many early pieces in the Dunbar tradition.[20]

Besides Dunbar and Chesnutt there were several other black writers who, while exhibiting significantly less talent than either of the Ohioans, nevertheless achieved some literary success before the Harlem Renaissance. They are interesting in spite of the overall poor quality of their writing, if only because their choice of subject matter and theme illustrates so clearly the derivative and unsophisticated nature of most black literature at the turn of the century and contrasts so greatly with the work of the Renaissance writers and poets. These writers generally attempted to produce dialect poetry that did not challenge either the plantation tradition or the accommodationist values of conservative black leadership. James Edwin Campbell's lone volume of poetry, *Echoes from the Cabin and Elsewhere* (1895), utilized dialect in an attempt to capture the southern black folk tradition, but failed both to match Dunbar's skill as a dialect poet and, more seriously, to avoid the stereotypes common to the minstrel stage. While it is possible to detect in Campbell's work antecedents to Langston Hughes's interest in black dance and musical rhythms, and the fascination of several Renaissance writers in black folkways, his failure to rid his work of outdated stereotypes and his inability to breathe any life into his version of black dialect limited the interest that Renaissance writers had in his work and prevented him from exerting any real influence on later black literature.[21]

The work of other would-be black dialect poets in the two decades preceding the Harlem Renaissance suffered from even greater flaws. Daniel Webster Davis's *'Weh Down Souf and Other Poems* (1897) consisted of undistinguished dialect poetry that depicted slavery as a blessing in disguise and asserted the Americanness of blacks while relying on overused and racially biased stereotypes such as the black man's love of watermelons. John Wesley Holloway's work reflected that of Dunbar, but demonstrated none of the latter's talent. His dialect verse was a pale imitation of Dunbar's, relying far too heavily on minstrel humor, while his standard English verse, which was his real interest, unfortunately displayed no literary merit. Both Joseph S. Cotter and Waverly T. Carmichael exhibited similar problems in their work. Carmichael's dialect verse is especially stilted, while Cotter's avid espousal of Booker T. Washington's politics of accommodation isolated him almost completely from later black writers. Raymond Dandridge did eliminate many of the minstrel stereotypes from his work, but his determination to present blacks only in a positive light made his work overly moralistic and unrealistic. However, he did occasionally capture some of the spirit of black life that would later be found in the Renaissance; his poem "Zalka Peetruza" expressed much of the same emotion as Claude McKay's "Harlem Dancer."[22]

The ability of minor black writers of limited talent to get their work published in the years preceding the Harlem Renaissance should not be misinterpreted. It certainly did not reflect the difficulties that most black writers experienced in attempting to get their work published, nor did it reflect the caution, and even the reluctance, with which most commercial presses approached the issue of publishing work by black authors. With the exception of Chesnutt and Dunbar, none of the writers discussed in this chapter were published by major or even minor commercial presses. Dandridge published his own work, while the others subsidized the publication of their work, used vanity presses, or used local or even black-owned publishing houses. None of them had the resources to adequately promote or distribute the books; at best, distribution was limited to advertisements which the publisher or the author placed in black newspapers or periodicals. Major publishing houses were willing to publish work by blacks if it was of reasonably high quality and if they thought that it would sell. Both Dunbar and Chesnutt found commercial publishers for their work. But it took Chesnutt five years from the time that he first approached Houghton Mifflin to produce a manuscript that the company was willing to risk publishing. After the relative success of his first collection of short stories, Chesnutt found it easy to get his second short story book and his first novel published. However, the failure of his first two novels to achieve commercial success cooled Houghton Mifflin's enthusiasm for black literature, and they rejected Chesnutt's third novel; Doubleday published it, but this would be Chesnutt's last publication by a major press.[23]

In addition to the black writers that have been cited already as planting the literary roots of the Harlem Renaissance, there were several others who made a slight name for themselves in literature before the 1920s.

James Weldon Johnson, besides serving in the American foreign service and with the NAACP, wrote a novel and several volumes of poetry (including some verse modeled on Dunbar's dialect pieces), and he collaborated with his brother on numerous songs and black musicals. Next to Dunbar he was the most widely known black literary figure before the Renaissance. However, his principal influence on black literature was not found in his poetry or his novel but in the fact that he emerged in the 1920s as one of the two or three leading figures who promoted the Harlem Renaissance, influenced the younger black writers of the 1920s, and helped them find an audience. W.E.B. Du Bois, without question the best-known black American following the death of Booker T. Washington, also included literature among his many accomplishments. During the first two decades of the twentieth century, he wrote poetry and several novels, but, like Johnson, his principal influence on the Harlem Renaissance would not be as a writer. Finally, William Stanley Braithwaite had established himself as a poet, literary scholar, and free-lance literary critic for the Boston *Transcript* well before the Harlem Renaissance began. Braithwaite's poetry was so far removed from the black experience in terms of both style and subject matter that few people were aware of his race. He never became actively involved in the Renaissance; instead, he remained outside and was more of a friendly critic of black literature than a participant.

Black literature before the Harlem Renaissance cannot be considered very successful. The two most accomplished black writers, Dunbar and Chesnutt, were silent after 1906; neither considered himself a literary success. A handful of other black writers occasionally managed to get their material in print, but their work could not be viewed as successful by any measure. Certainly they were not part of any kind of literary movement. Finally, there were several prominent blacks who dabbled in literature before the 1920s. Their ultimate importance to the Harlem Renaissance would be as critics and promoters rather than as writers. In short, while the Renaissance would not emerge from a total literary vacuum, neither would it build on a well-established black literary tradition. The Harlem Renaissance would represent more accurately the birth of black literature than its rebirth.

4   The Emergence of the Renaissance in Black Literature

The first stirrings of black literary activity that would foreshadow the Harlem Renaissance were evident in the years immediately before and shortly after World War I. During this period several black writers began publishing work that differed significantly from either the Chesnutt or the Dunbar traditions in black literature. These writers came from extremely diverse backgrounds and worked independently of one another in widely scattered areas of the country. Like Chesnutt and Dunbar, they published their initial work primarily in white magazines, and their initial literary contacts were generally with white writers and editors. They were not yet part of a literary movement, but their experiences and the direction that they took in their art served as an important prelude to the Harlem Renaissance. And, in the mid-1920s most of these writers, together with other young blacks, would meet in Harlem and be proclaimed as the founders of the new black literary movement.

The first of the new writers to publish was James Weldon Johnson. Johnson is especially important because, more than any other writer, he was a transitional figure whose early work was in the Dunbar tradition but who later became a significant poet and critic of the Renaissance. Chronologically Johnson, who was born in 1871, belonged to the generation of Dunbar and Chesnutt, and his first published work, a dialect piece patterned after Dunbar's popular poetry, was accepted in 1899 by *Century* magazine. By 1901, however, Johnson recognized the limitations of the Dunbar mold and began to pattern his verse on the free-verse model of Whitman's *Leaves of Grass*.[1]

James Weldon Johnson was born in 1871 in Jacksonville, Florida. His father was the headwaiter at one of the town's resort hotels, while his mother taught at Stanton School, the town's largest and best black grammar school. Johnson and his brother enjoyed a comfortable middle-class childhood; they were well fed and well clothed, and they lived in a nice house with intelligent parents who surrounded their children with books and good music. Johnson received his education at Stanton School and at Atlanta University's preparatory school and college. When he graduated in 1894, he returned to Jacksonville and assumed the prestigious position of principal of Stanton School. Johnson was not satisfied, however. While fulfilling his duties as principal, he attempted to publish a newspaper, and when this project failed he began to study law in the offices of Thomas Ledwith, a prominent white attorney. In 1898 he became the first black to be admitted to the bar in Duval County, Florida.[2]

Johnson began his literary career relatively late in life and with the caution and conservatism that characterized most of his endeavors. By 1897 Johnson had established himself securely in his hometown as a lawyer and an educator. That spring his brother, Rosamond, set to music several of the poems that Johnson had written in his spare time, and the two quickly achieved local success as songwriters. In the summer of 1899 they went to New York, hoping to further their musical careers. For the next three years Johnson spent his summers in New York collaborating with his brother and Bob Cole in writing songs for Broadway musicals, returning to Jacksonville every fall in time for the school term. During this period Johnson wrote the lyrics to a number of popular songs, including "Lift Every Voice and Sing," which became the unofficial black national anthem. Finally, after much hesitation and with many reservations, Johnson quit his teaching job and committed himself to a fulltime career as a songwriter.[3]

During the first decade of the twentieth century the area around 53rd Street became a center for black actors, prizefighters, and show people in New York. For the first time black performers and acting companies were being booked in first-class New York theaters. Most of this was in vaudeville, where black casts replaced black-faced ones and performed the minstrel show songs and dances to delighted white audiences. It was this scene that James Weldon Johnson, his brother Rosamond Johnson, and

Bob Cole broke into as successful songwriters and vaudeville performers, following in the footsteps of other black writing teams such as Dunbar and Cook. Even though his career gamble paid off economically, Johnson soon became discontented with this work for several reasons. First, although he collaborated with his partners in writing songs and skits, Cole and Rosemond were the performers, and James did not enjoy following them around the country as the business manager for their act. More important, Johnson quickly became disenchanted with writing strictly for Broadway. While in New York, he began graduate studies in English and drama at Columbia University and became interested in producing literary works more serious than songs or musicals. While at Columbia, he began work on his novel, *The Autobiography of an Ex-Colored Man.*[4]

During this period Johnson also began to dabble in politics, a decision that would have a significant impact on his career. As the result of his political interests, Johnson formed a friendship with Charles W. Anderson, a prominent associate of Booker T. Washington, who was New York City's most influential black politician and whom Theodore Roosevelt had named Collector of Internal Revenue for the city's financial district. By 1904 Johnson had become an officer in Anderson's Colored Republican Club, and through Anderson he had met Booker T. Washington. Washington was attracted to Johnson both because of his success as a songwriter and because of his political association with Anderson. In 1904 he invited Johnson, as a financially successful musician, to participate in the National Negro Business League. Johnson's association with the Tuskegeean came at a crucial time, when the black community was becoming politically divided and many young blacks were moving toward the more militant political philosophy of W.E.B. Du Bois. For Johnson, though, in 1904 Washington, not Du Bois, was the best model for the successful black. In 1907 Washington and Anderson used their patronage to reward this loyalty and persuaded Roosevelt to offer their protégé a position with the consular service. Again, with much hesitation and trepidation, Johnson made a career change. He dissolved the musical partnership and accepted a position in the Foreign Service as United States Consul at Puerto Cabello, Venezuela.[5]

During his seven years with the State Department, first in Venezuela and then in Nicaragua, Johnson began his serious writing. Like Dunbar and Chesnutt, Johnson's literary contacts were white editors and white magazines. While he was still at Columbia his friend and professor, Brander Mathews, introduced him to Harry Thurston Peck, who was the editor of *Bookman* and who accepted several of Johnson's poems for publication; and, before he left New York, Johnson established contact with the editors of *Century* magazine and the *Independent*. Johnson then used his spare time, which was plentiful in his consular position, to write, and his poems began appearing regularly in these magazines. His most important accomplishment during this period was the novel *The Autobiography of an Ex-Colored Man*, which Johnson published in 1912.[6]

The Autobiography of an Ex-Colored Man was the best novel written by a black before the Harlem Renaissance, and it is an important transitional piece between pre-Renaissance and Renaissance literature. The novel described the life of a light-skinned black and his attempts to live first as a black and then as a white man. Like Chesnutt, Johnson was especially interested in exposing the race problem, but he went far beyond this and endeavored to uncover and explain what it meant, both physically and psychologically, to be black in America. The racial prejudices of white society were important to Johnson, but of even greater significance was the attempt of blacks to come to terms with their blackness. In the novel Johnson's hero successfully overcame the racial prejudice of American society by passing for white. However, this victory was a shallow one, and Johnson clearly indicated that the freedom gained by being white did not offset the psychological damage resulting from passing.

The significance of the *Autobiography* was that in it Johnson began the process of turning inward which characterized black literature during the 1920s. The major problem that confronted blacks was no longer how to deal with prejudice but how to achieve racial identity; the major task of black writers was not to expose racial injustice but to uncover, describe, and possibly explain the life of American blacks. Johnson also pioneered the use of urban local color in black literature. Before the 1920s most black writers avoided detailed and realistic descriptions of the colorful life of lower-class urban blacks because they believed that depicting the squalor and vice of ghetto neighborhoods would only reinforce negative racial stereotypes. They usually described blacks in middle-class settings and emphasized the similarities between white and black society. Chesnutt was especially guilty of this. Dunbar though, in *The Sport of the Gods*, was the first to seriously attempt ghetto realism in American literature. In his novel Johnson expanded on this, with vivid descriptions of black life in the rural South and among the black actors and musicians of New York's 53rd Street district.

Johnson published *The Autobiography of an Ex-Colored Man* anonymously in 1912. Despite the quality of the work and the assistance of his friend, Professor Mathews of Columbia, Johnson had a very difficult time convincing a publisher to accept the work. Finally he arranged to have it printed in Boston by what he termed "one of those quasi publishing companies who are in fact only job printers for authors." The novel received little publicity and did not sell well until it was rescued from oblivion during the Renaissance. As Johnson himself observed, the novel suffered because it was written before its time.[7] The problems that Johnson faced in getting his novel accepted in 1912 were similar to those experienced by other black writers of that period but contrasted sharply with the seemingly insatiable appetite of the public for books by black authors only fifteen years later.

The same year that Johnson published his novel a young Jamaican, Claude McKay, published *Songs of Jamaica* and *Constab Ballads*, two collections of dialect poetry about life in rural and urban Jamaica. Following this early literary success in Jamaica, McKay came to the United States with a scholarship to study agriculture and with hopes of finding a larger audience for his poetry.

McKay was born in 1890 in a two-room, thatched-roof, frame house in the hilly midlands of Jamaica. However, McKay's early life was not that of a typical Jamaican peasant. His parents were relatively prosperous property owners who were literate, upwardly mobile, and occupied a position of considerable status in their community. McKay, the youngest of eleven children, went to live with his brother, Uriah Theodore McKay, when he was about seven. McKay spent his adolescence in the mountain villages where his brother taught school, and under his brother's guidance he read all the books he could find. By the age of fourteen he had become a confirmed "free thinker" and had begun writing poetry. Also during this period he met Walter Jekyll, an English folklorist, who became his literary and intellectual mentor. Jekyll directed the young McKay's reading, encouraged him to write dialect poetry of Jamaican peasant life, and promoted his literary career; Jekyll also may have introduced McKay to homosexuality, which would remain the Jamaican poet's sexual preference throughout his life.[8] By the time he was twenty-two McKay had achieved considerable success in his homeland as a poet. *Songs of Jamaica* and *Constab Ballads* were very popular in his homeland and earned him the title of "Jamaica's Bobbie Burns." In recognition of his accomplishments he received the medal of the Jamaican Institute of Arts and Sciences.[9]

Not really content to be Jamaica's greatest poet and desiring more widespread recognition, in 1912 McKay accepted an offer to continue his education in the United States. He chose Tuskegee for his studies because of his admiration for Booker T. Washington and his ambition to study agriculture. McKay never fit into Tuskegee's highly structured and disciplined program, so in October of his first semester, despite his continued respect for Washington, he transferred to Kansas State University. There, in addition to his courses in agronomy, he discovered W. E. B. Du Bois's *The Souls of Black Folk*, which he reported "shook me like an earthquake," and he became a member of a student socialist organization. After two years in Kansas he abandoned his ambition to study agronomy and moved to New York, where he married his Jamaican sweetheart, briefly operated a restaurant, and resumed his literary career.[10]

McKay's life in New York was not very successful, at least not at first. The restaurant that he opened in the Tenderloin district soon went bankrupt; after six months of marriage his wife, pregnant with what would be his only child, returned to Jamaica. During the next three years McKay held a variety of jobs, ranging from being a dishwasher in a boarding house to waiting tables in dining cars. Usually he worked just long enough to pay his bills and save enough to support his writing for several weeks. He had some difficulty getting material published. He submitted several poems to critic William Stanley Braithwaite in 1916 and sought his advice and criticism. However, most of his contacts during this period were with the handful of white editors and critics who were willing to consider material by black writers. He sent material to Oswald Villard, publisher of the *Nation*, but had no luck. Joel Spingarn was more helpful. In 1917 he helped McKay get two poems, "Invocation" and "Harlem Dancer," published in Joel Oppenheim and Waldo Frank's avant garde literary magazine, *Seven Arts*. McKay then met and became friends with Frank Harris, who published several of his poems in *Pearson's*. McKay's real break during this period came when Crystal and Max Eastman, publishers of the left-wing magazine *The Liberator*, befriended him. In Max Eastman, McKay found a mentor to replace Jekyll, who not only published his poems but also shared his political views.[11]

During this period McKay's poetry underwent transformation. He stopped writing dialect poetry and indicated in his correspondence with Braithwaite his intention to seek recognition as a poet, not just a black poet. In this vein he wrote a number of fairly formal and sentimental pieces about Jamaica and his longings for his homeland, a number of which appeared in *Spring in New Hampshire*, which he published in 1920 while he was in England. However, his strongest work explored his feelings as a black in a white-dominated world, and he would soon abandon his efforts to avoid racial themes. Some of this racially oriented work, such as "To the White Fiends," was essentially protest poetry written fairly skillfully and usually in a very tight and formal style. In other pieces, like "Harlem Shadows" and especially "The Harlem Dancer," McKay began exploring the spirit and pathos of black ghetto life:

> Applauding youths laughed with young prostitutes
> And watched her perfect, half-clothed body sway;
> Her voice was like the sound of blended flutes
> Blown by black players upon a picnic day.
> She sang and danced on gracefully and calm,
> The light gauze hanging loose about her form;
> To me she seemed a proudly swaying palm
> Grown lovelier for passing through a storm.
> Upon her swarthy neck black shiny curls
> Luxuriant fell; and tossing coins in praise,
> The wine-flushed, bold-eyed boys, and even the girls
> Devoured her shape with eager, passionate gaze
> But looking at her falsely-smiling face,
> I knew her self was not in that strange place.[12]

In 1917 McKay began publishing his poetry regularly, not in black periodicals but in white journals like *Seven Arts*, *Pearson's*, and *The Liberator*, and in 1922 Harcourt, Brace published his first American collection, *Harlem Shadows*.

During the period from 1918, when he met Frank Harris and the Eastmans, to 1922, when he left the United States for an extended stay in the Soviet Union, France, and North Africa, McKay was self-consciously a black poet, but most of his associations were with the black working class and the white left-wing intellectuals of Greenwich Village, not with Harlem's black middle class or emerging literary community. Although he had some contact with James Weldon Johnson and W. E. B. Du Bois, his closest intellectual association was with Max and Crystal Eastman, and for a time in 1921 and 1922 he supported himself by working as an associate editor of *The Liberator*. Ironically, one of his most militant sonnets, "To the White Fiends," was published in *Pearson's* after Du Bois earlier had rejected it for *Crisis*. [13]

McKay achieved his fame as a black poet in New York in the years immediately before the Harlem Renaissance, before there was any recognized black literary movement. His radical politics and self-consciously working-class orientation, plus the fact that he was a West Indian, not an American, made him comfortable with the black proletariat of Harlem and the white socialists at *The Liberator* but tended to isolate him from the black intelligentsia, whom he felt were too bourgeois for his taste. When he left New York late in 1922, there was not yet a black bohemia of writers and artists in Harlem to keep him in the city. In fact, as McKay observed, the city lost its appeal to him in direct proportion to the spread of his literary reputation:

> And now that I was legging limpingly along with the intellectual gang, Harlem for me did not hold quite the same thrill and glamour as before. Where formerly in saloons and cabarets and along the streets I received impressions like arrows piercing my nerves and distilled poetry from them, now I was often pointed out as an author. I lost the rare feeling of a vagabond feeding upon secret music singing in me. [14]

So McKay left Harlem before the Renaissance really began. By 1922, however, his poetry already embodied the spirit of the Harlem Renaissance. McKay was a self-proclaimed militant who consciously identified with the black masses, and he reflected both of these traits in his poetry. He protested against racial injustice and responded bitterly and angrily to the race riots of 1919 with "If We Must Die." He also looked deeply into the street life of Harlem and attempted to express the joys and sorrows of the everyday black life. This combination of militancy and introspection was central to the literature of the Renaissance. And, however alienated from Harlem's black intelligentsia McKay might have felt, they saw him as the finest young black poet of the early 1920s. As James Weldon Johnson proclaimed in 1924, of the young poets, "McKay shows the greatest range of imagination, the richest resources of material and the highest perfection of technique. He possesses both power and delicacy. He is both an Aframerican poet and a cosmic poet." [15]

While Claude McKay was involved with the socialist crowd at *The Liberator*, another young poet arrived in New York. Nineteen-year-old Langston Hughes had already published a poem, "The Negro Speaks of Rivers," in *Crisis* when he arrived in New York in the fall of 1921 to enroll at Columbia University.

Hughes was born in 1902 in Joplin, Kansas, and grew up in what can only be described as an impoverished but middle-class existence. Three figures—his father, his mother, and his maternal grandmother—exerted a major influence on his childhood and provided him with the intellectual stimulation of a middle-class home even though their economic situation was neither stable nor comfortable. Hughes's father, James Nathaniel Hughes, was an extremely bitter man contemptuous of blacks and all poor people. When discrimination prevented him from taking the bar exam in Oklahoma, he left the United States and his family and settled in Mexico, where he pursued a very successful career as a lawyer, rancher, and mine owner. Hughes's mother also spent much of her life in a battle against prejudice. She was well educated, having attended the University of Kansas, and she wrote poetry and participated in the literary affairs of Topeka. She also successfully resisted the attempt of the Topeka school system to place her son in segregated classes. However, her influence on her son was limited because she spent much of her time traveling in a fruitless search for a decent job. [16]

Hughes's grandmother, Mary Sampson Langston, exerted the greatest influence during his early years. For five years, beginning when he was seven, she provided a relatively stable home life. Except for occasional visits from his mother and one short stay with his father in Mexico, Hughes spent these years in Lawrence, Kansas, a few blocks from the University, under the strict control of his grandmother. Mary Sampson Langston was a powerful woman. Although she was stern, she left a deep impression on her grandson with her stories of slavery and the struggle for freedom. She had been born free in antebellum North Carolina and had attended Oberlin College. Her first husband, Lewis Leary, had participated in John Brown's raid on Harper's Ferry, leaving his widow a blood-soaked, bullet-riddled shawl as a memento of the adventure. Her second husband, Charles Langston, was a black abolitionist and active agent in the underground railroad. In spite of the poverty and instability of his life, the years Hughes spent with his grandmother were very enriching, and he enjoyed a stimulating childhood. His grandmother's stories excited his imagination and encouraged him to look more deeply into his past. In books he discovered an even more exciting world, and he made the public library his second home. The library became a welcome sanctuary from the strict rule of his grandmother's house, and a bastion of stability in an otherwise unstable life; there he found relief from the drab Kansas poverty in books, where "if people suffered, they suffered in beautiful language, not in monosyllables, as we did in Kansas."[17]

When Hughes was fifteen his grandmother died. For a few months he continued to live in Kansas with friends, but he soon moved, first to Lincoln, Illinois, and then to Cleveland, where he lived with his mother and stepfather. In Cleveland he attended high school and began writing poetry for the school literary magazine. Also, between his junior and senior years he endured what he later recalled as a traumatic reunion with his father. After a summer with his father in Mexico he concluded that James Hughes was interested only in making money, that he despised all blacks and Mexicans because he believed them all to be ignorant, backward, and lazy, and that he hated his family for remaining in the United States where they could be nothing but servants. Before he returned to Cleveland to finish high school, Langston Hughes decided that he hated his father.[18]

Hughes graduated from high school in 1920 and then returned to Mexico in hopes of convincing his father to send him to college. James Hughes scoffed at his son's ambition to become a writer, and refused to give him a penny to go to school in the United States. However, he offered to send him to college in Germany or Switzerland if he would study engineering and then return to Mexico and help manage the mines. This argument over education was never completely resolved. Hughes remained in Mexico for a year, teaching English to wealthy families and saving his money. Finally in a compromise with his father he decided to go to Columbia—but mainly because he wanted to be near Harlem and see the black musical *Shuffle Along*, which was then at the height of its popularity. In the late summer of 1921, Hughes left Mexico and enrolled at Columbia, not to study engineering but with the ambition of immersing himself in Harlem and trying to become a writer.[19]

Hughes did not get along well at Columbia. He quit after one unhappy year, and then worked at several odd jobs until he sailed for Africa as a mess boy on a freighter. During his brief stay in New York Hughes published a number of his poems in *Crisis*. Although his work attracted the attention of several prominent blacks, including W.E.B. Du Bois and Alain Locke, Hughes purposely avoided contact with them (primarily because he was shy) and isolated himself from contact with black intellectuals.[20]

Early in 1923 Hughes left New York and spent most of the next two years working on board ship or in Paris and Genoa. While in Europe he continued to publish material regularly in *Crisis* and corresponded with black poet and editor Countee Cullen, but otherwise Hughes had little contact with other black writers. In fact, when he returned to America in 1925 he settled with relatives in Washington rather than in New York, and he was still living in Washington when he received popular recognition and publicity as the "bus-boy poet," and, more important, won *Opportunity* magazine's annual poetry prize with "The Weary Blues." Even before Hughes returned from Europe, James Weldon Johnson counted him among the most promising young black poets on the basis of the material that he had published in *Crisis*.[21]

Like McKay, Hughes identified with the black lower classes and attempted to give voice to this class in his poetry. Hughes found the most basic expression of the black spirit in music, especially the blues and jazz, and attempted to capture this spirit, both in content and form, in his verse. "The Weary Blues" was one of the earliest and most successful examples of Hughes's experimentation with the blues as a pattern for his poetry.

> Droning a drowsy syncopated tune,
> Rocking back and forth to a mellow croon,
>   I heard a Negro play.
> Down on Lenox Avenue the other night
> By the pale dull pallor of an old gas light
>   He did a lazy sway. . .
>   He did a lazy sway. . .
> To the tune o'thost Weary Blues.
> .   .   .   .
>
> In a deep song voice with a melancholy tone
> I heard that Negro sing, that old piano moan——
>   "Ain't got nobody in all this world
>   Ain't got nobody but ma self.
>   I's gwine to quit ma frownin'
>   And put ma troubles on the shelf."
> Thump, thump, thump went his foot on the floor.

He played a few chords then he sang some more——
    "I got the Weary Blues
    And I can't be satisfied.
    Got the Weary Blues
    And can't be satisfied——
    I ain't happy no mo'
    And I wish that I had died."[22]

Like McKay, Hughes found subject material for his art in the streets and cabarets of Harlem. Also like McKay, as well as other poets of the Harlem Renaissance, Hughes used his art to search for the roots of the black experience. But, unlike the Jamaican poet, Hughes was far more innovative and experimental in terms of the style and form of his poetry.

Hughes also differed from McKay in another respect. Unlike the Jamaican, whose initial literary contacts were mainly with white magazines and white critics, Hughes's early poetry was published in *Crisis* and other black magazines, and his contacts were with the black intellectual community. Indeed, Langston Hughes was the first Renaissance writer to be discovered and promoted (initially, at least) by the black literary establishment that was emerging in New York in the early 1920s.

By far the most talented and promising black writer to surface in the early 1920s was Jean Toomer, whose experimental novel *Cane* created a sensation among black writers when it appeared early in 1923. *Cane* was a loosely connected series of sketches, poems, and vignettes that explored the black experience, first in the rural South and then in the urban North. *Cane*, together with McKay's *Harlem Shadows* which was published only a few months earlier, were the first full-length literary publications of the still-to-be-born Harlem Renaissance. *Cane* had a tremendous impact on the young black artists who read it. Langston Hughes, Countee Cullen, Zora Neale Hurston, Rudolph Fisher, and Wallace Thurman, who together made up the core of the young writers who launched the Renaissance, were just beginning their careers when they encountered *Cane*; all were deeply affected by it. Countee Cullen, whose first collection of poetry did not appear until 1925, praised *Cane* as "a real race contribution, a classic portrayal of things as they are." For most young black writers and would-be writers *Cane* was an incentive and a challenge which stimulated their literary ambitions.[23]

Jean Toomer was born in 1894 in Washington, D.C. He spent most of his childhood in a household dominated by his powerful grandfather, P.B.S. Pinchback, the former lieutenant governor of Reconstruction Louisiana. After the collapse of the Republican government in Louisiana, Pinchback had moved to the nation's capital, where for a time he held good government jobs and moved in the highest social circles. As time passed and his influence declined, the proud aristocrat became more and more of a tyrant in his household, which by that time included his daughter, Nina, and his grandson, Jean, as well as his wife and his unmarried son, Bismark. Jean Toomer's father had deserted his wife a few months after their son was born, and his mother died during a short and unhappy second marriage when Jean was fourteen. For all practical purposes Jean Toomer was reared by his grandparents.

Toomer's early life in Washington was hardly typical. At first he lived in a fine home in an all-white neighborhood (but attended the colored school); then, when his grandfather's fortunes declined, the family moved to a more modest dwelling in a black section of the city. This shift from a white world to a black one may explain Toomer's later ambivalent stance on the question of his race. As he recalled in 1922, "I have lived equally amid the two race groups. Now white, now colored." At first Toomer enjoyed the color and gaiety of his new life in the ghetto, but by the time he was a teenager, and especially following the death of his mother, he began to rebel. He got into minor scrapes in school and the neighborhood. Nevertheless, he graduated from high school and began college, intending to study agriculture.[24]

After he graduated from high school in 1914, Toomer began a lengthy period of wandering and soul-searching that included brief stays at the University of Wisconsin, Massachusetts College of Agriculture, a physical training college in Chicago, and the University of Chicago. For the most part he drifted without any real direction, unsure of what he wanted from life, dropping out of one college after another; in turn he became a socialist, a student of sociology at New York University, and a student of history and then psychology at the City College of New York. After being rejected for the draft, he tried his hand at a series of odd jobs. He sold cars in Chicago, taught physical education and lectured on politics and philosophy in Milwaukee and Chicago, and worked for ten days in a New Jersey shipyard. This lack of direction and inability to commit himself to any course of action was more than the indecisiveness of youth—it would characterize Toomer's behavior throughout his life. The most significant development during this period was that Toomer began reading, lecturing, and writing.[25]

In 1920 he returned to Washington, a failure, to face the disappointment of his grandfather. Feeling bitter and rejected, Toomer embraced literature in the first of a life-long series of largely unsuccessful attempts to find himself. As he recalled in one of his unpublished autobiographies:

> Though I was living at the time much to myself in out of the way Washington, something of the literary renaissance that centered in New York and Chicago touched and kindled me, and my interest in the literature of that day became absorbing. Now I felt that creative writing might be my means, my way. For I felt that I too had something to say about America. Besides, it seemed to me that writing was the only means whereby I could make good use of my varied experiences, giving value to much that otherwise would be wasted. By writing I thought I might build myself into the man I wanted to be.
>
> The decision was made. I wrote—that is, I tried to write. Day and night I did hardly anything else. Never before had I dedicated myself so thoroughly, in fact so desperately to any work—and it was more difficult than I had imagined.[26]

In 1921 Toomer took a temporary break from writing and accepted a position as substitute principal at the all-black Sparta (Georgia) Agricultural and Industrial Institute. This brief foray into the South had a tremendous impact on Toomer and stimulated him for a time to embrace the black side of his heritage. As he wrote to his close friend Waldo Frank, "there for the first time I really saw the Negro, not as a ps[eu]do-urbanized and vulgarized, a semi-Americanized product, but the Negro peasant, strong with the tang of fields and soil. It was there that I first heard the folk-songs rolling up the valley at twilight, heard them as spontaneous and native utterances. They filled me with gold, and hints of an eternal purple." While Toomer did not subscribe to "plantation school," he undoubtedly romanticized the South and the black folk spirit that he perceived there. However unrealistic his view of the black South was, it did provide him with the material and much of the inspiration for his one period of literary productivity.[27]

For about two years, during 1921 and 1922, Toomer actively pursued his literary career—and to a large degree he did so as a black writer. His brief exposure to the South triggered a passionate interest in his black heritage. In 1922 he returned to the South with writer Waldo Frank. The two young men spent a week in Spartenburg, South Carolina, where Toomer guided his white friend through the world of southern blacks—a world that Toomer had experienced only during his two months in Georgia the previous fall. Nevertheless, Toomer again found the black South invigorating, and he would use his experiences there as the basis for much of his writing.

Toomer also established contacts during this period with the central figure in Washington's black intellectual and literary community, Alain Locke of Howard University, and other blacks who later would be involved in the Harlem Renaissance. Locke was especially helpful. He introduced Toomer to other young black poets, including Countee Cullen, and helped arrange for *Crisis* to publish "Song of the Son," Toomer's first piece of work that appeared in a major magazine. Toomer also corresponded with Claude McKay, who placed several of his southern pieces in *The Liberator* in late 1922.[28]

Despite these connections with black writers and critics, and the fact that in his writing he self-consciously embraced his blackness, Toomer never moved into the mainstream of the black literary Renaissance. Instead, he found his closest friends, his principal literary contacts, and his literary philosophy and style principally among the white writers, editors, and critics of Greenwich Village, and to a lesser degree with small southern literary magazines. Waldo Frank was his best friend during this period. Throughout 1921 and 1922 the two corresponded regularly, critiqued each other's manuscripts, and shared a vision of a new American literary aesthetic. After Toomer introduced his friend to the black South, Frank reciprocated, introducing him to the Greenwich Village literary scene. The contacts that Toomer made there included poet Hart Crane, editor Gorham Munson, and a bit later photographer Alfred Stieglitz and artist Georgia O'Keeffe. Toomer's efforts to find a southern outlet for his writing led him to John McClure, editor of *Double Dealer*, who published several of his manuscripts and also put him in contact with northern literary magazines like *Dial* and *Broom*, which could handle material with racial content that might be offensive to *Double Dealer*'s southern patrons, and introduced him to Sherwood Anderson and several other white writers.[29]

These were the literary contacts that had the major influence on Toomer's work. From his Greenwich Village associates, especially Waldo

Frank, Toomer's literary aesthetic evolved. He became involved in Frank's efforts to redefine American culture by focusing on the "buried cultures"—the American Indians for Frank and southern blacks for Toomer—and adopted Frank's vision of art as a spiritual force which motivated people and defined the symbols that give life meaning. He evolved his literary style, which was reflected in the unorthodox structure of *Cane*, from the experimental literature of Crane, Frank, and, most important Sherwood Anderson's *Winesburg, Ohio*.[30]

The culmination of Toomer's literary activities was the publication of his experimental novel, *Cane*, by Lippincott in September 1923. Waldo Frank wrote the introduction and helped Toomer find his publisher. The book was well received, with generally favorable reviews among white literary critics. Allen Tate, who reviewed the book in the Nashville *Tennessean* and personally wrote Toomer about the book, was especially impressed with *Cane*'s innovative style and its realistic portrayal of the South.[31] Black critics were even more enthusiastic in their praise for their new black literary star. Alain Locke praised Toomer for possessing both the feelings and the technique of a poet, congratulated him for the novel's publication, and offered to help promote the book by writing a favorable review. William Stanley Braithwaite, the most respected black critic of the pre-Renaissance period, was even more unrestrained in his praise:

> In Jean Toomer . . . we come upon the very first artist of the race, who with all an artist's passion and sympathy for life, its hurts, its sympathies, its desires, its joys, its defeats and strange yearnings, can write about the Negro without the surrender or compromise of the artist's vision. . . . *Cane* is a book of gold and bronze, of dusk and flame, of ecstasy and pain, and Jean Toomer is a bright morning star of a new day of the race in literature.[32]

Despite the positive reception of *Cane* by white critics, the book did not sell well; despite the enthusiastic reception of both *Cane* and its author by the black community, Toomer, even more than Claude McKay, remained detached from the emerging black literary world. Nevertheless, Toomer had a significant impact on the Harlem Renaissance, an impact that went beyond the mere example of his artistic achievement. In *Cane* Toomer pioneered much that would define the artistic quest of the Harlem Renaissance. He asked the questions that other black writers would echo: What is the meaning of our slave heritage? Where do I find the meaning of my life, in the urban North or the rural South? How can I make myself whole and become a real man? These questions would preoccupy the literature of the Renaissance; these were the questions that Toomer tried, without real success, to answer in *Cane*.

After *Cane* Toomer never published any other work of significance to the Harlem Renaissance or to black literature. The reasons he turned his back on literature are not entirely clear. He was both exhausted by the effort to write and deeply disappointed by the failure of his book to find a wider market. Also, shortly after the publication of *Cane*, Toomer became estranged from Waldo Frank, his literary mentor. More seriously, Toomer was very uncomfortable that *Cane* had identified him as a black, and began to consciously distance himself from his race—not only turning his back on the black literary movement but also denying his own blackness. In 1924 Toomer went to France to study under the mystic, Georges Gurdjieff; for the rest of his life he would drift from one mystical enthusiasm to another, concerned far more with philosophy, psychology, and religion than with literature. Finally, Toomer's brief literary career was typical of his behavior throughout his life. He was far more of a searcher than a doer; he constantly changed his life's direction from one career to another, never sticking with anything long enough to savor real success or risk real failure. Still, his single novel cast a shadow over the Harlem Renaissance, and Jean Toomer, despite his shortcomings, was one of the most influential black writers of the decade.[33]

By the mid-1920s the stage was set for the birth of the Harlem Renaissance. Langston Hughes, Claude McKay, and Jean Toomer had laid the literary foundations. By 1925 they had been joined by numerous aspiring young black writers who had come to Harlem looking for excitement, color, and camaraderie, and hoping for literary fame. Langston Hughes, Wallace Thurman, Rudolph Fisher, and Zora Neale Hurston became the nucleus of a black literary bohemia that, together with other young writers such as Countee Cullen and Jessie Fauset, would dominate black literature for a decade.

The only thing needed to launch the Renaissance was for someone or some event to make the birth announcement. Between the spring of 1924 and the fall of 1926 three events occurred which served this purpose. Each was especially significant because it symbolized an awareness on the part of both the black intelligentsia and black writers themselves that a literary movement had been born. The Harlem Renaissance was, more than anything else, a state of mind among black writers and critics that they were the founders of and participants in a new era of black literature.

It was one of the black critics who first announced the movement to the world.

On March 21, 1924, Langston Hughes, Countee Cullen, Jessie Fauset, and a small group of other young black writers and poets joined professor Alain Locke, W.E.B. Du Bois, James Weldon Johnson, and a number of white writers, editors, and literary critics for a dinner hosted by Charles S. Johnson of the Urban League at New York's Civic Club. The dinner, initially conceived as a small gathering to celebrate the publication of Jessie Fauset's first novel, was transformed by Johnson into a major literary event that introduced the emerging black literary renaissance to New York's white literary establishment. Notably absent from the gathering were Jean Toomer, who had been invited but did not attend, and Claude McKay, who had already left Harlem and the United States by 1924. However, more than one hundred did attend the gathering, which one observer labeled the "dress rehearsal" of the Harlem Renaissance.[34]

One of those in attendance at the Civic Club dinner was Paul U. Kellog, editor of *The Survey Graphic*. He was so impressed that night with the potential of the black literary movement that he decided to devote his entire March 1925 issue to black literature and art. Alain Locke, named as guest editor of the "Harlem issue," used this forum to present a sample of the new black writing to a largely white audience. Later that year he expanded this issue into a book of black art, literature, and critical comment which he entitled *The New Negro* and dedicated to the younger generation whom he believed represented a new vitality never before seen in black literature. He used the book to introduce the Harlem Renaissance, which he saw as the cultural embodiment of a "New Negro" and the hope of the black race:

> Negro life is not only establishing new contacts and founding new centers, it is also finding a new soul. There is a fresh spiritual and cultural focusing. We have, as a heralding sign, an unusual outburst of creative expression. There is a renewed race-spirit that consciously and proudly sets itself apart. Justifiably then, we speak of the offerings of this book embodying these ripening forces as culled from the first fruits of the Negro Renaissance.[35]

For the most part *The New Negro* was concerned with what Locke christened the "Negro Renaissance," and especially the works of the young poets and writers who became this Renaissance. Locke was unrestrained in his praise for the young men and women whom he felt were the

heart and soul of the movement: "the Younger Generation comes, bringing gifts. They are the first fruits of the Negro Renaissance. Youth speaks
and the voice of the new Negro is heard." Locke presented a fairly
representative survey of the early work of the Renaissance writers. The
short stories of Rudolph Fisher, Jean Toomer, and Zora Neale Hurston,
and the poetry of Toomer, Langston Hughes, Claude McKay, and Countee
Cullen dominated the section devoted to literature. Locke also included
articles from critics that evaluated the early literary accomplishments and
optimistically predicted a new era of black literary creativity and black
racial progress. The most significant accomplishment of both *The New
Negro* and *The Survey Graphic* issue was that they identified and publicized the literary developments of the Harlem Renaissance and for the
first time made this work easily available to the reading public.[36]

The third event which marked the birth of the Harlem Renaissance was
the publication in the fall of 1926 of *Fire!!*, the only magazine both
produced by and devoted to the artists and writers of the Harlem Renaissance. The Civic Club dinner and *The New Negro* signaled the black
intelligentsia's awareness of a black literary movement, while *Fire!!*
demonstrated that the black writers themselves both accepted the existence of such a movement and were committed to it. Although the
magazine went bankrupt after a single issue, it nevertheless symbolized
the growing consciousness of the young Harlem writers that they were the
vanguard of a black literary movement—it represented the birth of that
state of mind that was the Harlem Renaissance.

As a literary magazine, *Fire!!* accurately mirrored the literary movement which created it. *Fire!!*, like the Harlem Renaissance, blended a
somewhat militant and avowedly independent, bohemian outlook which
emphasized freedom of expression and the quest for black identity with a
more moderate attempt at literary success and middle-class respectability. It almost seemed as though the young writers who put the magazine
together, while determined to be daring, radical, and honest in their
portrayal of life as they saw it, were at the same time glancing over their
shoulders for some sign of approval from the very literary establishment
that they mocked and scorned. This strange dichotomy was clearly apparent in the contrast between the content of the magazine and its style, and
was nowhere better reflected than in the title itself. Across the cover in
oversized, striking black on red print blazed the word "Fire!!" while on
the title page the very formal subtitle, "A Quarterly Devoted to the
Younger Negro Artists," toned down the radicalism of the cover. The

remainder of the magazine continued in this ambiguous manner. The cover consisted of a strikingly primitive black on red print, featuring an African theme, by Aaron Douglas. The other illustrations were equally intense portrayals of nude Africans and jungle scenes by Douglas and Richard Bruce. This contrasted sharply with the very formal table of contents and equally formal list of patrons and appeal for financial contributions; the foreword, however, returned to radical style and rhetoric:

> FIRE . . . flaming, burning, searing, and penetrating
> far beneath the superficial items of the
> flesh to boil the sluggish blood.
> FIRE . . . a cry of conquest in the night warning
> those who sleep and revitalizing those who
> linger in the quiet places dozing.
> FIRE . . . melted steel and iron bars, poking livid
> tongues between stone apertures and burning
> wooden opposition with a crackling chuckle of
> contempt.
> FIRE . . . weaving vivid hot designs upon an
> *ebon* bordered loom and satisfying
> pagan thirst for beauty unadorned—
> the flesh is sweet and real—the soul
> an inward flush of fire. . . . Beauty? . . .
> flesh on fire—on fire in the furnace
> of life blazing. . .
>   "Fy-ah,
>   Fy-ah, Lawd,
>   Fy-ah gonna burn ma soul!"[37]

Wallace Thurman edited *Fire!!* in association with Langston Hughes, Zora Neale Hurston, Gwendolyn Bennett, Aaron Douglas, Richard Bruce, and John Davis. It included work by all of its editors plus contributions by other young black writers, including Arna Bontemps and Countee Cullen. *Fire!!* then represented a joint effort by most of the writers who had associated themselves with the Harlem literary movement by 1926. However, the magazine, like the Renaissance itself, had difficulty binding together in any kind of permanent association a group of writers and poets who had a propensity to scatter in all directions. Notably absent from the pages of *Fire!!* were Jean Toomer, Rudolph Fisher, and

Claude McKay; Hughes claimed that he expected to obtain material from the first two (although Toomer had clearly disassociated himself from black literature by this time), and McKay was in France, far removed from the Harlem literary scene.[38]

Fire!! also reflected the lack of a clearly defined (and uniformly accepted) aesthetic in the Harlem Renaissance and the differing priorities of various Renaissance participants. The magazine was a curious mixture of conservative form and radical content. Hughes especially was determined that the radical element be preserved in future issues. He wanted to make the black on red color scheme a permanent feature of the cover and felt that the editorial page " 'Fire Burns' should really be kept burning,—a department of clever, satirical comment on the vices and stupidities of the race. Make it hot!" Wallace Thurman wanted to keep the publication strictly under black control and questioned the wisdom of including white novelist Carl Van Vechten among the patrons.[39]

In literary content *Fire!!* vacillated between militancy and introspection, and between formal, traditional literary styles and literary experimentation. Countee Cullen contributed his bitter sonnet, "From a Dark Tower":

> We shall not always plant while others reap
> The golden increment of bursting fruit,
> Nor always countenance, abject and mute,
> That lesser men should hold their brothers cheap;
> Not everlastingly while others sleep
> Shall we beguile their limbs with mellow flute,
> Not always bend to some more subtle brute;
> We were not made eternally to weep.
>
> The night whose sable breast relieves the stark
> White stars is no less heavenly being dark,
> And there are buds that cannot bloom at all
> In light, but crumple, piteous, and fall.
> So in the dark we hide the heart that bleeds,
> And wait, and tend our agonizing seeds.

Langston Hughes's "Elevator Boy" contrasted sharply in style with Cullen's piece, and it was more philosophical than bitter in its depressing, but pre-Depression, picture of Harlem's working class:

> I got a job now
> Runnin' an elevator
> In the Dennison hotel in Jersey,
> Job ain't no good though.
> No money around.
> Jobs are just chances
> Like everything else.
> Maybe a little luck now,
> Maybe not.
>
> .   .   .   .
>
> I been runnin' this
> Elevator too long.
> Guess I'll quit now.[40]

The public reaction to *Fire!!*, especially among the black middle class, reflected the ambiguity that many blacks felt toward the literature of the Harlem Renaissance. While there had been near-unanimous approval by all elements of the black intelligentsia at the Civic Club dinner, *Fire!!* was another story. It deeply offended and shocked the more conservative black literary critics, who were extremely sensitive about any writing that depicted blacks in a less than favorable light or focused attention on unsavory elements of activities in the black community. Benjamin Brawley was especially vocal in opposition. He felt that its preoccupation with "unseemly" topics reflected the influence of Van Vechten and accused its editors of confusing vulgarity with art. At Craig's, a popular restaurant frequented by Harlem's literary set, *Fire!!*'s editors were given the silent treatment, while the literary critic of the Baltimore *Afro-American* merely noted that he had "tossed the first issue of *Fire!!* into the fire."[41]

This negative reaction is not surprising, since it was the self-conscious intention of the magazine to shock—especially to shock the black middle class. The editors of *Fire!!* were the core of the young writers of the Harlem Renaissance, who created the magazine because they wanted their own journal as an outlet for their work, free from the restrictions of other magazines, and as a vehicle that would "burn up a lot of the old, dead, conventional Negro-white ideas of the past" and force the middle class to recognize their existence as writers and artists. The members of the editorial board each contributed fifty dollars toward publication costs, but Thurman, who insisted that they produce a quality magazine, ran up bills much higher than that. The hostility of much of the black middle class hurt sales, distribution was poor, and consequently few issues got into circulation. Ironically, the death blow to the magazine came when most copies were destroyed by a fire that swept through the building where they were being stored. By that time the journal was already being smothered beneath a mountain of unpaid bills. As Hughes recalled, "that taught me a lesson about little magazines. But since white folks had them, we Negroes thought we could have one, too. But we didn't have the money." This failure would leave a permanent mark on the Renaissance. After the demise of *Fire!!* black writers would be tied to white publishers and to the already established black and white journals.[42]

Although *Fire!!* failed as a magazine, it did succeed in igniting the literary Renaissance in Harlem by welding together its major participants. The sense of community and the belief that there was indeed a Negro Renaissance flourished in the ashes of *Fire!!*. By 1926 the Harlem Renaissance was in full swing. The early writings of McKay, Toomer, Hughes, and James Weldon Johnson excited the imagination of other black writers and encouraged them to write. The Civic Club dinner, *The New Negro*, and *Fire!!* represented the public debuts of a literary movement that would flourish for the rest of the decade. During this period Harlem would be the literary and cultural capital of black America.

5   Black Bohemia: When the Negro Was in Vogue

By early 1926 the basic ingredients that gave rise to the Harlem Renaissance had been assembled. The literary foundations had been laid, and a generation of young black writers was ready to join those who had already established themselves. *Fire!!* symbolized the spirit and self-consciousness of these writers. The black intelligentsia, alerted by Charles S. Johnson's Civic Club dinner and Alain Locke's *The New Negro*, stood waiting like anxious parents to applaud the artistic endeavors flowing from the pens of their young writers. As the Renaissance took root, Harlem was transformed, at least in the popular mind, into a bohemia which not only housed a literary movement but which offered excitement and entertainment to those whites daring enough to venture uptown and directly sample the primitive and exotic pleasures that abounded there; this image of black bohemia also could be packaged and delivered to those less daring, who were content to experience Harlem vicariously through art, literature, and popular culture. The writers of the Harlem Renaissance would explore this bohemia in both their lives and their writings, and it would influence the literature that many of them produced. It gave birth to a fascination with black life and black culture that certainly helped account for the success of the Harlem Renaissance.

Popular fascination with black life was directly related to the emergence of the black bohemia in Harlem. In 1922 Claude McKay left New York partially because his growing literary reputation isolated him from the street life that he enjoyed so much. Most of the writers who remained in Harlem overcame this isolation by creating their own community there. What they produced was a strange blend of Greenwich Village bohemia and Harlem cabaret life with jazz and the blues thrown in for good measure.

In a number of ways the Harlem Renaissance owed much to the cultural movement that had blossomed in the Village a decade earlier. For example, Carl Van Vechten, Max Eastman, DuBose Heyward, Frank Harris, and a number of other white intellectuals, each of whom had personal ties with black writers in the early twenties, were products of Mable Dodge's "23 Fifth Avenue" salon. Many Village intellectuals, including Mable Dodge herself, as well as Waldo Frank and his circle of writers and artists, concluded that in order to deal adequately with American culture, race must be considered. This attitude lay behind the efforts of many of the white writers and intellectuals to forge links with the black community and stimulated their interest in black writers and their work. In turn, the Harlem writer shared with his downtown counterpart a bohemian lifestyle and a rejection of conventional morality, but he was distinguished by the fact that the reality of economic necessity frequently forced him to adjust the tempo of his living and maintain hours and habits compatible with his need to earn a living. In addition the Harlem writers avidly embraced the music and nightlife of Harlem's cabarets.[1]

By the mid-1920s Harlem contained a thriving colony of black writers and artists who worked, partied, and played in association with each other. They reflected attitudes similar to other writers of the twenties, but they also possessed characteristics unique to the black experience and to the fact that their bohemia was located in the heart of the black metropolis.

At the center of Harlem's black bohemia stood Wallace Thurman and a small circle of writers that included Langston Hughes, Rudolph Fisher, and Zora Neale Hurston. Loosely associated with this inner circle were the other Renaissance writers who lived in Harlem during the late 1920s—Countee Cullen, George Schuyler, Arna Bontemps, Jessie Fauset, and Nella Larsen. All were equal participants in the Renaissance, but the inner circle made up the hard core of the black bohemia. They set the pace and perfected the lifestyle that characterized the Harlem Renaissance.[2]

Of the four who made up the inner circle, Wallace Thurman was the central and dominant character. Thurman was born in 1902 in Salt Lake City but grew up in a number of western and midwestern towns, from

Chicago and Omaha to Boise, Idaho, and Pasadena, California. He attended the University of Utah, but after apparently suffering a nervous breakdown he moved to California, where he continued his studies at the University of Southern California. While on the West Coast Thurman became aware of the new stirrings in black literature, and he tried to foment a similar movement in California by publishing his own literary magazine. When this venture failed, Thurman gave up trying to bring New York to California and instead packed his bags for Harlem.

In New York Thurman found lodging in a rooming house with Arna Bontemps, a young black writer he had met in California. Initially Thurman found work as a night elevator operator a few blocks from Harlem. Originally he had planned to get a job with the Customs House, but by the time his civil service rating came through he had "discovered" Harlem and was reluctant to tie himself down to such a mundane job. Instead he found a literary position as a reader with Macaulay, where, to the best of Langston Hughes's knowledge, he was the only black to hold such a prominent position with a major publishing firm during the Renaissance. By the summer of 1926 Thurman lived in the same 136th Street rooming house with Hughes and was the managing editor of *The Messenger*, a black journal which was sometimes radical and sometimes just a society magazine, depending on who was paying its bills at the time. He also supported himself by selling Irish, Jewish, and Catholic "true confessions" to magazines such as *True Story* under outlandish pseudonyms such as Ethel Belle Mandrake and Patrick Casey, and he became a ghost writer of several short stories and popular novels.[3]

By the mid 1920s Thurman had emerged as a leader among the writers and poets of Harlem. He helped organize *Fire!!* and was elected editor of the journal by his colleagues in the venture; meanwhile, his apartment, a rent-free room on 136th Street, infamous among Harlem's young writers as "263 house," and mockingly referred to as "Niggerati Manor" by Thurman and Hurston, had become the meeting place and social center for the inner circle of Renaissance participants. Thurman himself was both the model for and the severest critic of the bohemian lifestyle that was popular among Harlem's young artists. He was also one of the principal victims of this lifestyle. In spite of his popularity Thurman was a tragic figure, undermined by self-doubt and unfulfilled ambitions, and weakened and ultimately destroyed by alcoholism and tuberculosis. Langston Hughes remembered him as a "strangely brilliant black boy, who had read everything, and whose critical mind could find something wrong with everything he read" and as a man who passionately wanted to be a great writer but was never satisfied with anything he wrote. Thurman's public image was that of a self-proclaimed hedonist, a "professional New Yorker," and leader of the "shock-proof young sophisticates." Hughes saw him more tragically as a man who compensated for his feelings of failure by "writing a great deal for money, laughing bitterly at his fabulously concocted 'true stories'; creating two bad motion pictures of the 'Adults Only' type for Hollywood, drinking more and more gin, and then threatening to jump out of windows at people's parties and kill himself." It was Thurman who sardonically branded the pretentious black literate the "niggerati."[4]

Harlem offered its bohemians a variety of opportunities for entertainment and amusement. Thurman, Hughes, and others frequented the parties and joined in the night life both of the ghetto elite and of its masses and occasionally journeyed downtown to the Van Vechten mansion or to the home of some other patron of the black arts. At one extreme were the Harlem parties of A'Lelia Walker, heiress of the Madam Walker Hair Straightening fortune and the woman who came closest to establishing a salon atmosphere in Harlem. At A'Lelia Walker's and at similar parties given by other members of Harlem's upper crust, black poets and black numbers bankers mingled freely with black and white celebrities, business people, and commercial bankers. Typically, several hundred persons would crowd into a single apartment, creating the crush of the New York subway at rush hour. Geraldyn Dismond, society reporter for the black *Interstate Tattler*, vividly described one of these gatherings:

> What a crowd! All classes and colors met face to face, ultra aristocrats, Bourgeois, Communists, Park Avenue galore, bookers, publishers, Broadway celebs, and Harlemites giving each other the once over. The social revolution was on. And yes, Lady Nancy Cunard was there all in black (she would) with 12 of her grand bracelets. . . . And was the entertainment on the up and up! Into swell dance music was injected African drums that played havoc with blood pressure. Jimmy Daniels sang his gigolo hits. Gus Simons, the Harlem crooner, made the River Stay Away From His Door and Taylor himself brought out everything from "Hot Dog" to "Bravo" when he made high C.[5]

The average Harlemite, of course, never attended a party like this. However, he was familiar with the house-rent parties that mushroomed in Harlem during the mid-twenties. These gatherings, originally conceived as a way to raise rent money, soon became a regular item in the social life of the ghetto working class. Brightly colored cards posted in the front windows of apartments announced the party. For the price of an inexpensive ticket, usually twenty-five cents, the party-goer gained admission to a stranger's apartment, where he found the rug rolled back for dancing, a piano or small combo in the corner, bootleg whiskey, fried fish, a steaming pot of chitlings for sale in the kitchen, and plenty of company. As the popularity of the house-rent party spread, some entrepreneurs (occasionally even small-time pimps and madams) cashed in on the fad by setting up house-rent parties, often as a front for their more illegal activities, and advertised them among truck drivers, Pullman porters, traveling salesmen, other transients, and especially among the thousands of unattached men and women who thronged Harlem's streets at night looking for excitement.[6]

The house-rent party, legitimate or otherwise, grew in popularity as the fame of Harlem spread downtown. They remained one of the few places where the average Harlemite could relax and dance the black-bottom out of sight of the curious white tourists who flocked to the ghetto every Saturday night looking for the wild, primitive night life reputed to be found there. Blacks were happy to cash in on the white tourists, who were so willing to spend money on black exotica. Some Harlem night spots so catered to their white clientele that they refused to admit blacks. The Cotton Club, on Lenox Avenue and 143rd Street, was for whites only, although light-skinned blacks could sometimes slip past the imposing doormen who stood guard at the entrance. The entertainment was all black, of course, although its famous chorus line featured "high yaller" dancers; a job in this chorus was so desirable and lucrative that it was rumored that white girls occasionally tried to pass for black in order to join its ranks.[7]

While the Cotton Club and its many imitators attracted the socialites and celebrities from Park Avenue who wanted to experience Harlem without confronting the dangers they imagined would result from race mixing, the house-rent party remained the staple entertainment for the majority of the black working class, and it also became a favorite hangout for many of the writers of the Renaissance. As Langston Hughes recalled:

Almost every Saturday night when I was in Harlem I went to a house-rent party. I wrote a lot of poems about house-rent parties, and ate many a fried fish and pig's foot—with liquid refreshments on the side. I met ladies' maids and truck drivers, laundry workers and shoe shine boys, seamstresses and porters. I can still hear their laughter in my ears, hear the soft slow music, and feel the floor shaking as the dancers danced.[8]

Less spectacular than the extravaganzas of Harlem's aristocracy and less colorful than the house-rent parties were the regular gatherings hosted by a number of the Renaissance writers and critics. Novelist and *Crisis* literary critic Jessie Fauset's parties were attended by editors, students, social workers, "and serious young people who liked books and the British Museum," who entertained themselves by discussing literature, reading poetry, and conversing in French. Walter White, a writer and an officer with the NAACP who lived in Harlem's tallest and most exclusive apartment house, frequently extended dinner invitations to "hungry literati," while at artist Aaron Douglas's parties in the same building the guests contributed to the fund that was used to purchase refreshments from the local bootlegger. Finally, at the James Weldon Johnsons' the elite of the black and white intelligentsia met and fraternized. A memorable scene from one of these parties featured Clarence Darrow, sitting under the only lighted lamp, reading aloud passages from his book, *Farmington*, to an attentive audience that included Ruby Darrow, Carl Van Vechten, and his wife, actress Fania Marinoff. Later that night Paul Robeson held the group spellbound with a reading from "The Creation."[9]

No matter how formal and sedate or how gay, Harlem parties usually adjourned to one of the nearby cabarets to finish the evening. It was these ghetto nightclubs and speakeasies that provided the most attractive features of its night life and which for a time served as a melting pot for all classes of New Yorkers. Blacks of all types gathered in these nightspots to debate politics, religion, sex, and the "race problem"; black writers entertained their white friends as well as their patrons and sponsors there. These were the places that made Harlem special in the 1920s.[9]

One of the most popular of the Harlem cabarets was the Sugar Cane Club at 135th Street and Fifth Avenue. The Sugar Cane was located down a flight of stairs in a damp, dimly lit cellar, crowded with tables that framed a tiny dance floor. Atmosphere consisted of a single spotlight which reflected off the many facets of a mirrored chandelier and provided just enough distorted light over the dance floor. Entertainment was provided by a five-piece combo, none of whose members were able to, or seemed to need to read music as they improvised the jazzy but soft "swing" music that the crowds demanded. The music drew patrons to the crowded dance floor, where they would just stand and shuffle their feet, "dancing on a dime" it was called; the popular dances were the Bump and the Mess Around.[11] Black performers such as Bessie Smith, Ethyl Waters, Duke Ellington, and Louis Armstrong entertained at the Sugar Cane Club and dozens of similar Harlem nightspots long before fame sent them downtown. Langston Hughes remembered Gladys Bentley working in a small Harlem bar while she was still an unknown singer:

> For two or three amazing years, Miss Bentley sat, and played a big piano all night long, literally all night, without stopping—singing songs like "The St. James Infirmary," from ten in the evening until dawn, with scarcely a break between the notes, sliding from one song to another, with a powerful and continuous underbeat of jungle rhythm. Miss Bentley was an amazing exhibition of musical energy—a large, dark, masculine lady, whose feet pounded the floor while her fingers pounded the keyboard—a perfect piece of African sculpture, animated by her own rhythm.[12]

Harlem's black bohemia formed the essential backdrop to the black literary Renaissance. Young black writers submerged themselves in the primitive black culture that flourished in the ghetto's speakeasies, ginhouses, and jazzrooms. There all of Harlem converged: the prostitute, the washwoman, the petty gangster, the poet, and the intellectual shared the blues and swayed to the beat of the jazz musicians. On a more refined level the gatherings hosted by Harlem's literary and intellectual elite brought black writers into contact with black intellectuals such as James Weldon Johnson and W.E.B. Du Bois and with white liberals such as Alfred Knopf, Clarence Darrow, and Carl Van Vechten. In short, Harlem in the mid-1920s provided a cosmopolitan setting where black writers had easy access to all levels of life. As Langston Hughes summarized the social scene:

> At the James Weldon Johnson parties and gumbo suppers, one met solid people like Clarence and Mrs. Darrow. At the Dr. Alexander's, you met the upper crust Negro intellectuals like Du Bois. At Wallace

Thurman's you met the bohemians of both Harlem and the Village. And in the gin mills and speakeasies and night clubs between 125th and 145th, Eighth Avenue and Lenox, you met everyone from Buddy de Silva to Theodore Dreiser, Ann Pennington to the first Mrs. Eugene O'Neill. In the days when Harlem was in vogue, Amanda Randolph was at the Alhambra, Jimmy Walker was mayor of New York, and Louise sang at the old New World. [13]

The glamour and excitement that made Harlem a mecca for black writers also attracted the attention of white New Yorkers who began regular pilgrimages to the ghetto in search of its exotic night life. New York's interest in black life can be traced back to the turn of the century, when black songwriters (including James Weldon Johnson, his brother Rosamond, and Paul Laurence Dunbar), singers, dancers, and actors first achieved success in Broadway musicals and vaudeville. (See the discussion of this phenomenon on pages 65–66). In the 1920s, however, this interest became a fascination, then almost an obsession, as Harlem and blacks in general became the latest fad for middle-class America.

Langston Hughes and James Weldon Johnson dated the beginning of this era, when the Negro was in vogue, at 1921 when the musical *Shuffle Along* became a major Broadway hit. *Shuffle Along* was followed by Eugene O'Neill's *Emperor Jones*; next came *Green Pastures* and a number of lesser-known plays featuring black actors and black themes. By the middle of the decade an extravagant musical production featuring black singers and dancers was one of the formulas for commercial success on Broadway. At the same time white audiences were experiencing these innovations in theater, they discovered another aspect of the ghetto world—music. White audiences flocked into night-clubs and concert halls to hear Roland Hayes, Paul Robeson, Bessie Smith, Ethyl Waters, and Louis Armstrong. Black music, both the blues and jazz, swept New York, America, and western Europe. [14]

Ironically, though, and with great symbolic significance, the most important single event in creating the Negro craze and sending thousands of whites into Harlem's speakeasies and clubs was the appearance in 1926 of Carl Van Vechten's sensational bestseller, *Nigger Heaven*. Carl Van Vechten, who was instrumental in forging ties between Greenwich Village and Harlem, also, more than any other single individual, created the Negro vogue. Following the publication of his book, white middle-class America eagerly devoured anything with a black flavor to it. Black writers and poets suddenly found themselves pursued by publishers, exhibitions of African art brought crowds to museums and galleries, *Amos 'n' Andy* became a hit radio show, and slumming in Harlem became a favorite pastime for those looking for a sensual, exotic, and primitive thrill.

Both Carl Van Vechten and his novel *Nigger Heaven* played an extremely important role in the Harlem Renaissance. It is somewhat ironic that it was a white writer who first popularized Harlem local color; it is also significant that the controversy that this novel generated in the black community anticipated a similar reaction toward the works of black writers and poets.

Carl Van Vechten was born in 1880 in Cedar Rapids, Iowa. His parents were both well educated, and he grew up in a stimulating and liberal intellectual environment. Early in life he was exposed to the women's rights movement, and his parents were always sympathetic to Negro rights.[15] In 1906 Van Vechten graduated from the University of Chicago and moved to New York, where he became a music critic for the *New York Times*. For the next ten years he worked for various New York newspapers, primarily as a music and drama critic, and during World War I he published three volumes of music criticism. During this period Van Vechten was active in the literary and cultural circles of Greenwich Village, where he frequented Mabel Dodge's salon and became friends with Gertrude Stein, and more important, with Alfred Knopf. Also in 1914 Van Vechten married actress Fania Marinoff.

It was not until the 1920s, after he turned forty, that Van Vechten shifted the focus of his career from critic to artist. Beginning in 1922 with *Peter Whiffle: His Life and Works*, he published six novels in rapid succession. Van Vechten's greatest literary strength was his ability accurately and sardonically to describe American society in the 1920s. One critic, in fact, has labeled Van Vechten's work as "the most concentrated example in the American novel of the satiric comedy of manners" in the tradition of Fielding, Huxley, and Waugh.[16] His novels enjoyed considerable popular success largely because of his ability to portray sophisticated society with insight, humor, and literary craft. Van Vechten did quite well during the twenties. In addition to the income from his writing, he inherited a sizable fortune from his brother. This economic independence enabled him to move freely in the circles he described in his novels and to pursue his more serious interests, which included promoting the careers of promising black writers. In 1932 Van Vechten published his last novel and shifted his creative energies from literature to photography.

Nigger Heaven, Van Vechten's fifth novel, is by far his best known and most controversial. Also it was his most serious work, and the one with which he was most emotionally involved. *Nigger Heaven* did share characteristics with Van Vechten's other novels—it was in many ways a black version of his exposés of New York society. However, although the novel did uncover several levels of Harlem society, its tone was far less comic and its outlook far more tragic than in Van Vechten's other novels. *Nigger Heaven* was the fruition of Van Vechten's long fascination with black life and the Negro race. Years before he began the novel he had been interested in the Negro theater, had been an enthusiastic fan of Bessie Smith, and had tried to get blacks admitted to Mabel Dodge's salon. By the early 1920s Van Vechten had gained a reputation for mixing blacks and whites at his parties and spending many evenings in Harlem's bars and cabarets. He had also become good friends with Walter White of the NAACP, and James Weldon Johnson, and through them gained access to most of Harlem's celebrities. When he began to research *Nigger Heaven*, even though he was white, he found few obstacles in his path. [17]

Nigger Heaven was, among other things, a sympathetic white observer's examination of Harlem life at the onset of the Harlem Renaissance, at a moment when the "Harlem vogue" was in its infancy. In the novel Van Vechten exposed a cross-section of Harlem life, describing the activities of the richest and most colorful as well as the most ordinary middle-class inhabitants. He divided the novel into two sections and a short prologue. In the prologue he introduced two of the most colorful characters, Anatole Longfellow, better known as the Scarlet Creeper, who was Harlem's most notorious ladies' man, and Ralph Pettyjohn, the Bolito King, a wealthy numbers racketeer. In just a few pages Van Vechten dramatized the color and exotic atmosphere of Harlem's cabaret and underworld life. In sharp contrast, Book One focused on Mary Love, a middle-class black girl living a fairly sheltered life in a Harlem filled with young doctors, lawyers, writers, artists, and teachers (indeed, when purged of its bohemian element, the life experienced by many of the Renaissance writers and their friends). Mary Love's Harlem was distinctly middle class, and she and her friends lived essentially middle-class lives. The only thing that distinguished the lives of these Harlemites from the rest of New York's middle class was their regular encounter with racial prejudice.

This racial conflict was a strong undercurrent running throughout the novel.

In Book Two Van Vechten finally focused on his major character, Byron Kasson. Kasson, who had been introduced early in the novel as Mary's lover, was an aspiring young writer who had recently arrived in Harlem after graduating from a white university. Kasson was a tragic figure whose moral downfall was the central theme of the novel. Van Vechten was a novelist of the naturalist school, and Kasson's destruction is clearly reminiscent of that of Clyde Carrington in Dreiser's *An American Tragedy*, published just a year earlier. Kasson was never able to come to terms with being black. He lost Mary and was seduced and morally destroyed in an orgy of sex and drugs with the amoral, hedonistic Lasca Sartoris. Finally, in a scene that recaptured the cabaret atmosphere of the prologue, Kasson stood impotent, accused of a murder he wanted to commit but was incapable of carrying out.

Nigger Heaven was far more than just the story of the decline and fall of Byron Kasson. Van Vechten wanted to depict all facets of black life, and, more importantly, he endeavored to shed some light on the complicated question of what it meant to be black in America. This was a bold and rather risky undertaking, especially for a white writer, but Van Vechten did not choose to be cautious. Neither did he attempt to be objective or dispassionate. Instead he openly undertook to expose racial injustice, and at the same time to educate his readers about the nature of black Americans and their struggles with themselves and with white society. There were two, somewhat conflicting, aspects of Van Vechten's portrait of blacks. First, he insisted that blacks were just people—people who differed very little from other people of similar social and economic background. He went to great lengths to demonstrate that Mary Love and her circle of friends were no different in their attitudes, values, or behavior from any other group of young urban professionals. They shared the same tastes, read the same books, went to the same theater, and behaved the same at dinner parties. In one scene Van Vechten took obvious pleasure in describing the surprise of a white writer at his first mixed party when he discovered that the black guests were cultured, refined, educated, and quite capable of carrying on dinner table conversation in French as well as English.[18]

Against this background the day-to-day discrimination encountered by these cultivated blacks (such as wondering what restaurant they could eat in while shopping downtown) cast American prejudice in a distorted, absurd, and even monstrous role and clearly accounted for the impatience and bitterness voiced by blacks against their country's racial policies. The bitterness generated by prejudice was compounded by the fact that, as one character pointed out, Harlem readily picked up and accepted the discriminatory stereotypes of white America:

> Try Harlem, will you? Dick's lip curled cynically. I guess you won't find that much easier. Howard here is a lawyer, but the race doesn't want colored lawyers. If they're in trouble they go to white lawyers, and they go to white banks and white insurance companies. They shop on white One hundred and twenty-fifth Street. Most of 'em, he added fiercely, pray to a white God. You won't get much help from the race.[19]

The similarities that Van Vechten drew between middle-class blacks and whites was only one aspect of his picture of the black race. He also underscored the differences between the races. In doing so he exposed a dilemma which faced American blacks and concerned all of the Renaissance writers. Should blacks merge their identity with that of the majority white society as a means of achieving equality, or should they strive to preserve those attributes in their character that were unique and distinctive? For Van Vechten, as well as for a number of Renaissance writers, the distinctive element in the black character was a primitiveness, a close tie to jungle rhythms, a sensuality. According to Van Vechten, these were the traits that the advent of civilization and the dependence on technology had refined out of Western civilization, traits that the West now was seeking to reacquire. These were the gifts that the black race could restore to the West.[20]

In *Nigger Heaven* this conflict between the primitive and the civilized was centered in the character of Mary Love. Mary was conscious that she faced a dilemma that seemed irreconcilable. On the one hand she was the most "civilized," the most solidly middle class of all of Van Vechten's black characters. While she took pride in her education and her ability to mingle comfortably in the most refined social circles, she was also deeply disturbed because civilization seemed to have alienated her from her African birthright. She wished that she was not so prim and proper and felt an urgent need to recapture her savage and pagan heritage.

> She [Mary] cherished an almost fantastic faith in her race, a love for her people in themselves, and a fervent belief in their possibilities.

She admired all Negro characteristics and desired earnestly to possess them. Somehow, so many of them, through no fault of her own,
eluded her. . . . How many times she had watched her friends
listening listlessly or with forced or affected attention to alien music,
which said little to the Negro soul, by Schubert or Schumann,
immediately thereafter loosing themselves in a burst of jazz or the
glory of an evangelical Spiritual, recognizing, no doubt, in some
dim, biological way, the beat of the African rhythm. . . . To be sure,
she, too, felt this African beat— it completely aroused her emotionally, but she was conscious of feeling it. This love of drums, of
exciting rhythms, this naive delight in glowing colour—this warm,
sexual emotion, all of these were hers only through a mental understanding.[21]

In Van Vechten's view Mary Love's problem was the same problem that
confronted all people of the twentieth century. Civilization must be hu-
manized; there must be a blending of the primitive with the tech-
nologically advanced civilization of the West. In this process, America
had much to learn from the Negro.

Although Van Vechten's objective in writing *Nigger Heaven* had been
to engender a deeper understanding of and appreciation for American
blacks, the response to his novel was not exactly what he had anticipated.
To put it simply, *Nigger Heaven*, like *Fire!!*, precipitated anger and
resentment in the black community; Van Vechten was utterly dismayed by
the furor that greeted his novel. George Schuyler recalled that of all the
black reviewers only he, James Weldon Johnson, and Alice Dunbar
Nelson had approved of the novel without reservations, and he further
noted that most blacks who damned the novel did so without even reading
it. Although he was upset, Van Vechten was not entirely caught off guard
by the negative response. Several months before he published *Nigger
Heaven* he wrote, perhaps as a warning to himself, that the Negro had a
tendency "to be sensitive concerning all that is written about him, particularly by a white man, to regard even the fiction in which he plays a role
in the light of propaganda." With these concerns in mind Van Vechten
took the precaution of clearing the manuscript through both James
Weldon Johnson and Rudolph Fisher before publication, but this gesture
did not win black acceptance of or even tolerance for the novel.[22]

The debate over *Nigger Heaven* within the black community mirrored
many of the conflicts over the appropriate nature of black literature that

would divide the Harlem Renaissance. W.E.B. Du Bois led the attack on *Nigger Heaven*. In a review in *Crisis* he argued simply that "Carl Van Vechten's 'Nigger Heaven' is a blow in the face. It is an affront to the hospitality of black folk and to the intelligence of whites." Du Bois went on to object to the title and to accuse Van Vechten of painting a distorted and grossly misrepresentative picture of Harlem life. Finally, he contended that Van Vechten, in creating his "cheap melodrama," had eliminated all decent human feelings from his characters and had depicted life as "just one damned orgy after another, with hate, hurt, gin, and sadism."[23]

Nigger Heaven split Harlem into two opposing groups: those who opposed Van Vechten and those who supported him. Van Vechten's critics generally accepted Du Bois's argument that the novel had done a disservice to blacks by exposing the seamy side of Harlem rather than concentrating on the more respectable elements of the black community. Richetta Randolph, James Weldon Johnson's secretary at the NAACP, wrote to Johnson that the novel had both disappointed and depressed her. She felt that Van Vechten had written "just what those who do not know us think about all of us," and she urged Johnson to write something that would counteract the evil that had been done. Benjamin Brawley sadly acknowledged that *Nigger Heaven* was the most significant novel written about blacks and that its influence on the young black writers of the twenties was tremendous, but he argued that Van Vechten, while presenting only factual information, nevertheless had drawn a distorted picture of Harlem.[24]

While Brawley, Du Bois, and others severely criticized Van Vechten, most of the young writers were more tolerant. Harold Jackman, a schoolteacher friend of poets Countee Cullen and Claude McKay, wrote to McKay about the furor generated by the publication of the novel:

> His book has been through some twelve or thirteen editions. Needless to say you know it has stirred a lot of comment. Some like it (I am one who likes it although I don't think the writing is as brilliant as in his other books—I continue to say that that particular phase in Negro life in Harlem is done well and I happen to know because I frequently travel in those sets) very much and others loathe it—Washingtonians can't see it.[25]

Wallace Thurman wrote perhaps the most balanced review in *Fire!!*. He criticized Van Vechten for letting sentimentality overcome his sophistication in his descriptions of Harlem life, but he was much more concerned with those critics who would restrict Van Vechten and other writers in their selection of subject matter and prevent them from portraying the more colorful elements of ghetto life. Thurman urged all writers to ignore such "ignoramuses" and freely choose the subject for their art from whatever phase of life that seemed most interesting. Of the younger writers Langston Hughes most clearly demonstrated his support of Van Vechten by writing the jazz lyrics which were used in the seventh and later editions of the novel.[26]

If the black reaction to *Nigger Heaven* bewildered Van Vechten, he was even more surprised by the response of whites. Although a number of white readers criticized the book as being pure fantasy, it was generally well received in the white press, and more significantly it achieved tremendous popular success, running through numerous editions and being translated into a number of foreign languages. Its popularity fueled the rapidly growing white fascination with black art and literature and further stimulated the white influx into Harlem's bars and cabarets. More important, though, *Nigger Heaven* tended to establish stereotypes about the nature of black life that thrill-seeking white audiences would expect to be fulfilled when they visited ghetto nightspots or bought books written by black authors. This situation would have both positive and negative effects on the Harlem Renaissance.[27]

The most important result of this increased fascination with black life was that the white public became interested in the works of black writers and poets and was eager to buy books by or about blacks. Publishers, aware of this new market, actively sought manuscripts from black writers, and literary patrons opened their purses to promising young artists. The growing popularity of Harlem and Harlem life in general, and the popularity of Van Vechten's *Nigger Heaven* in particular, did much to create the Harlem vogue, which in turn generated the market for black literature and made the Harlem Renaissance possible. There was, however, a negative aspect of this phenomenon. If black writers found that suddenly the world was ready for them, they also often discovered that the world had certain preconceptions about what the true nature of black literature should be. So, while it became much easier for blacks to publish their works and occasionally even to support themselves with their writing, they also felt some pressure, either from their publishers or from their perception of what it took to achieve literary success, to make their work conform to the Van Vechten model.

6 The Black Intelligentsia: Promoters

lthough the Negro Vogue, Harlem's famous nightlife, and Van Vechten's notorious novel did much to launch the Harlem Renaissance and to define its nature, equally important was the relationship between the black writers and Harlem's intellectual community. While the writers produced the literature, the intelligentsia served as critics who helped define the movement and give it direction, and they acted as liaison between the creative artist and his or her publishers, patrons, and public. A major critic of the Harlem Renaissance, Harold Cruse, castigated the movement for its dependency on white financial support and accused black intellectuals and the black middle class of failing to provide adequate support and guidance for the Renaissance. To some extent these concerns were valid—especially the complaint that the black middle class did not adequately support its writers. However, the involvement of black intellectuals in the Harlem Renaissance was both considerable and complex.

The black intelligentsia of the 1920s was a diverse group of men and women scattered throughout the country who were associated with colleges and universities, newspapers, periodicals, black churches, and black political and civil rights organizations like the Urban League and the NAACP. While most black intellectuals, and especially those who resided in Harlem, were deeply concerned about the developments in black literature in the mid-1920s, only a handful including James Weldon Johnson of the NAACP, Alain Locke of Howard University, and Charles S. Johnson of the Urban League can be characterized as major boosters of the movement. These three men were highly visible promoters of the Renaissance whose commitment to and support of black writers was considerably greater than that of any white patron and who were as involved in the movement as any of the black writers. These three men, with assistance from a few other men and women, were the principal black proponents of the Harlem Renaissance, who, more than any other blacks of this period, attempted to define the nature of the movement while encouraging the endeavors of the young black writers and poets.

It is difficult to determine which black intellectual played the most important role in the Renaissance. Each of the three mentioned above made an important contribution to the movement. However, James Weldon Johnson, if not actually the most significant, was strategically placed to make the greatest contribution, because he, far more than any other black intellectual, was able successfully to bridge the gap between artist and critic or promoter. He was an accomplished poet and novelist in his own right, and he was one of the pioneers of the black literary revival that emerged during and just after World War I and helped lay the foundations for the Renaissance. At the same time, he was one of the principal supporters and critics of the Renaissance, an officer in the NAACP, and one of the most respected black intellectuals of the period.

In 1914 Johnson returned to New York and to his literary career after having served seven years overseas with the State Department.[1] An old friend, Charles Anderson, helped him secure a job as editorial page editor of the New York *Age*, one of the best-known black weeklies in the country. In 1907 Fred Moore (with financial assistance from Booker T. Washington) had acquired the *Age* and quickly made it one of the major organs for the Tuskegeean faction. Consequently, when Johnson accepted a position with the paper, he was renewing his political association with Anderson and the Bookerites. However, his even-handed management of the editorial page and his effective use of his weekly column to attack any incident of discrimination or racial injustice which came to his attention soon won the respect of a broad cross-section of the black community, including W.E.B. Du Bois. In fact, although Johnson remained quite friendly with Anderson and the other Bookerites, the political stance that he took in his editorials often aligned him with the Du Bois camp, and in 1915 he joined the NAACP. Indeed, his popularity as an editorial writer was due primarily to his ability to take a strong position on important issues without committing himself to either of the factions that divided black America.[2]

Johnson's association with both the Washington and Du Bois factions made him an important figure in the attempts to restore unity in the black intellectual community following Washington's death in 1915. This consideration prompted Joel Spingarn, board chairman of the NAACP, to nominate Johnson for the position of field secretary of the Association. In 1916 Johnson accepted this position, which made him responsible for increasing the size and vitality of NAACP branches across the country. Throughout the 1920s Johnson worked for the NAACP, first as field secretary, then as secretary to the Association and director of its campaign against lynching.

The NAACP was only one of Johnson's many concerns during the 1920s. He also became a fairly popular public speaker on the subject of civil rights and the cultural contributions of black Americans, and he continued his literary career. During the Harlem Renaissance he published several volumes of poetry and edited three anthologies of black literature. Both his personal literary experience and resulting literary contacts and his position with the NAACP placed him in a strategic position to promote the emerging Renaissance, and by the mid-1920s he assumed an active role assisting a number of young writers and attempting to influence the development of the movement.[3]

One of the tactics Johnson used to promote black literature was to publicize it during his many lecture tours. As field secretary of the NAACP, he constantly received invitations to speak on the question of the race problem in America. Since his speeches were primarily political in nature, he fashioned them carefully for the audience he was addressing. For example, when speaking to white audiences, he emphasized that in spite of Constitutional guarantees to the contrary, blacks continued to exist as second-class citizens who suffered daily from the indignities of segregation, job discrimination, and the threat of racial violence. On the other hand, when addressing blacks, he felt there was no need to chronicle racial injustice. Instead, he called upon blacks to unite and assume the "power" that their numbers should bring them.[4] Then, during the mid-1920s he began to introduce the emerging literary movement to his audiences as a factor that would help blacks win their struggle for equality. For example, in an address at Howard University in 1924 Johnson outlined his hopes for the Renaissance. "It is through the arts," Johnson proclaimed, "that we may find the easiest approach to the solution of some of the most vital phases of our problem as a particular group in this country. It is the path of least friction. It is the plane on which all men are more willing to meet and stand with us." This hope, that black cultural achievements provided blacks with a weapon against racism, was a consistent component of Johnson's attitude toward the Renaissance, and in the attitude of most other black intellectuals as well. Occasionally this attempt to link the literary aspirations of black writers with the political aspirations of the black intelligentsia led to bitter conflict over the use of literature as propaganda and the freedom of literary expression. James Weldon Johnson, largely because he was a poet as well as a politician, tolerated even the more controversial works of the Renaissance and defended the right of black writers to be free from political pressures as they fulfilled their literary ambitions. Nevertheless, Johnson still championed the Harlem Renaissance primarily for political rather than aesthetic reasons.[5]

Johnson first expressed his views on the relationship between culture and the racial situation in 1921 in the preface to his collection, *The Book of American Negro Poetry*. He suggested that "the status of the Negro in the United States is more a question of national mental attitude toward the race than of actual conditions. And nothing," he continued, "will do more to change that mental attitude and raise his status than a demonstration of mental parity by the Negro through the production of literature and art." Three years later he echoed these sentiments at Howard University: "I can conceive of nothing that will go further to raise the status of the Negro in America than the work done by great Aframerican creative artists." Back in 1916, when Johnson first considered accepting the post at the NAACP, he had worried about how he could combine his literary ambitions with a political job. W.E.B. Du Bois even wrote to assure him that his new position and the wide variety of people he would meet would be an asset, not a liability to his literary work. By the mid-1920s, though, Johnson had reversed his priorities. Black literature, and the Harlem Renaissance in particular, became the means to a political end. Art would be the most effective solution to the race problem in America.[6]

Because he saw black literature within the context of the struggle for civil and political rights, Johnson was sensitive about both the content and the literary form of the works of the Renaissance. In terms of content he insisted that the major focus of black poetry must be race consciousness. One aspect of racially conscious poetry was, of course, protest poetry. In 1924 Johnson singled out Claude McKay's "If We Must Die" and "To the White Fiends" as classic examples of this genre, and he quoted from his own work, "Brothers," to illustrate the techniques of using poetry to express protest. In this poem Johnson vividly depicted one of the horrors confronting blacks in America:

Enough, the brute must die!
Quick! Chain him to the oak! It will resist
The fire much longer than this slender pine.
Now bring the fuel! Pile it 'round him! Wait!
Pile not so fast or high, or we shall loose
The agony and terror in his face.
And now the torch! Good fuel that! the flames
Already leap head-high. Ha! hear that shriek!
And there's another! wilder than the first.
Fetch water! Water! Pour a little on
The fire, lest it should burn too fast. Hold so!
Now let it slowly blaze again. See there!
He squirms! He groans! His eyes bulge wildly out,
Searching around in vain appeal for help!   ·

·   ·   ·   ·   ·   ·   ·   ·   ·   ·   ·   ·

And now his fiendish crime has been avenged;
Let us back to our wives and children—Say.
What did he mean by those last muttered words,
"Brothers in spirit, brothers in deed are we"?[7]

Johnson maintained that the strength of this poem came from the fact that
he did not simply attack the inhumanity of lynching:

> I do not inveigh against lynching. I do not appeal for mercy or
> justice. I do not obviously denounce the lynchers. Nor do I hold the
> lynching victim to be innocent and by that make the appeal of the
> poem through pathos. I keep the poem hard and biting. I admit the
> victim's guilt of the revolting crime of which he is accused, then I
> make him place the blame where it rightly belongs; and at the end of
> the poem I try to drive home this truth—that the crime of the
> lynchers shows them to be lower on the human scale than the
> victim.[8]

If Johnson's purpose was to prompt young black writers to follow his
example and produce high-quality protest poetry, he was largely unsuccessful. For the most part Renaissance poets rejected this formula for
race-conscious poetry. In fact, as Johnson himself later observed, by and
large they disavowed such obvious protest in favor of a more subtle
approach to race in their literature. He went on to note, however, that
while the younger poets eschewed propaganda and the "race problem"

poetry in an attempt to transcend racial barriers and emerge as simply poets (instead of black or Negro poets), they still produced race-conscious poetry that was often more racially oriented than that of the overt protest poets. To his credit Johnson was not especially concerned that the Renaissance poets largely ignored his call for protest poetry. Indeed, he recognized and admitted that the real strength of the young black poets lay in their less direct, but more effective portrayal of black life. However, he also insisted that their greatest failures came when they tried to ignore race and racial problems. But he never went so far as to stipulate that black poets had an ironclad responsibility to confine their art to racial themes, and he refused to discredit totally all nonracial writing by blacks. Instead, he merely noted that black poets seemed to possess more artistic power when they concentrated on racial themes, and then he concluded:

> [All of this] is merely a confirmation of the axiom that an artist accomplishes his best when working at his best with the material he knows best. And up to this time, at least, "race" is perforce the thing that the American Negro poet knows best. Assuredly, the time will come when he will know other things as well as he now knows "race," and will, perhaps, feel them as deeply; or, to state this in another way, the time should come when he will not have to know "race" so well and feel it so deeply. But even now he can escape the sense of being hampered if, standing on his racial foundations, he strives to fashion something that rises above mere race and reaches out to the universal in truth and beauty.[9]

Johnson's attitude toward the Renaissance, then, was fairly complex. First, he recognized the propaganda value of literature and urged black writers to use their craft as a weapon in the struggle for racial equality. He pursued these ends himself in several of his own poems and generally applauded the efforts of others in this area, although he always demanded that propaganda complement, not replace, literary merit. In terms of the Renaissance, Johnson approved the more subtle and indirect approach to racial problems that the younger writers often adopted. Furthermore, in spite of his commitment to a political agenda, he was surprisingly tolerant of the subject matter chosen in a number of books by (or about) blacks. He did not object to books like Carl Van Vechten's *Nigger Heaven*, Claude McKay's *Home to Harlem*, or Langston Hughes's ghetto poetry. He disagreed with those black intellectuals who denounced these and similar works because they feared that literature which portrayed the sordid elements in black life undermined racial progress by exposing the less-than-desirable aspects of black America to an overly critical white public. Johnson, while never backing away from the political struggle, accepted the ghetto realism of many of the younger writers as an accurate and valid portrayal of the exotic and lusty aspects of Harlem life.[10]

The key to James Weldon Johnson's toleration of diverse literary works was his firm belief that the fundamental problems facing black writers were to produce first-rate literature, get these works published, and find an audience. He was very familiar with the problems earlier black writers such as Charles W. Chesnutt had faced finding publishers and markets for their books. After all, he faced similar difficulties with his novel, *The Autobiography of an Ex-Colored Man*. As long as a black writer examined racial themes, Johnson was satisfied. His tastes encompassed a wide range of black literature, from the ghetto realism of *Home to Harlem* to the more conventional, middle-class novels of Jessie Fauset. Furthermore, he was deeply committed to the principle that all black poets and novelists must have the freedom and opportunity to express themselves. After all, he argued, it was far more important that a black writer find a publisher than that his works embrace middle-class standards of morality or that they consciously seek to uplift the race. Indeed, Johnson acknowledged that the "lower levels" of black life generally presented the writer with "greater dramatic and artistic potentialities than the so-called higher classes, who so closely resembled the bourgeois white classes." Finally, he maintained that literature did not have to resort to propaganda to benefit the race. Instead he felt that any writer who honestly portrayed any aspect of black life would promote the cause of racial equality. The mere presence of black literature on the shelves of libraries and book shops would constitute a victory against racial prejudice and ignorance.[11]

Consistent with this attitude, most of Johnson's activities in promoting the Harlem Renaissance focused on helping young black writers get their work published. By the mid-1920s Johnson occupied a very powerful position within the black literary community and had established strategic contacts among white literati. His endorsement could open the doors to white publishing houses and white patronage; he could lead an unknown black writer down the path that led to the fame (if not the fortune) that awaited in those years when the Negro was in vogue.

Johnson, perhaps more than any other black of his day, was well situated to accomplish these goals. First, through his varied career in the arts and politics he had acquired the credentials which enabled him to contribute a great deal of support to the Renaissance. Through his work at the NAACP he earned a position of respect and prominence within the black community. Meanwhile, his experiences as a songwriter, poet, and novelist made him appreciate the needs of young writers and established his credentials as a qualified critic of black literature. More important, though, by gaining the respect of both black intellectuals and writers, he was in an ideal position to act as a spokesman and exert a guiding influence on the Harlem Renaissance.

In addition to his role in the black community, Johnson's friendships in the white community increased his ability to aid the Renaissance. Through the NAACP and his own literary activities he met a number of white liberals, including Joel and Arthur Spingarn, Alfred and Blanche Knopf, and Carl Van Vechten. Johnson often worked in concert with them, channeling funds into the Renaissance and helping black writers find publishers. To a large degree he served as an intermediary between interested whites and black writers. His relationship with the Knopfs was especially important. They frequently sent manuscripts from unknown black writers to Johnson for his evaluation before they would accept them for publication. Johnson's opinion was often sufficient to determine acceptance or rejection of a manuscript. On other occasions Johnson lobbied to get young writers published whom he had discovered, often working with Arthur Spingarn, Van Vechten, and the Knopfs. Throughout this period, and indeed even after the Renaissance had run its course, Johnson continued to use his contacts in the white literary and intellectual community to promote black literature.[12]

Despite the influence he wielded, Johnson's relationship with the Renaissance was defined to a large degree by his personality. James Weldon Johnson was exceptionally cautious, socially conservative, and very aloof and formal in his relationships with others. Even with his closest associates he maintained an air of dignity and a sense of propriety that contrasted sharply with the general informality that characterized the demeanor of most other participants in the Renaissance and the whites who were involved with them. The clearest example of this is found in Johnson's correspondence with his friends. No matter how informal and chatty his friends were in their letters, Johnson's responses were always meticulously formal in style and tone.[13] This formality, which verged on stuffiness, clearly set him apart from the younger members of the Renaissance, especially the bohemian element. Although he attended many of the same parties and frequented the same cabarets, his aloofness prevented him from forming any close, informal relationships with Renaissance writers. (Johnson's wife, Grace Nail Johnson, whom some labeled the social dictator of Harlem, steadfastly refused to attend any of hair-straightening heiress A'Lelia Walker's notorious Harlem parties, although most other literary figures could be found there.)[14] Throughout this period Johnson maintained his distance from the active participants in the Renaissance, where he could serve more effectively as an adviser to and critic of the movement. He was far more of a father figure (or perhaps a friendly uncle) to the younger writers than a colleague or an intimate friend. It must be stressed, though, that his formality and aloofness did not anger or alienate the young writers. Instead it created the barriers that enabled him to function in a special role. Johnson's personality ideally suited his position as a fatherly adviser and friendly critic of the Harlem Renaissance. He could not have maintained the distance necessary for him to serve in this capacity if he had attempted to be an active participant in the literary activities or the bohemian lifestyles that abounded in Harlem in the 1920s.

Johnson was extremely effective as a promoter of the Harlem Renaissance. He was quite successful in helping a number of black writers find publishers and patrons, and he introduced several to the literary community in the early 1920s through his column in the *Age* and in both the 1922 and 1931 editions of his collection, *The Book of American Negro Poetry*. Langston Hughes and Claude McKay were especially indebted to him. Johnson helped launch Hughes's literary career in 1925 when he read aloud "The Weary Blues" at the *Opportunity* awards banquet. As a result of Johnson's assistance, that evening Hughes met Carl Van Vechten who read his poems and arranged for them to be published by Alfred Knopf. In 1922 Johnson had helped Claude McKay sell copies of his just-published collection of poetry, *Harlem Shadows*, and helped him raise money for his trip to Europe and the Soviet Union. Eleven years later when McKay, who had never been an American citizen, was down and out in North Africa and having difficulty getting permission from immigration officials to return to the United States, Johnson contacted an old friend at the State Department who arranged McKay's readmittance to the country. Throughout the 1920s and the early 1930s Johnson provided similar assistance to many other Renaissance writers. Although he remained aloof from the participants in the movement and although he did not always share their literary views, he was so committed to black literature that he did everything possible to promote the Harlem Renaissance.[15]

In 1931 Johnson resigned his post with the NAACP, left New York, and accepted a position as writer-in-residence at Fisk University. The principal advantage of this job change was that it gave him a great deal of free time to devote to literary activities, even though it removed him from the center of black literary activity. However, by the early 1930s Johnson's reputation was so widespread that prospective writers regularly sent him manuscripts and requested his advice, criticism, and help in finding a publisher. Johnson claimed that he was still very much interested in the Renaissance, which was slowly waning in the early 1930s, and he devoted much attention to it in his Fisk lectures on black literature. However, as he became more and more the elder statesman of the movement, his tendencies toward aloofness grew, increasing his isolation in both distance and spirit from the young generation of black writers.

This development was clearly reflected by Johnson's involvement at Fisk. John Hope Franklin, who was a student there in 1931, recalled the excited anticipation of students awaiting Johnson's arrival. This excitement faded into disappointment, and Johnson was remembered as one of the campus's elite professors who dressed impeccably but maintained a distant relationship with his students. Black writers shared these experiences and found it increasingly difficult to get his ear. In fact, as Owen Dodson discovered, an unknown writer was very fortunate if Johnson took time to look at his manuscript at all. When Dodson sent several poems to Fisk in 1933, Johnson's secretary replied:

> For the past year or so Mr. Johnson has received so many manuscripts from young authors all over the country that he has found it impossible to accommodate all of them, and so he has instructed me to return all manuscripts received in the future with his regrets. You will note, however, that Mr. Johnson has made a few marginal notes on your work. I feel sure that if it were possible, Mr. Johnson would be glad to assist you further.[16]

Ironically Johnson's reputation as a promoter and friend of black literature ultimately isolated him almost completely from those he was committed to helping.[17]

James Weldon Johnson, then, always remained somewhat apart from the Renaissance even though he was its most significant promoter. Although he was a writer and a critic himself and knew virtually every participant in the Renaissance and although he lived in Harlem throughout the 1920s, he never participated fully in the community of writers there. At the same time he was equally isolated from the life of the average Harlemite. As his biographer, Eugene Levy, observed, Johnson was as far removed from the life of the average resident of Harlem as his white friends Alfred Knopf and Carl Van Vechten and probably gained most of his knowledge about the lower levels of ghetto life from the writings of Van Vechten, Hughes, and McKay. And, although he was cold and formal in his personal relations, in many ways he was something of a dreamer. After all, he envisioned the birth of a black metropolis in Harlem, even as the neighborhood deteriorated into a slum. And, he, more than anyone else, saw the Harlem Renaissance as a vital literary movement which would help blacks win political and social equality. [18]

James Weldon Johnson, of course, was not the only major black promoter of the Harlem Renaissance. He shared this honor with two scholars, philosopher Alain Locke and sociologist Charles S. Johnson. While James Weldon Johnson initially became involved in the Renaissance through his own literary activities, Locke and Charles S. Johnson were interested principally in scholarship and literary criticism. Neither demonstrated any personal literary ambitions. However, both became active boosters of the Harlem literary movement and contributed a great deal to its success.

Alain Leroy Locke was born in 1886 in Philadelphia. His parents were both schoolteachers and members of what Locke described as Philadelphia's "smug gentility." Although his father died while he was an infant, Locke enjoyed a stable middle-class childhood with his mother in Philadelphia, and at a very early age he began to be groomed for an academic career. Alain Locke possessed the most impressive academic credentials of any black of his generation. Always a brilliant student, Locke graduated from public high school when he was fifteen and then attended a teacher-training institution. In 1904 he entered Harvard, where he majored in English and philosophy, and in 1907 he graduated Phi Beta Kappa. He gained the further distinction of being named the first (and until 1962, the only) black Rhodes Scholar. Between 1907 and 1910 he studied at Oxford and then spent a year at the University of Berlin. In 1911 he accepted a position as assistant professor of philosophy at Howard University. Except for the two years he spent back at Harvard, where he earned his Ph.D. in philosophy in 1918, he spent the rest of his career in the Philosophy Department at Howard. It was while serving in this position that he became involved with the Harlem Renaissance.

Like James Weldon Johnson, Locke made his principal contribution to the movement as a promoter, or, as John Hope Franklin observed, the "liaison officer of the Negro Renaissance." He helped young writers find patronage, introduced them to the reading public through reviews and essays in black periodicals, criticized and promoted their literature, and boosted the movement in general. He made his greatest contribution when he guest-edited the March 1925 issue of *The Survey Graphic*—an issue that was titled "Harlem—The Mecca of the New Negro"; later that same year he published *The New Negro*, an expanded and more polished version of the *Survey Graphic* issue that also contained material that had been presented at the *Opportunity* literary contest. Locke used the term "New Negro" to denote the new vitality and racial pride that had appeared among young blacks in the early 1920s and which was reflected in their literature. In these anthologies Locke introduced the Renaissance to the reading public and outlined his views about the literary movement. According to Locke, the Harlem Renaissance reflected a new group psychology that had surfaced among young blacks in the 1920s. As he saw it, the young writers now rejected the sentimental appeal against racial injustice that had motivated earlier black writers and instead embraced the more positive attitudes of self-respect and self-reliance. They repudiated the doctrine of social dependence and strongly asserted their racial pride.[19]

Like James Weldon Johnson and most other black intellectuals, Locke had a clear idea about the direction that he wanted black literature to take. Locke agreed with Johnson that black writers should enjoy full freedom of expression, but, while Johnson essentially viewed black literature in terms of political objectives, Locke's concerns were almost totally aesthetic. Consequently he applauded the "lusty vigorous realism" adopted by most of the young writers, and he praised their struggle to free themselves from the dictates of their elders who "felt that art must fight social battles and compensate social wrongs." Instead, Locke observed with approval, writers such as Rudolph Fisher, Jean Toomer, Zora Neale Hurston, and Langston Hughes chose "their material objectively with detached artistic vision; they have no thought of their racy folk types as typical of anything but themselves or of their being taken or mistaken as racially representative." It is not the purpose of art, Locke maintained, to produce stereotypes—instead, art should explore the uniqueness and variety of life. The Renaissance, he insisted, should be racial, not for the sake of politics or propaganda, but "purely for the sake of art," and race should become an idiom of experience for the artist, "a sort of added enriching adventure and discipline, giving subtler overtones to life, making it more beautiful and interesting," which deepened rather than narrowed social vision. A quarter of a century later, Locke still found these arguments valid. Looking back on the Harlem Renaissance from the perspective of mid-century America, he observed that when "racial themes are imposed upon the Negro author either from within or without, they become an intolerable and limiting artistic ghetto, but . . . accepted by choice, either on the ground of best known material or preferred opportunity, they stake off a cultural bonanza."[20]

In encouraging black writers to view themselves as artists rather than polemicists, Locke consistently went farther than other black intellectuals in protecting artistic freedom and eschewing literary propaganda, and consequently he did a great deal in this area alone to strengthen the Renaissance. This, however, was not his only concern. As much as was consistent with his commitment to artistic freedom, he urged black writers to mine the rich vein of their racial heritage for its literary wealth. Black artists, Locke urged, should carry their search for literary material both to Africa, which had already inspired Europeans such as Pablo Picasso and Georges Braque, and to the South, where poets like Jean Toomer were already examining closely the "racy peasant undersoil of the race life."[21] He saw the fruits of merging art and black traditions already beginning to blossom in a number of the works of the early Renaissance:

The interesting experiment of Weldon Johnson in *Creation: A Negro Sermon*, to transpose the dialect motive and carry it through the idioms of imagery rather than the broken phonetics of speech is a case in point. In music such transfusions of racial idioms with the modernistic styles of expression has already taken place; in the other areas of art it is just as possible and likely. Thus under the sophistications of modern style may be detected in almost all our artists a fresh distinctive note that the majority of them admit as the instinctive gift of the folk spirit. Toomer gives a musical folk-lilt and a glamorous sensuous ecstasy to the style of the American prose modernists. McKay adds Aesop and peasant irony to the social novel and folk clarity and naivete to lyric thought. Fisher adds the tenseness and emotional raciness of Uncle Remus to the art of Maupassant and O. Henry. Walrond has a tropical color and almost volcanic gush that are unique even after more than a generation of exotic word painting by master artists. Langston Hughes has a distinctive fervency of color and rhythm, and a Biblical simplicity of speech that is colloquial in derivation, but full of artistry. Roland Hayes carries the rhapsodic gush and depth of folk-song to the old masters. Countee Cullen blends the simple with the sophisticated so originally as almost to put the vineyards themselves into crystal goblets.[22]

Although some of his images are muddled and others somewhat overstated, Locke's intent was clear. He urged black writers to merge their racial experience into the sophisticated mainstream of art and literature in order to rejuvenate Western culture.

Like Johnson, Locke devoted a lot of time and energy to helping promote the Renaissance and assisting young black writers launch their literary careers. In 1922, for example, Locke became interested in Jean Toomer. He frequently invited Toomer to his home, where he met other young black writers, he helped Toomer publish his poetry in *Crisis* and included his play "Balo" in an anthology that finally came out in 1927, and he offered to prepare an advance review of *Cane*. In a 1924 article (which Locke coauthored with W.E.B. Du Bois) he featured Toomer as an example of the potential of the young black writers.[23]

Locke also became interested in Langston Hughes's career after he saw several of his poems in *Crisis* in 1922. That winter he contacted the young poet and attempted to arrange a meeting. At the time Hughes was working on a fleet of mothballed Liberty ships tied up on the Hudson and was intimidated by educated people, so he avoided the Howard professor. Two years later, while Hughes was working in a Paris restaurant, Locke looked him up and arranged to publish several of his poems in the New Negro issue of *The Survey Graphic*. Locke also introduced the young poet to several art patrons and took him on a tour of Venice. During this same period Locke became interested in another of the young Harlem poets, Countee Cullen. He met Cullen while the poet was still a student at New York University and was deeply affected by his work. Cullen, perhaps more than any other Renaissance writer, was impressed by the sophistication of the Howard professor and captivated by his sense of a black literary aesthetic; Locke, in turn, praised Cullen's poetry and, as he did for Hughes and other poets, included several examples in *The Survey Graphic*.[24]

Locke assisted a number of other black writers besides Toomer, Hughes, and Cullen. He published their work in *The Survey Graphic* and *The New Negro*, often bringing them to the attention of the white reading

public for the first time. He also helped them find publishers and introduced them to potential patrons. In addition he consistently defended
their right of freedom of expression and generally did everything within
his power to promote the movement. In spite of this he was not particularly
liked by most of the Renaissance writers. In fact only Countee Cullen,
who was strongly attracted to Locke, and Langston Hughes, who came to
sincerely admire the Howard professor after he got over his initial feeling
of intimidation, publicly expressed friendship or admiration for him. Two
writers, Zora Neale Hurston and Claude McKay, were especially sharp in
their criticisms, even though Locke had included the work of both in *The
New Negro* and had done a great deal to help Hurston launch her career.
Hurston was especially venomous in her denunciation. She characterized
him as a "malicious, spiteful little snot" who attempted to dominate the
Renaissance on the basis of his academic credentials. She claimed that
he ran a "mental pawnshop," lending out patronage in exchange for ideas
which he took in and "soon passes off as his own." Finally she warned,
"God help you if you get on without letting him 'represent' you."[25]

Zora Neale Hurston, who was extremely colorful if not always accurate
in her observations, repeated and expanded on these charges in a letter
she tried to get published in *Opportunity* in 1937. She repeated her
charge that Locke aspired to be the "race leader" and that he had stolen
most of his ideas from others. In addition she accused him of insincerity
and hypocrisy, recalling that at Howard University:

> he was one of the leaders in the hullabaloo against the singing of
> Negro spirituals. That was before so many people in high places had
> praised them. Now he tootches his lips all out ans [sic] shivers with
> ecstasy when he speaks of "those beautiful and sensitive things." I
> remember him trembling with emotion over "the faithfulness to
> Negro religion" in "The Green Pastures": Which is anything you
> want to call it but the truth. But nobody was going to catch Dr. Locke
> not chiming in with anything so popular as that.[26]

Apparently the hot-tempered Hurston cooled off after a time. Not surprisingly, her letter was not published. Furthermore, in her autobiography,
published five years later, there is no repetition of the anti-Locke tirade.
Instead she attacked him indirectly by barely mentioning him at all even
though he was a major influence early in her literary career. She claimed
that Charles S. Johnson, not Locke, was the real force behind the Renais-

sance, and she even implied that Johnson had collected most of the material that Locke published (and took credit for) in *The New Negro*.[27]

Hurston's anger with Locke probably arose, at least in part, because of his review of her novel *Their Eyes Were Watching God*. Consequently it would be easy to dismiss her criticisms, except for the fact that others shared her antipathy toward the Howard professor. Jean Toomer, who, like Hurston, owed much to Locke for his early assistance with his literary career, later accused Locke of reprinting selections from *Cane* without permission. These charges, which came at a time when Toomer was attempting to distance himself from black literature and, indeed, the whole black race, were probably accurate, but there is no evidence to suggest that they were anything but inadvertent slights made with only good intentions. Wallace Thurman and Claude McKay, while not nearly so hostile or bitter, questioned Locke's credentials to lead the literary movement. Thurman satirized him and his efforts to define the aesthetics of black literature in *Infants of the Spring*. McKay, who first met Locke in Berlin in 1923 and then again in Paris in 1929, was amused by the fact that the dapper professor, who had been so shocked by the brutal realism of George Grosz's *Ecce Homo* when they first met, had since become a leading authority on African sculpture (which McKay believed shared a close affinity with Grosz's work). Although McKay admitted that Locke had done much to assist black literature, he did not think that the Howard professor had a sufficient understanding of or appreciation for the black Renaissance:

> Yet I must admit that although Dr. Locke seemed a perfect symbol of the Aframerican rococo in his personality as much as in his prose style, he was doing his utmost to appreciate the new Negro that he had uncovered. He had brought the best examples of their work together in a pioneer book. But from the indication of his appreciation it was evident that he could not lead a Negro Renaissance. His introductory remarks were all so weakly winding round and round and getting nowhere. Probably this results from a kink in Dr. Locke's artistic outlook, perhaps due to its effete European academic quality.[28]

At first glance it seems a little strange that a man who enthusiastically supported the Renaissance and defended the artistic freedom of black writers would draw their ire rather than their applause. However, the contempt that many black writers felt toward Locke is not really all that difficult to understand. First, Hurston accused him of displaying favoritism in bestowing his support on black writers, and, more seriously, she claimed that he made damaging statements about one writer to build up the career of another. Whether these charges were true or not is not the issue; the fact is that they were believed (at least by some) and they alienated a number of younger writers from Locke. McKay, on the other hand, was angry because Locke had altered the title of one of his poems without permission for purely political reasons. Locke did change "The White House" to "White Houses" when he published it in *The New Negro*, apparently to make sure that no one thought the poem referred to the residence of the President. McKay was still furious twelve years later when in his autobiography he accused Locke of arbitrarily tampering with the whole symbolic intent and meaning of the poem. Behavior like this was almost guaranteed to alienate black artists who were especially sensitive about any form of censorship or meddling with their literary creations.[29]

Perhaps even more than any overt action on Locke's part, his personality and style offended many black writers (and offended them in a way that James Weldon Johnson's aloofness did not). Most observers described Locke as a small, fastidious, and even dapper man who openly cultivated the polish usually associated with a Harvard Ph.D. and Rhodes scholar. Of course, James Weldon Johnson and W.E.B. Du Bois could be described in similar terms. But Renaissance writers, most of whom were in rebellion against this sort of formality, particularly singled out Locke as a symbol of those upper-middle-class Negroes who were stuck up, "dicty," or putting on airs. In a sense they resented Locke because he reminded them too much of themselves and reflected many of the problems and inherent contradictions of the Renaissance. On the one hand, Locke recognized the need for literary freedom and the need to free the artists' attention from a preoccupation with the racial attitudes and prejudices of white Americans; on the other hand, he reflected the problems that an essentially bourgeois literary movement faced as it attempted to understand and accurately express the life and aspirations of the black masses.[30]

The black intelligentsia and virtually all of the Renaissance writers came from thoroughly middle-class backgrounds. However, a number of the writers tried, not always successfully, to reach out to the black masses and especially to capture the spontaneity they felt characterized the black lower classes. Many of their most successful novels were set against the life of the lower classes in the urban ghettos; much of their poetry borrowed the rhythms and themes that the black working class had brought to its music and religion. But the most attractive feature was the supposed spontaneity of the black masses—a spontaneity that stood in stark contrast to the cold formality that characterized most of the black intellectuals, including James Weldon Johnson and W.E.B. Du Bois. Johnson and Du Bois, however, had earned the respect of the Renaissance writers for their political activity and, for the former at least, his own literary endeavors. Alain Locke, on the other hand, the small, dapper Rhodes scholar, perfectly epitomized those rejected bourgeois traits.

Finally Locke attracted criticism because he assumed a very vulnerable position in the Renaissance. More than any other figure, he represented the attempt of the black intelligentsia to define and label the Renaissance as a literary movement. Beginning with his essays in *The Survey Graphic* issue and *The New Negro* Locke was determined to define the aesthetic nature of the Harlem Renaissance. This made him a target for writers who resented being defined, categorized, or labeled, who, although emotionally attached to the Renaissance, also were thoroughly individualistic in their literary philosophy. Wallace Thurman in his satire of the period, *Infants of the Spring*, described the resentment toward Locke. In the novel Dr. Parks, a thinly disguised caricature of Locke, wanted to establish a permanent salon where black writers and intellectuals could meet and exchange ideas. Although his intentions were noble and his literary ideas valid, Parks simply could not impose order on anarchy. The preliminary meeting of the salon degenerated into a chaotic argument about the nature of art.[31]

This was the problem that Locke faced. Thurman and the other writers of the Renaissance rejected all artificial standards, whatever they were, whoever defined them. They insisted instead on a more personalized and individualistic approach to art. Locke supported the Renaissance and the demand of its writers for the freedom to express reality as they perceived it; and he did a great deal to promote the movement and the careers of many of its participants. However, when he attempted to define the nature of black literature, he came into conflict with those who resented being defined. This, together with the fact that he had became the symbol of rejected middle-class values and mores, made it difficult for Locke to relate to black writers. Nevertheless Alain Locke made a major contribution as the "liaison officer" of the Renaissance.

The third major promoter of the Renaissance, Charles S. Johnson, approached the Renaissance from a perspective different from either James Weldon Johnson's or Alain Locke's. For example, he was not known primarily for his contributions to the Harlem Renaissance. Instead he earned his reputation principally for his work as a sociologist and from the fact that he was the first black president of Fisk University. Johnson was born in 1893 in Bristol, Virginia, into a fairly secure middle-class family. His father was a well-educated Baptist minister. He introduced his son to most of the classics of Western literature, theology, and history, and saw to it that he received a good education, first at Wayland Academy in Richmond and then at Virginia Union University. Johnson graduated from college in just three years and then went to Chicago to study sociology under Robert E. Park. The First World War interrupted his graduate studies, but by 1919 Johnson was back in Chicago and deeply involved with the Chicago Commission on Race Relation's study of the 1919 Chicago race riot. Johnson gained a national reputation in the field of race relations for his work in this investigation. With his Ph.D. from the University of Chicago in hand, he received a number of offers to participate in similar studies of race relations and racial violence. In 1921 he accepted a position as Director of Research and Investigations for the Urban League in New York.[32]

Johnson arrived in New York in time to witness the emergence of the literary renaissance, and through his position with the Urban League he was strategically situated to assist in its birth and development. Not surprisingly, Johnson's background in sociology played a major role in determining his attitudes toward the Renaissance. Robert Park was in the process of revolutionizing the discipline's approach to the study of race relations. Traditionally social scientists had approached the subject of race already committed to two basic assumptions: blacks belonged to an inferior race, and because of this fact it was impossible for blacks to assimilate totally into the mainstream of American life. Park rejected both of these premises. He shifted the focus of the discussion away from an examination of racial differences or racial traits and instead viewed the subject in terms of class and status conflict. In the process he utilized two concepts that had been developed by the Chicago School. First, Park used his theory of "social disorganization" to argue that the process of rapid migration of blacks from rural to urban areas, together with the rapid social mobility and depersonalization of life in the city, resulted in the breakdown of social mores and community sanctions. This in turn led to the disintegration of the family and a growth in antisocial behavior. The victim of this process was the "marginal man," a concept initially developed by William Isaac Thomas but utilized by Park to characterize the figure caught between two cultures. In Park's analysis of race relations in America, blacks caught between the rural South and the urban ghetto exhibited the characteristics of the marginal man. As such they were situated in a strategic position where they could stand apart and evaluate both worlds—the one they were leaving and the one they were entering; but they also suffered from not belonging to either world and must endure a conflict of values that often threatened to tear apart one's personality as he or she wavered between the two cultures. In spite of this rather dismal picture of the black situation in the early twentieth century, Park remained optimistic, convinced that ultimately the inevitable result of the interaction of two cultures or two races was assimilation.[33]

Charles S. Johnson adopted the concept of the marginal man as the basis of his sociological views. In his analysis of the racial situation in America he stressed the negative side of the problem—the fact that the marginal man was trapped in a situation that led to social deterioration and disorganized, counterproductive, or even antisocial behavior. In the process of shifting from the folk culture of the rural South to the industrial culture of urban America, blacks found that discrimination and segregation prevented them from completing the transition, and consequently it left them semi-permanently suspended in the marginal situation. Their rural heritage did not survive transplantation to the city; urban white culture, on the other hand, did not prepare them to cope with a racially segregated situation. As a result, they developed intense frustrations and hostilities, including a deep-seated feeling of inferiority. Johnson's solution to this problem was fairly simple—blacks must concern themselves with reality and real possibilities, not impossible dreams. They must recognize that they are caught between two cultures and must adjust their outlook accordingly. Their education should reflect this by preparing them to relate to two levels of culture, the one they were in and the one toward which they are heading. But most important, according to Johnson, blacks must learn to value their experiences as marginal men and appreciate the record of their race in America.[34]

It was for this purpose that Johnson turned to the Harlem Renaissance. The young black writers appealed to him because they also were engaged in a search for the meaning of the black experience. In addition many of them focused their literature on the black experience in the real world—

the ghettos and slums of Harlem—and they urged blacks to investigate and understand all facets of their racial heritage. In other words, they were investigating through their literature the very issues that Johnson had identified as crucial to understanding the black experience through his studies in sociology and his work at the Urban League.

In the mid-1920s Johnson was well situated to aid black writers and their literary efforts. For slightly more than five years, beginning in 1923, he edited *Opportunity*, the monthly journal of the Urban League. The magazine had been established originally as a semi-scholarly sociology journal dedicated to depicting "Negro life as it is with no exaggerations" by publishing scientific research on race relations. As Johnson became convinced of the importance of art and literature in assisting blacks to come to terms with their difficult situation in urban America, he shifted the magazine's focus to the analysis and promotion of the cultural life of black America. Under his guidance the periodical played a key role in the Harlem Renaissance. He opened its pages to unknown black writers, and he took the leadership in organizing many of the contests and literary dinners that effectively publicized and rewarded the more successful black writers.[35]

Opportunity was not the only black journal to play a part in the Harlem Renaissance, but it was the most important. *Crisis*, edited by W.E.B. Du Bois, also published the work of a number of black writers, but it never really captured the spirit of the movement. Although for a time *Crisis* employed novelist Jessie Fauset as its literary editor and published a number of pieces by Renaissance writers, the magazine's tone and emphasis remained political, not literary. According to Harold Jackman, a minor figure in the Renaissance, it never enjoyed the reputation among black authors that *Opportunity* did. While *Opportunity* never totally abandoned its commitment to political and sociological reporting, it found its greatest success in the 1920s reporting and promoting black culture. Under Johnson's direction the magazine devoted entire issues to topics such as African art and the art of the Caribbean basin, it published work by virtually unknown black authors, and it regularly reviewed every novel or volume of poetry written by a black.[36]

Besides publishing the work of black writers, Johnson also organized the *Opportunity* contests and literary awards banquets. In this role he achieved his greatest success in promoting and publicizing the movement by bringing together white publishers and black writers. Indeed, in March 1924 it was Johnson who arranged the Civic Club literary banquet that helped give birth to the Harlem Renaissance, inaugurated the literary association between Renaissance writers and white publishers, and even more significantly signaled the active involvement of the black intelligentsia in the movement. For example, the "Harlem" edition of *The Survey Graphic* (which evolved into *The New Negro*) grew out of a meeting between Paul U. Kellogg and Alain Locke at the literary banquet.[37]

Within six months of the literary banquet Johnson launched the second phase of his literary operation when he established the first of a series of annual *Opportunity* literary contests. When he announced the first contest in September 1925, he used the occasion both to explain the guidelines for the award and to outline his views on the literary movement in general. Unlike Alain Locke, Charles S. Johnson did not see black literature in purely aesthetic terms. Instead, like James Weldon Johnson, he argued that a flourishing black cultural movement was an effective means of combating racism and advancing the political objectives of the black race. Indeed, he initiated the literary contests to achieve these ends by encouraging artistic expression and creative effort. As he explained:

> The purpose, then, of *Opportunity*'s literary contest can thus be stated in brief: it hopes to stimulate creative literary effort among Negroes; to locate and orient Negro writers of ability; to stimulate and encourage interest in the serious development of a body of literature about Negro life, drawing deeply upon these tremendously rich sources; to encourage the reading of literature both by Negro authors and about Negro life, not merely because they are Negro authors but because what they write is literature and because the literature is interesting; to foster a market for Negro writers and for literature by and about Negroes; to bring these writers into contact with the general world of letters to which they have been for the most part timid and inarticulate strangers; to stimulate and foster a type of writing by Negroes which shakes itself free of deliberate propaganda and protest.

The ultimate result of the Renaissance would be to create a body of black literature that would articulate honestly and openly the black experience, and in doing so would help free blacks from their marginal status and heal the wounds they had suffered during their slow transition into the mainstream of American society.[38]

Although he was principally interested in the political and social benefits that would be reaped from the Renaissance, Johnson insisted that black literature must transcend the limitations of propaganda and exhibit the highest artistic merit. Like Alain Locke and James Weldon Johnson, he demanded that Renaissance writers must be free to describe black life as they saw it. This, he argued, would result in first-class literature free from overt protest or propaganda but realistically expressing all facets of the black experience in America. This was the type of literature that he hoped to uncover by opening the pages of *Opportunity* to black literature and by sponsoring the annual literary contests.

Johnson's promotional activities were quite successful. The first *Opportunity* contest attracted more than eight hundred entrants, and the winners included some of the major figures in the emerging Renaissance. Langston Hughes, Zora Neale Hurston, Countee Cullen, and Sterling Brown were among the prize-winners of the first contest. The awards banquet of this contest and the two that followed continued the successful tradition of the 1924 Civic Club dinner in generating broad-based support within the black middle class for the literary movement. He even arranged for a black patron, Casper Holstein, to fund the second and third literary contests. From 1925 to 1927 Johnson's contests and banquets were a prominent feature of the Harlem literary scene and were responsible for assisting a large number of black writers. Even more importantly these events successfully publicized the high quality of black literature. Johnson noted with pride that several award-winners went on to achieve further acclaim. One prize-winning story from the first contest was recommended to the O. Henry Memorial Prize committee for consideration in its competition, and Edward J. O'Brien included several contest entries in his selection of the best short stories of 1925. Johnson could also point with pride to the effect of these banquets and contests on the careers of young black writers. Arna Bontemps would recall that winning *Opportunity*'s Pushkin Prize for poetry in 1925 and 1926 was what really launched his career as a writer, while Langston Hughes was a virtual unknown until his "Weary Blues" was read at the first Civic Club banquet.[39]

Although Johnson made a major contribution to the development of black literature, his principal concern was the political and social position of blacks in America. Literature was only a means to an end, a way for blacks to survive their ordeal as marginal men and a way to facilitate their ultimate acceptance into the majority society. Consequently, he tried to direct black literature into channels that would accomplish these ends. On the one hand he believed that literature was an effective means of bringing blacks into direct confrontation with their blackness, thereby helping to create a sense of racial pride. To this end he restricted the *Opportunity* contests to subjects that directly or indirectly related to the black experience, and he praised works such as Jean Toomer's *Cane* as an example of the type of literature that blacks should produce. In addition he viewed the Renaissance as a means of bridging the gap between the races. While he rejected the use of literature as propaganda, he did see it as a legitimate means of furthering interracial communication and understanding. Therefore, he cautioned black writers against using race for its exploitable or salable features. Johnson also insisted that mediocre literature should not be permitted to hide behind race. Rather, he demanded that black literature be judged by the same aesthetic standards that were applied to white literature.[40]

Johnson best expressed his views on black literature in *Ebony and Topaz*, an anthology of black literature and essays similar to *The New Negro*, which he edited for the Urban League in 1927. In his introduction he praised the maturity of writers who were more interested in portraying the black experience than in the response of their critics or the public. He also applauded them for avoiding some of the racial stereotypes that had ensnared their predecessors. As he observed, black writers "are now much less self conscious, less interested in proving that they are just like white people, and, in their excursions into the fields of letters and art, seem to care less about what white people think, or are likely to think about race. Relief from the stifling consciousness of being a problem has brought a certain superiority to it."[41]

In other words, just like his two colleagues, James Weldon Johnson and Alain Locke, Charles S. Johnson supported the efforts of black writers to concentrate on literature as art, not as propaganda, and he strongly defended their right to freedom of expression against those critics, white or black, who would limit the themes or subject matter appropriate to black literature. Each of these men saw literature as a means of addressing the racial problems blacks faced, but they rejected the premise that political concerns should take precedence over literary ones. Instead they agreed that the honest and realistic literary examination of the social and psychological experiences of black Americans was, in itself, the greatest service that black writers could provide for their race and the most valuable contribution that they could make to the efforts of blacks to adjust to life in urban America and to achieve self-respect.

In 1927, after devoting five years to the Urban League and the Harlem

Renaissance, Johnson left New York and moved to Nashville, where he joined the social science department at Fisk University. Following his departure, and facing financial problems, *Opportunity* partially abandoned its commitment to black culture. Although the magazine continued to publish material by black writers, cultural concerns once again took second place to economic and sociological issues. More important the literary contests and banquets, which had been "temporarily" suspended with Johnson's departure, were never resumed.[42]

Charles S. Johnson spent the rest of his life at Fisk and eventually became the institution's first black president. Unfortunately his academic career effectively ended his active involvement in the Harlem Renaissance. This was a great loss to the movement because during the few years he spent in New York Johnson had made a valuable contribution to black literature. As Langston Hughes recalled, "Mr. Johnson, I believe, did more to encourage and develop Negro writers during the 1920s than anyone else in America. He wrote them sympathetic letters, pointing out the merits of their work. He brought them together to meet and know each other. He made the *Opportunity* contests sources of discovery and help."[43] Hughes could not have been more flattering in his praise. While Johnson may not have been the most important black intellectual associated with the movement, he did make a significant contribution to the Renaissance during its crucial formative years. Perhaps more than any other single individual he served as the midwife of the Harlem Renaissance.

While James Weldon Johnson, Alain Locke, and Charles S. Johnson clearly were the most influential and important black promoters of the Harlem Renaissance, other blacks also contributed to the movement. Casper Holstein and A'Lelia Walker, while neither literary critics nor intellectuals, recognized the importance of black literature and provided much-needed financial support to the movement. Even though they were never closely connected to the mainstream of the Renaissance, and some even resented their involvement in the movement, their patronage was essential and appreciated by most black writers.

Casper Holstein, a West Indian immigrant who helped organize and then made a fortune from Harlem's numbers racket, was considered too unsavory by most respectable Harlemites to be included in the social life of the community. However, Holstein, who was concerned about the suffering of West Indians and who linked the plight of his people to the racial situation in America, used his wealth to improve the status of West Indians in New York. He and one or two other successful West Indian businessmen began quietly to advance the businesses and careers of promising Islanders. Holstein also began writing articles about the conditions in the West Indies for papers like the *Negro World*. Eric Walrond, a West Indian short story writer who was a participant in the Renaissance and worked for a time with Charles S. Johnson on *Opportunity*, arranged for Holstein to write a detailed exposé on conditions in the Virgin Islands for the magazine. Following this opening, the numbers banker became a patron of black literature, contributed the thousand dollars which made possible the 1926 *Opportunity* contest, and generally supported the Renaissance.[44]

A'Lelia Walker, the daughter and heiress of the Madam Walker hair-straightening fortune, also attempted to promote black literature. The parties at her mansion at Irvington-on-the-Hudson were a central feature of Harlem's social scene, although some boycotted them because of her origins as the daughter of a washerwoman. In 1928 she self-consciously set out to become a patron of the literary Renaissance. She opened her house to young writers, and she provided them with food and support. Her efforts to become the "patron saint" of Harlem's writers and artists culminated with the establishment on one floor of her mansion of a literary salon named the "Dark Tower," which was envisioned as a place where Harlem's literary community could gather informally, discuss their plans and projects with their friends, and find a meal and refreshments that even those of limited means could afford. Unfortunately this vision never became a reality. The Dark Tower opened after many delays, not as an informal gathering place for writers and artists but as a rather expensive club for cafe society, filled with well-dressed celebrities from downtown, and complete with a hatchecker and a formal tearoom with prices few writers could afford. Despite the dismay of most of the young writers, for two years the Dark Tower remained a gathering place where the black intelligentsia met influential whites, especially publishers, critics, and potential patrons, and occasionally a young writer like Countee Cullen or Langston Hughes. Although the original plan was never realized, the Dark Tower did help publicize black art and literature.[45]

Occasionally the line dividing the artist and intellectual was not very clear. Several participants in the Renaissance also served as critics or promoters of the movement. Langston Hughes, for example, spent several months in the fall and winter of 1931–1932 touring the South reading his poetry, mainly at black schools and colleges, promoting black literature, and encouraging the black writers that he encountered. Hughes also identified black writers to Nancy Cunard for possible inclusion in her anthology on black literature and art. Countee Cullen, Gwendolyn Bennett, and Eric Walrond held positions on the editorial staffs of *Crisis* and *Opportunity*, while Wallace Thurman briefly served as the editor of *The Messenger* in 1926 and then spearheaded the short-lived literary magazine *Fire!!*. Cullen also edited a "Negro Poets" issue of the avant-garde poetry magazine *Palms* in 1926 which included the work of a number of Renaissance poets as well as a critical evaluation of the movement.[46]

The individual who epitomized the role of the writer as promoter and critic was novelist Jessie Fauset. She was so effective in promoting the careers of young black writers that Langston Hughes credited her (along with Alain Locke and Charles S. Johnson) of having "midwifed" the Harlem Renaissance into being. Jessie Redmon Fauset came to New York in 1919 after teaching high school for fourteen years in Washington, D.C. She was better educated than the other Renaissance writers, having graduated Phi Beta Kappa from Cornell with a major in classical languages and from the University of Pennsylvania with an M.A. in French. From 1919 to 1926 she served as literary editor of *Crisis* (and actually edited the magazine during Du Bois's many travels). In this capacity she identified and promoted the careers of many talented black writers, including Langston Hughes, whom she first published in 1921, and Jean Toomer, whose work she felt proved that black literature could focus on race without resorting to propaganda.[47]

Jessie Fauset's age (she was in her early forties when the Renaissance began), her essentially conservative demeanor, and the fact that she had no worries about money tended to isolate her from the bohemian element of the Renaissance. If James Weldon Johnson was a father figure to many of the younger black writers, Jessie Fauset was their older sister. If she did not frequent the bars, cabarets, and house rent parties, she was active in the literary activities centered in the Harlem branch of the New York Public Library, was one of the first to become interested in organizing contests and prizes for Harlem writers and artists, and for a time, at least, effectively used her position as literary editor of *Crisis* to promote the Renaissance. Furthermore, she transformed the large apartment that she shared with her sister into a center for Renaissance activities. She occasionally sheltered newly arrived writers and frequently hosted literary forums and discussion sessions, which, although rarely relaxed or informal, were an important part of Harlem's literary scene. Finally, what added to her credibility among the younger writers and distinguished her from the other promoters of the Renaissance was the fact that in addition to her editorial duties she was also the most prolific black novelist of the Renaissance period.[48]

In 1926 Fauset severed her ties with *Crisis*. In part this might have occurred because of growing friction between Fauset and Du Bois over an unpaid loan of $2500 that the Fauset sisters had made to Du Bois. More likely the rift occurred because of a conflict about the editorial direction of *Crisis*. Fauset, who was deeply involved in the Renaissance by 1926, was impressed by the involvement of *Opportunity* in literary activities and wanted *Crisis* to give the arts parity with economic and political reporting. Du Bois, however, disillusioned with the direction that the Renaissance had taken, especially with the publication of *Nigger Heaven*, but impressed with the Bolshevism that he had observed on his trip to the Soviet Union, announced his intention to focus *Crisis* on the history and significance of the labor movement in the modern world. Fauset's departure from *Crisis* did not end her involvement as a promoter of the Renaissance, but it seriously undermined her effectiveness.

There were, of course, scores of other blacks who contributed to the success of the Harlem Renaissance. Arthur Schomburg, who established the black collection at the Harlem branch of the New York Public Library, Walter White of the NAACP, who was especially effective in finding publishers for black writers, as well as virtually every publisher of a black newspaper or periodical who reported on black literary activity and reviewed the works of black writers and poets helped to promote the movement. But the three major figures, James Weldon Johnson, Alain Locke, and Charles S. Johnson (the politician, the aesthetic, and the sociologist), dominated these activities and set the tone for the relationship between black writers and those black intellectuals who supported the movement. Although each of these men had his own agenda for the Renaissance, and James Weldon Johnson and Charles S. Johnson in particular expected that the movement would positively affect the racial situation in America, all three were very tolerant and supportive of all manifestations of black literary activity and made no effort to impose their political concerns on the movement. Consequently, black writers generally appreciated their assistance and owed a great deal to their efforts to open doors to publishers and patrons and to their support of black literary freedom. And the Harlem Renaissance itself would not have emerged as a coherent movement without the efforts of these black intellectuals to create the movement, promote it, define it, and give it direction.

7   The Black
Intellegentsia:
Critics

Despite the crucial role that James Weldon Johnson and other black intellectuals played in supporting the Harlem Renaissance, it would be a mistake to assume that the entire black intellectual community was uniformly elated about the movement. For example, the two most prominent black literary critics of the period, William Stanley Braithwaite and Benjamin Brawley, did not view the movement enthusiastically at all. Neither did the most prominent black intellectual of the period, W. E. B. Du Bois. Each of these men had serious misgivings about the nature of much of the Renaissance literature. While they generally supported black literary endeavors and encouraged and assisted a number of young writers, they were highly critical of a number of the Harlem writers, especially those closely identified with ghetto realism, and they were more inclined than others to view art in terms of its propaganda potential. Marcus Garvey, perhaps the most influential spokesperson for the urban black masses in the early 1920s, also viewed literature in terms of its political potential and had an even more strained relationship with the movement. Quite clearly, the black intelligentsia was not unanimous in its commitment to the Harlem Renaissance.

William Stanley Braithwaite was the first of these men to emerge as an unequivocal critic of the Renaissance, although he was also the least concerned about using black literature as a propaganda weapon in the struggle for racial equality. Braithwaite was born in Boston in 1878 and attended public school there and in Newport, Rhode Island. Although he was largely self-educated, he had become one of the leading scholars of American poetry by the second decade of the century. After publishing two small volumes of his own work, he became the literary critic of the Boston *Evening Transcript* and contributed literary essays to a number of magazines. In addition he edited several volumes of poetry, and each year from 1913 to 1929 he edited the annual *Anthology of Magazine Verse*. In 1934 he became professor of creative writing at Atlanta University. Braithwaite, then, had already established his credentials as a poet, critic, and literary scholar several years before the Renaissance began. He had also earned a reputation for identifying, befriending, and assisting young black writers. Indeed, before the 1920s he was the most important black promoter of black literature.

The black writer who benefited most from Braithwaite's support was James Weldon Johnson. Indeed, according to Johnson's biographer, Braithwaite was the closest thing to a literary adviser that he ever had. In 1911 Johnson began corresponding with the Boston critic about publishing a volume of poetry. Braithwaite responded enthusiastically and included one of Johnson's poems in his anthology that year. He advised Johnson to collect his better poems, arrange them into sections of racial, nonracial, and dialect poetry, and then submit them to a publisher. Meanwhile, he helped Johnson place his poems with several magazines. Finally, in 1917, after several years of negotiations, Braithwaite arranged for the publication of Johnson's first book of poems, *Fifty Years and Other Poetry*, through a publishing house in which he held a major financial interest. He then tried to promote the book's sales. In a review for the *Evening Transcript* he compared Johnson's dialect pieces favorably to those of Dunbar, praised the "intellectual qualities" of his work, and observed approvingly that his poetry was free from the "sensuality" that had marred the poetry of Dunbar and earlier black poets.[1]

In spite of Braithwaite's assistance, Johnson's first volume of poetry was not well received either by critics or by the public. In part its weakness lay in precisely the qualities that the Boston critic praised—the absence of emotion or sensuality. Also, there was no unifying theme to the collection. Instead, the book was a hodgepodge of dissimilar poems with nonracial verse combined with dialect pieces and rather mild protest poetry. Eugene Levy suggested that Johnson's failure to settle on a single theme and more important, his failure to concentrate on racially oriented poetry was due largely to Braithwaite's influence. If this was true, it certainly foreshadowed the difficulty that Braithwaite would have in dealing with the Renaissance poets. The Boston critic simply was not in tune with the New Negro movement or the resurgence of racial pride that defined much of the intellectual content of the Renaissance. Furthermore, he never accommodated himself to the new developments in Harlem literature in the mid-1920s, especially the concentration on ghetto realism and the fas-

cination with the lower levels of ghetto life that characterized the work of a
number of the young black writers. Braithwaite feared that if these
tendencies were not restrained, the Renaissance would stereotype blacks
as immoral. Ghetto realism, he claimed, praised degradation. In a very
real sense Braithwaite, in his own poetry, in his attitudes toward literature, and in his racial views, was more in tune with the nineteenth than
the twentieth century.[2]

In spite of these difficulties and the misgivings that Braithwaite would
have toward much Renaissance writing, he continued to offer assistance
to black writers, especially those like Johnson whose work did not violate
his sense of what was appropriate. In the summer of 1918 he provided
Johnson with constructive criticism and friendly encouragement for his
poem "The Creation," the first in a series of poems patterned after black
sermons. He was one of the most enthusiastic in his praise of Jean
Toomer's *Cane*, describing the young writer as a "bright morning star of a
new day of the Race in literature." However, it was his relationship with
Claude McKay that best illustrated the positive features and the limits of
his association with Renaissance writers.[3]

Braithwaite came into contact with McKay in January 1916, when the
Jamaican sent him several poems, asked for advice about the quality and
content of his poetry, and queried him about the appropriateness of
racial poetry. Braithwaite offered McKay friendly advice, and several
years later in a review of black literature that he wrote for *Crisis* in 1924,
he devoted considerable attention to the Jamaican poet. Braithwaite
argued that McKay's potential as a poet was unsurpassed, but he also
expressed his concern that the poet would never realize this potential.
The problem, as he saw it, was that McKay too often turned away from
pure and lofty ideas and became instead the "violent and angry propagandist, using his natural poetic gifts to clothe arrogant and defiant
thoughts." Braithwaite praised McKay's nonracial poems, such as
"Spring in New Hampshire," and even some of his racial verse like "The
Harlem Dancer," but he rebuked McKay for his racial protest pieces like
"If We Must Die."[4]

Braithwaite clearly had no appreciation for the ghetto realism that was a
part of so many Renaissance works. The Boston critic's taste in literature
was, frankly, old-fashioned. He preferred the novels of Jessie Fauset,
which described the lives of middle- and upper-class blacks, to the novels
and poetry of McKay, Langston Hughes, and other black writers who
explored the lower levels of the black experience. In this context McKay

would characterize Braithwaite as attempting to impose a timid, play-it-safe attitude on black literature.[5]

If possessing conservative literary taste had been his only sin, Braithwaite would not have so alienated the young black writers. Political protest, such as that which he criticized in McKay's poetry, was never a major thrust of the Renaissance; in addition a number of the younger writers, Countee Cullen and Jessie Fauset, for example, shared his conservative literary taste. Far more serious, though, was the charge, widely believed by many Renaissance writers, that Braithwaite hoped to channel black literature away from racial themes. This, if it was true, ran counter to the commitment to literary freedom, realism, and racial pride, which were essential ingredients of the movement. In his autobiography McKay recalled sadly his initial contacts with the Boston critic. He had written to Braithwaite in 1917 because he had been experiencing difficulty in getting his poetry published. McKay remembered that in his reply Braithwaite had complimented him for his work but had warned him that most of his poems revealed his race. He advised the Jamaican to accept the realities of racial prejudice and only submit poems that did not betray his racial identity. In fairness to Braithwaite it is important to note that in his correspondence McKay had expressed his ambition to succeed as a poet, not simply a black poet, and his frustration over the lack of interest in his nonracial poetry. Nevertheless, Braithwaite's advice, though given with the best of intentions, addressing the problems that McKay expressed at this early stage in his career, and responding to the realities of the racial situation in 1917, was totally incompatible with the spirit of the Renaissance.[6]

In spite of his conservative literary preferences, his distaste for the ghetto realism of *Nigger Heaven* and a number of other Renaissance works, and the fact that his attitudes about the relationship between race and literature alienated most of the young black writers and poets, Braithwaite did not sever all contacts with the Harlem literary movement. Indeed, Braithwaite even attempted gently to divert black literature into channels he felt were more appropriate and more beneficial to blacks as a whole. However, perhaps because his own experiences as a writer made him sensitive to the demands of most creative people for artistic freedom, perhaps because he had learned a lesson from his conflict with McKay and other Renaissance writers, or perhaps because it was simply compatible with his conservative personality, Braithwaite was cautious in his dealings with the movement. Consequently, even his efforts to wean black literature away from its fascination with Harlem local color and redirect its focus to the black middle class were never heavy-handed.

In his efforts to influence the direction of black literature, Braithwaite basically relied on his influence as one of the foremost black literary critics. His strategy was to make it clear in his many book reviews and literary columns the type of literature that he preferred. For example, in comments that he wrote to Alfred Knopf regarding Nella Larsen's novel *Passing*, he advised, "let others do the color, the riot, the childish abandon of Harlem life, in 'Passing' there is a quality that will survive when that glitter and tinsel have grown stale and perished." Braithwaite then argued that works like *Passing* would be far more effective than the ghetto realism of a McKay or a Van Vechten in improving racial conditions in America. "The country," he continued, "cannot afford to laugh at what 'Passing' reveals, as it laughs at the jazzy tales about the 'Black City.' It is such literature as 'Passing' typifies that will make America take an inventory of its prejudices and liquidate [them] for the credit of democracy."[7]

Braithwaite had another opportunity to influence the direction of Renaissance literature in late 1928 when he served as the only black judge for the annual William E. Harmon Foundation Award for Distinguished Achievement in black literature. This was one of the more prestigious honors established for blacks during the mid-1920s; gold medal winners received a five hundred dollar prize. In his tenure as a judge for the contest Braithwaite again attempted to promote literature that reflected his aesthetic standards. Two novels of the black middle class, Nella Larsen's *Quicksand* and Jessie Fauset's *Plum Bun*, received his votes for the gold and bronze Harmon medals, while he only recommended McKay and his novel of the Harlem lower classes, *Home to Harlem*, for an honorable mention. Interestingly, even though *Home to Harlem* represented everything that Braithwaite disliked about many of the works associated with the Renaissance, he still was willing to accord it an honorable mention.[8]

In spite of his general dissatisfaction with the black literature of the Renaissance and his alienation from most of the young writers, Braithwaite nevertheless maintained some contact with the movement. In particular he continued his close friendship with James Weldon Johnson and his active interest in black literature. In 1934, during the last days of the Renaissance, he approached Johnson with a plan to revive the waning literary movement. His proposal focused on a strategy to make the race "book-conscious" in order to generate a permanent market for black literature and black writers among the black middle class. First, he proposed to edit an "Omnibus of Negro Literature" that would include all of the great literary achievements of the American Negro. This publication would be accompanied by a promotional campaign that would seek to place the volume in 100,000 black homes and to establish an annual "Negro Book Week," which, under the slogan "Buy a Book by a Negro Author," would be the centerpiece of a national effort to increase the literary awareness of black Americans. Braithwaite's proposal is fascinating because it squarely addressed the major weakness of the Harlem Renaissance—its failure to create a black book-buying public that would continue to purchase books by black writers after all of the hype and hoopla of the Renaissance died down. Unfortunately this suggestion came at a time when the Renaissance was already fading and the Great Depression had undermined the ability of blacks to purchase many books. In any case Braithwaite's suggestions were never implemented.[9]

Benjamin Brawley was an even more outspoken critic of the Renaissance. He took an uncompromising stand against the tendency of Renaissance writers to concentrate on the exotic and colorful aspects of lower-class black urban life rather than on the more sedate lifestyles of the black middle class. Brawley took this position because he firmly believed that black writers had a responsibility to select their subject matter and themes with an eye toward countering the prevailing prejudices and depicting the race in a favorable light. Ghetto realism and Harlem local color, he feared, would provide bigoted whites with ammunition to use in their struggle against racial equality.

Benjamin Brawley was born in 1882 in Columbia, South Carolina. He attended Morehouse College and then did graduate work at the University of Chicago and at Harvard. After completing his education, he taught English at Howard University, Morehouse College, and finally at Shaw University in Raleigh, North Carolina. He also was a minister in the Baptist church. An extremely successful academician, Brawley was one of the most prominent black historians and literary critics during the first half of the twentieth century. By the time the Renaissance began, he had already published several volumes of social history and literary criticism, including his best-known work, *The Negro in Literature and Art* (1918). The revised edition of this book, *The Negro Genius* (1934), contained the most complete statement of Brawley's views on black literature and the Harlem Renaissance.

Like William Stanley Braithwaite, Brawley approached the Renaissance with ambivalence. While he approved of and encouraged the development of black culture, he had serious reservations about the specific literary developments that characterized the Harlem movement. He outlined most of these reservations, as well as his praise for certain aspects of the movement, in *The Negro Genius*. Unfortunately, Brawley was never very analytical in his study of black literature. His book was essentially an encyclopedia, listing and briefly summarizing the major works of everyone who made any contribution to black art, literature, drama, or music, but attempting little critical evaluation of these accomplishments except to point out those works or artists he felt were inappropriate. He did express clearly his likes and dislikes, especially toward Renaissance literature.

By the very nature of the book, and particularly by the title that he chose, Brawley indicated his conviction that the artistic accomplishments of blacks contributed significantly to their position in America. As he stated in his introduction, the "distinction so far won by members of the race has been most frequently in the arts." But, just as clearly he expressed his reservations about the new direction that some black writers had taken in the 1920s. In particular he questioned what he considered to be the obsession of some black writers with Harlem and the Negro vogue, especially the influence of Van Vechten:

> That literature, like most produced in America in recent years, has been realistic and to some extent analytical. In subject-matter there was influence from some writers who were not of the race and who were disposed to exploit it. Harlem began to be attractive, also anything suggesting the primitive. The popular demand for the exotic and exciting was met by a strident form of music originating in Negro slums and known as jazz. Along with this was a mood that was of the essence of hedonism and paganism. Introspection and self-pity ran riot. [10]

Although Brawley acknowledged the positive effect of the Renaissance in freeing the black genius, and while he applauded serious collections of black literature such Alain Locke's *The New Negro* and Charles S. Johnson's *Ebony and Topaz*, he was alarmed by the growth of other factors which he felt detracted from these accomplishments. First, he worried about what he saw as the total lack of regard for any accepted standards of prose or poetry, especially the indifference toward training and technique. The young writers, he observed, had been led to believe "that they did not need any training in technique"; consequently the "popular form of poetizing known as 'free verse' was most acceptable because most unrestrained. In prose the desired outlet was found in a sharp staccato form of writing that some well known authors used as a medium but that attacked the very foundations of grammar." Brawley also was alarmed by the preference for sordid, unpleasant, and forbidden themes that he felt dominated the movement. This ghetto realism, he argued, was usually so contrived, blatant, and so obviously done for effect that it ended up being artificial rather than realistic. Finally, he questioned the efforts of some black writers to capture the essence of the black folk or the black masses. "In general the writers were closer to the heart of the folk, . . . but while Uncle Tom and Uncle Remus were outmoded, there was now a fondness for the vagabond or roustabout, so that one might ask if after all the new types were an improvement on the old."[11]

In his survey of the work of individual Renaissance writers Brawley expressed mixed reactions. The more conservative black writers, especially those who described the lives of middle-class blacks in their literature, fared quite well. Walter White, an officer in the NAACP who wrote several novels during the decade, earned a fairly positive assessment, even though Brawley had to acknowledge his rather mediocre literary talents. He was even kinder to Jessie Fauset, whose four novels certainly addressed the subject matter that Brawley favored. While he observed that not one of her books was a great novel, he commended them for containing "strong situations, and much of tenderness and beauty," and for directing their attention to the black middle class, "a phase of life, that except for the work of Chesnutt, had been almost untouched in American fiction." Brawley reserved his highest accolades for the work of William Stanley Braithwaite and James Weldon Johnson, both of whom he praised without reservation.[12]

Most other black writers did not fare so well. Countee Cullen, for example, who basically shared Brawley's conservative literary philosophy, received a surprisingly mixed review. Brawley praised the young poet for displaying a "delicate perception and a keen instinct for beauty," but he also argued that much of his work was marred by an "artificiality, a thinness of substance," that he suffered from occasional "lapses in taste," and that there was a "sophomoric note" in his work that he found hard to outgrow.[13]

Brawley saved his strongest criticism for Langston Hughes. Although he acknowledged that Hughes had achieved a certain significance in black literature, primarily for his honest and consistent commitment to racial themes, he was not pleased with the fact that the young poet rebelled more than others against conventional patterns, both in literature and in his personal lifestyle. Brawley found little to applaud in Hughes's literary innovation. *The Weary Blues*, with poems set to the rhythm of jazz, he dismissed as "popular in its hour." However, he saved the brunt of his criticism for Hughes's second collection of poems, *Fine Clothes for the Jew*. This book, he argued, exaggerated the faults while possessing none of the merits of the first book and demonstrated sadly what could happen to a "young man of ability who has gone off on the wrong track altogether." He found absolutely no merit in this volume, concluding "it would have been just as well, perhaps better, if the book had never been published. No other ever issued reflects more fully the abandon and vulgarity of the age." No other black writer had his work so unequivocally damned by Brawley.[14]

Most of Brawley's criticism of the Harlem Renaissance was based on his aversion to what he considered the poor taste of much of the black literature produced during the movement. Initially he had been enthusiastic about the black literary activity that surfaced following World War I. Like James Weldon Johnson, he felt that black artistic achievement could help the race realize its potential and gain equality. This potential, he argued, had been betrayed by the young writers, who, trying to cash in on the demand for exploitative literature that had been stimulated by *Nigger Heaven*, turned their talents in the wrong direction and did their race a disservice by focusing their art on the crime, open sexuality, and immorality of ghetto life. Brawley could point out many manifestations of this trend. *Fire!!*, for example, he found disgusting, and he predicted that the federal government would ban it from the mails. However, he singled out Claude McKay as both the principal offender and the principal victim of the preoccupation with ghetto realism. Like Braithwaite, Brawley waxed enthusiastic about the talent that the Jamaican had displayed as a poet but despaired at the direction that he had taken in his novels, and he accused him of trying to cash in on the market Van Vechten had uncovered:

> For years he [McKay] had been writing exquisite or dynamic verse, and the favor of the public, judged at least by commercial standards, was but luke-warm. Now there was a change of tone and emphasis. It is impossible for him to write incompetently; on everything he puts

the stamp of virility. After the success of *Nigger Heaven*, however, he and some other authors seemed to realize that it was not the poem or fine touch that the public desired, but the metal of a baser hue; and he decided to give them what was wanted. The result was a novel, *Home to Harlem*, that sold thousands of copies but that with its emphasis on certain degraded aspects of life hardly did justice to the gifts of the writer.

Brawley acknowledged that in *Home to Harlem* and his subsequent novels McKay displayed his strengths as a writer, but he also felt that the preoccupation with slum and ghetto life prevented the Jamaican from producing the truly great novel he was capable of writing.[15]

McKay's career epitomized the tragedy and failure of the Harlem Renaissance, as Brawley saw it. The creative energies of McKay and other young black writers had been seduced into producing literature that sold fairly well but did, first, a disservice to the race by stressing the unsavory elements in the black community and, second, a disservice to the literary talents of black writers by directing them away from the subject matter and themes from which great literature could be made. As an expression of his distaste Brawley remained aloof from the Renaissance and critical of Harlem's sway over black culture. Although he continued to be active and influential as a critic, he did so more out of a sense of duty as a teacher of black youth than out of commitment to Renaissance literature. In fact Brawley refused even to acknowledge the existence of a Harlem Renaissance and never mentioned the term in any of his books on black literature.[16]

The difficulty that Brawley and Braithwaite had relating to the Renaissance was primarily because they were both deeply concerned about the racial situation in America in the 1920s and because they feared that ghetto realism portrayed blacks in a manner which would intensify white prejudice. It is easy to understand their apprehension. Both men were born in the 1880s and witnessed during their youth and early adulthood the steady deterioration of the position of blacks in American society. However, their reaction to the black political situation—to denounce any negative, critical, or even unsavory depiction of black life in black literature—was in essence an attempt to impose censorship on black literature and was incompatible with a vital literary movement. Most black writers recognized this and were unhappy with the criticism that Brawley and Braithwaite levied against their work, especially when it centered on their choice of subject matter. Langston Hughes, who was one of the most vocal of the Renaissance writers in his demand for literary freedom, explained the problems that critics like Brawley and Braithwaite faced when they tried to deal with the Harlem Renaissance:

> The Negro critics and many of the intellectuals were very sensitive about their race in books. (And still are). In anything that white people were likely to read, they wanted to put their best foot forward, their politely polished and cultured foot—and only that foot. There was a reason for it, of course. They had seen their race laughed at and caricatured so often in stories like those by Octavus Roy Cohen, maligned and abused so often in books like Thomas Dixon's, made a servant or a clown always in the movies, and forever defeated on the Broadway stage, that when Negroes wrote books they wanted them to be books in which only good Negroes, clean and cultured and not-funny Negroes, beautiful and nice and upper class were presented. Jessie Fauset's novels they loved, because they were always about the educated Negro—but my poems or Claude McKay's *Home to Harlem* they did not like, sincere though we might be.[16]

Never able to convince most black writers to view the racial situation in their way and to convince them to restrict their writing skills to topics that would improve the racial situation, Benjamin Brawley and William Stanley Braithwaite remained alienated from the Renaissance.

If Langston Hughes's observations reflected the direction that the more conservative black intellectuals wanted the Renaissance to take, it is probably fortunate that there was little that they could do beyond damning the work of Hughes, McKay, and others of their ilk, or bemoaning the fact that talented black youth seemed to be falling under the influence of *Nigger Heaven* and Harlem's cabaret and bawdy life. However, one black intellectual, W.E.B. Du Bois, attempted to take more positive action and redirect the creative energies of Renaissance writers into more politically effective channels.

During the 1920s W.E.B. Du Bois was in a strategic position to exert a great deal of influence on black literature. He was one of the founding members of the NAACP and editor of its widely read monthly, *Crisis*, and without question the best known and most influential black intellectual of the decade. He had also pioneered the militancy associated with the New Negro, and he had expended considerable energy trying to improve the position of blacks in America by creating a new society based on social and racial equality. As his biographer Elliott Rudwick noted, the Harlem Renaissance was, in many ways, the crowning glory of the Negro society that Du Bois had worked to create. However, the Renaissance would not follow the path that Du Bois had charted, and Du Bois's own political and social views were themselves evolving. As a result Du Bois would become one of the most outspoken critics of the Renaissance.[18]

There were several factors that affected Du Bois's relationship with the Harlem Renaissance. First, Du Bois's position as intellectual leader of the black community was coming under attack during the 1920s, much the way Booker T. Washington's leadership had been challenged two decades earlier. Although Du Bois had become a virtual institution for most younger blacks, several black intellectuals only ten to twenty years his junior were less willing to accept his leadership. As early as 1920 William H. Ferris anticipated much of the criticism of Du Bois that would surface during the Renaissance when he suggested that Du Bois was "too aristocratic and hypercritical, too touchy and too sensitive, too dainty and fastidious, too high and holy to lead the masses of his race." Furthermore, he argued that Du Bois was too eager to "referee" the work of other blacks in an effort to dictate " 'who was who' in the Negro race." Ferris's criticism was shared by three prominent black scholars: Carter G. Woodson, founder of the Association for the Study of Negro Life and History and editor of *The Journal of Negro History*; and, more importantly for its impact on the Renaissance, Alain Locke and Charles S. Johnson.[19]

Du Bois's conflicts with these three black intellectuals, based on both personal and philosophical differences, mirrored similar conflicts within the NAACP that would culminate, ultimately, with his resignation from that organization in 1934. The petty jealousies which marred Du Bois's relationships with other black intellectuals, his growing fascination with Marxism and intolerance for those who did not share his political views, his strong belief that aesthetic issues were secondary to political ones in black literature, and finally his near-prudish hostility to ghetto realism drove a wedge between Du Bois and the more traditional leadership of the NAACP, while at the same time isolated him from most elements of the Harlem Renaissance.

A second factor that affected Du Bois's relationship with the Renaissance was his own experience as a novelist and a poet, an experience which he tried to use as a model for the direction that black literary creativity should follow. Du Bois had first expressed his literary talents quite some time before the Renaissance began. Indeed, some scholars consider one of his early poems, "Song of Smoke," published in 1899, to be a direct precursor of the Harlem movement. His two novels are somewhat more difficult to categorize. The first, *In Quest of the Golden Fleece* (1911), does not shed much light on his attitudes towards black literature. Using Frank Norris's *Octopus* as a model, he examined the cotton industry and the roots of southern racial prejudice. The novel and Zora, one of its characters, illustrated clearly both the problem that Du Bois had in dealing with the black lower classes and how far removed his standards of morality were from those of Langston Hughes, Claude McKay, and other young black writers. Zora, who had been been forced to submit to the sexual advances of her former master, symbolized the moral degradation blacks suffered because of the heritage of slavery; although she escaped from this relationship, in Du Bois's eyes she still had far to go before she could gain respectability and her life could be salvaged. This dated view of morality that characterized much of Du Bois's work was starkly out of step with the values of most Renaissance writers.

Du Bois, whom Arna Bontemps described as a fastidious gentleman of aristocratic leanings, always found it difficult to embrace the black masses unless they had been thoroughly regenerated and cleansed of all traces of the curse of their slave heritage. In his second novel, *Dark Princess* (1928), which he wrote at the height of the Renaissance, he underscored both his alienation from the literary movement and his distaste for the preoccupation of many young writers with ghetto realism and the life of lower-class blacks. Du Bois, who was sixty when he wrote the novel, was firmly attached to the Victorian tradition in American literature. It was not surprising, then, that his literature was so conservative in flavor and that it contrasted so sharply with the work of most of the Renaissance writers. However, in spite of its conservative tone and style, the theme of *Dark Princess* was quite modern. It focused on a group of Asian and African revolutionaries who planned to liberate the nonwhite areas of the world from Western colonialism, clearly anticipating the third-world revolutions of the mid-twentieth century. In contrast to its modern theme, in terms of style, characterization, and sexual morality Du Bois's conservatism shone through. The characters were upper class, well educated, and cosmopolitan; their language and dialogue were exceptionally formal. In addition, in contrast to the radical political content of the novel, its moral tone and style were much closer to a Harold Bell Wright than a Langston Hughes or a Claude McKay.[20]

Perhaps because of his own literary interests, Du Bois was an early supporter of black art and literature. However, it is also possible to detect very early the attitudes that would alienate him from much of the Renaissance. For example, as early as 1905 he had proposed the establishment of a "Negro Journal," which was to be "a literary digest of fact and opinion concerning the Negro" and which would attempt to portray black life "on its beautiful and interesting side." Two decades later he would castigate Rudolph Fisher, Claude McKay, and other young black writers for neglecting the beautiful in their rush to depict ghetto life. And yet in 1912, he applauded developments in black music from the pages of *Crisis*, in the early 1920s he became an active promoter of black drama, and as late as 1925 he defended artistic freedom against those who wanted "no art that is not propaganda."[21]

Du Bois also greeted with enthusiasm the early stirrings of the Renaissance. In 1924 he sang the praises of what he termed "the younger literary movement," especially commending Jessie Fauset and Jean Toomer for their new novels but also noting with pleasure the work of young black poets like Langston Hughes, Countee Cullen, and Claude McKay. Basically, though, Du Bois's literary tastes were as conservative as those of Braithwaite and Brawley. However, he was in a better position to express his views, both by promoting the literature that he admired, and by strongly criticizing works and writers that he did not approve of. Throughout the 1920s Du Bois's forum for his literary views was *Crisis*. Like Charles S. Johnson, he attempted to use his editorship to promote and influence black literature. Although *Crisis* continued to focus primarily on social and political issues and was never as committed to black literature as *Opportunity* was, it nevertheless gave Du Bois a vehicle through which to express his literary views.

Du Bois's activities as a literary promoter took several forms. First, he employed several black writers on the staff of his magazine. Jessie Fauset, as mentioned in the previous chapter, served as literary editor of *Crisis* during the mid-1920s, and she was largely responsible for bringing the work of several of the poets and writers of the emerging Renaissance into the magazine. Along with Countee Cullen, who was briefly married to Yolanda Du Bois, Fauset wrote a number of articles for *Crisis* and helped Du Bois make the magazine a major force in the early years of the Renaissance. Indeed, in the mid-1920s *Crisis* briefly challenged *Opportunity* as the most important black journal of literature and the arts.

As early as 1920 *Crisis* had informed its readers that recent black literary activity held the promise of "a renaissance of American Negro literature." For the next several years it devoted considerable energy to making that promise a reality. In August 1924, following the lead of *Opportunity*, the magazine announced its own literary contest with prizes in a number of categories, including illustration and song. These initial awards included a $300 award donated by Amy E. Spingarn to "promote the contribution of the American Negro to American art and literature." The most impressive features of the *Crisis* contest were its distinguished panel of judges, headed by Rene Maran and including H.G. Wells, Sinclair Lewis, along with Chesnutt, Braithwaite, and Brawley, and the size of its prizes. By 1928 it was awarding fifty-dollar-a-month Charles Waddell Chesnutt honoraria to promising young writers, and it had persuaded a number of black banks and insurance companies to fund "economic" prizes for literary and artistic creations that portrayed black economic development.[22]

The close association between Du Bois's magazine and the Renaissance reached its peak in the spring and summer of 1926, when it published the responses of a number of prominent black and white writers, patrons, and publishers to the question, "The Negro in Art: How Shall He Be Portrayed." The purpose of this symposium in print was to make sure that the fledgling Renaissance did not get off "on the wrong foot." Contributors to the discussion ranged from veteran black writers like Chesnutt to youngsters like Cullen and Hughes; also included were white literary figures like Sherwood Anderson, Carl Van Vechten, Vachel Lindsay, Alfred Knopf, and H.L. Mencken. While a number of issues were probed, the dominant theme centered around the appropriate subject matter for black art, literary propaganda, and literary freedom.[23]

Du Bois failed in his efforts to use this symposium to define the proper direction for Renaissance literature to take. Indeed, the very attempt to define the appropriate nature of black literature offended many of the young writers. McKay described it as the attempt of that "NAACP crowd" to turn itself into a "Ministry of Culture for Afro-America." However, it was the publication of Carl Van Vechten's *Nigger Heaven* in August 1926, halfway through the symposium, that shattered any consensus that may have been emerging. This, together with the publication of McKay's *Home to Harlem* and the rise of ghetto realism, divided the black intellectual community.[24]

Du Bois clearly sided with the conservatives. By the end of the year he had published his very critical review of *Nigger Heaven*, in which he called the novel a "blow in the face" and recommended that those of his readers who might be tempted by a "sense of duty or curiosity" to try the novel, instead "drop the book gently in the grate" and read the *Police Gazette*. In December 1926 Du Bois also criticized the approach to black literature taken by James Weldon Johnson and Alain Locke. He implied that those like Johnson who felt that black literary achievement would lead to political gains were instead deterring racial progress by diverting energies away from protest and agitation. Likewise, he rejected Locke's focus on the aesthetics of black literature. He saw the pursuit of beauty for its own sake (or art for art's sake) as an empty and meaningless philosophy. He demanded that the artist consciously link beauty to truth, and he concluded:

> Thus all Art is propaganda and ever must be, despite the wailing of the purists. I stand in utter shamelessness and say that whatever art I have for writing has been used always for propaganda. . . . I do not care a damn for any art that is not used for propaganda.

These sentiments were clearly out of step with those voiced by most contributors to the symposium, who would agree with Mary White Ovington that stereotypes and propaganda had no place in art.[25]

In the late 1920s Du Bois became an increasingly outspoken critic of the Renaissance. Like Brawley and Braithwaite, he objected to black writers who concentrated their art on lower-class blacks and ghetto life. Instead, he urged black writers to choose subjects that would present the race in the most favorable light. Du Bois expressed these views in his regular column, "The Browsing Reader," in which he personally surveyed virtually every work published during the Renaissance. For example, he characterized Rudolph Fisher's novel, *The Walls of Jericho*, as another story of Harlem following in the footsteps of *Nigger Heaven* and *Home to Harlem* and then asked, "Why does Mr. Fisher fear to use his genius to paint his own kind. . . . the glimpses of better class Negroes which he gives us are poor, ineffective make believes." Du Bois saved his most vicious review for Claude McKay's first novel. Although he had listed the Jamaican poet as one of the most promising young talents in 1924, four years later he wrote that *Home to Harlem* "nauseates me." He accused McKay of catering to the "prurient demand on the part of white folk for a portrayal in Negroes of that utter licentiousness which conventional civilization holds white folk back from enjoying. . . . and after the dirtier parts of its filth, I felt distinctly like taking a bath."[26]

Du Bois was not offended by all black writing, only that which was mired in ghetto realism. He was much friendlier toward writers like Countee Cullen and Jessie Fauset, who generally shared his literary tastes. Nearly a year after he lambasted McKay, he used his review of Fauset's *Plum Bun* to illustrate what he considered a positive step in black literature and to underscore his concern about recent developments in the Renaissance: "*Plum Bun* talks about the kind of American Negroes that I know. I do not doubt the existence of the debauched tenth, but I cannot regard them as characteristic or typical. . . . [*Plum Bun*] will not attract those looking for filth in Negro life, but it will attract those looking for the truth."[27]

Du Bois also tried to use the *Crisis* literary prizes in an effort to control the content and orientation of black literature. In 1924 the contest rules required only that entrants be black; poetry submitted did not even have to deal with race. Two years later the rules incorporated a statement of philosophy which stressed that the contest organizers rejected the concept of art for art's sake and that "Life and Truth" took precedence over beauty—sentiments that Du Bois had outlined more fully that year in his essay "Criteria of Negro Art." In 1927, at the time Du Bois was becoming alienated from the Renaissance, he took greater control over the contests. No longer was there a published list of judges—the editor had become the sole judge; no longer were prizes announced at an awards banquet—checks were just mailed to the winners. This practice was continued in 1928, after which *Crisis* suspended the competitions.[28]

In 1931 Du Bois reinstituted the literary contests under a new format and with a new source of funding. That year he met Mrs. Edward Mathews, the granddaughter of abolitionist Patty Thayer, who offered to fund an annual Du Bois literary prize of $1000. The purpose of this prize, according to Du Bois, would be to draw black writers away from sensationalism and back into "a normal, human, and truthful channel." More specifically he hoped "that this substantial prize, as the years go by, will draw the thought and genius of our young writers away from the school of Van Vechten and the later McKay to a more human and truthful portraiture of the American Negro in the twentieth century. I do not want a Prunes and Prism School, but I want writers frank and unafraid, daring to produce things that are true and beautiful, and thinking last of all of the wealth which books and poems seldom bring."[29]

Du Bois, however, did not realize these objectives. No prize was awarded for fiction in 1932, because the contest judges decided that no book had been published that was worthy of the award. Apparently

Wallace Thurman's bitter satire of the Renaissance, *Infants of the Spring*, was not the type of novel that Du Bois wished to encourage. The following year the prize was awarded in nonfiction to James Weldon Johnson for his history of Harlem, *Black Manhattan*. No prize was presented after 1933; in the summer of 1934 Du Bois resigned his position with *Crisis* and withdrew from the NAACP after an ideological dispute with the rest of the Association leadership. Du Bois's efforts to influence the rapidly waning Harlem Renaissance ended when he departed from the NAACP.[30]

Although Du Bois, Brawley, and Braithwaite were more critics than promoters of the Harlem Renaissance, they remained clearly within the mainstream of the black literary and intellectual community. However, another major black figure during the postwar period did not enter this mainstream. His impact on the black community in general was considerable and is well documented; his impact on the Harlem Renaissance, however, is not so well understood. On the whole, despite some claims to the contrary, Marcus Garvey was not a major factor in the movement.

At least on the surface Garvey was as well positioned in the early 1920s as either James Weldon Johnson or W.E.B. Du Bois to exert a major influence on the Renaissance. He was the leader of the Universal Negro Improvement Association (UNIA), which in the years immediately following the First World War seemed destined to overshadow the fledgling NAACP, at least in terms of its influence among the black masses.

Garvey also had a forum for his views and for his efforts to influence black literature. In 1918, two and a half years after he arrived in New York, he established *Negro World*, a black weekly newspaper that became the principal publication for his organization. Regular features of the paper included a front-page editorial addressed to "Fellowmen of the Negro Race" and signed from "Your obedient servant, Marcus Garvey, President General" and a very popular literary section devoted to "Poetry for the People." Although George Schuyler spoke for many Garvey critics when he ridiculed *Negro World* as the "bulletin of the Imperial Blizzard," others like Claude McKay, who was not always a supporter of his fellow Jamaican, rated the paper as the best-edited black weekly in New York. It was certainly one of the most popular. It was distributed nationally (indeed, even worldwide) and had a circulation that at its peak was estimated to be between 60,000 and 200,000.[31]

Finally, Garvey was well positioned to aid the Renaissance because of his own well-publicized literary interests. In the early 1920s the editors of *Negro Age* included William H. Ferris, a historian and literary critic, and

Eric Walrond, a short story writer later involved in the Harlem Renaissance who between 1921 and 1923 served as assistant and then associate editor of the paper. The years of Walrond's involvement with the paper corresponded with the peak of Garvey's literary activity, some of which anticipated the developments several years later that launched the Harlem Renaissance. During this period, the paper published poetry, short stories, and literary essays by writers such as Zora Neale Hurston, Eric Walrond, Alain Locke, and Claude McKay. *Negro World* helped launch Zora Neale Hurston's literary career when it published three of her poems in April 1922; in late 1921 it anticipated *Opportunity* and *Crisis* literary contests when it staged an elaborate Christmas literary contest with thirty-six prizes in the areas of poetry, short stories, and essays. Walrond, who won $100 (and a job offer with *Negro World*) for his short story "A Senator's Memoirs," also owed a great deal to Garvey's activities as a booster of black literature. *Negro World* also promoted black writing by giving away books by black authors to subscribers to the paper.[32]

Garvey and his followers were also active participants in Harlem's organized literary activities in the years preceding the Renaissance. Speakers from the UNIA or *Negro World* regularly addressed the "Book Lover's Club," organized at the Harlem branch of the New York Public Library, and the "Electric Club," a Harlem literary and artistic society. Eric Walrond and other *Negro World* literary figures were members of the latter organization; Claude McKay entertained them in April 1922 with selections from his forthcoming book of poetry, *Harlem Shadows*. The Garveyites dreamed of nurturing a full-fledged literary community in Harlem several years before the Renaissance took root. The UNIA hoped to make its Phyllis [sic] Wheatley hotel a gathering place for artists and writers as well as "one of the literary forums and social centers of Harlem." Likewise, the White Peacock, a tea parlor strategically located on 135th Street a few doors down from UNIA headquarters, served for a time as a literary gathering place. Walrond described this cafe for the readers of *Negro World* as a place where amid avant-garde paintings and furnishings poets, artists, and musicians, along with students, flappers, and professionals met well into the night to discuss the issues of the day— "love and death, sculpture and literature, socialism and psychoanalysis. . . .[it was] Harlem's Greenwich Village!"[33]

Garvey and the UNIA seemed poised in the early 1920s to take the lead in promoting and perhaps directing and dominating black literature. However, this did not occur. The Harlem Renaissance, which arose in

Garvey's very back yard and which undoubtedly benefited from the literary climate that the Garveyites had helped to foster, had no real links to the UNIA. Indeed, participants in the Renaissance, both writers and intellectuals, were careful to distance themselves from Garvey, and Garvey, in turn, became one of the harshest critics of the movement.

Garvey's estrangement from the Harlem Renaissance is remarkably easy to document. Far more than even Du Bois, Garvey demanded that literature be subordinated to politics and valued art and literature primarily for its propaganda potential. In addition, he rejected the arguments advanced by James Weldon Johnson that literary accomplishments would help blacks win their struggle for equality. He scoffed at the idea that "the solution to the race problem depends on our development in music, in art, in literature." Garvey's approach was much more basic—in fact reminiscent of that of Booker T. Washington: "You talk about music, art, and literature, as such men like Du Bois and Weldon Johnson take pride in doing. A nation was not founded first of all on literature or on writing books, it is founded first upon the effort of real workers." Garvey stated these views even more succinctly in an article in the *Negro World* in March 1923. Again he stressed that black workers with practical skills that could be translated into economic success were the real keys to racial progress, while "philosophy and the ability to write books were not going to bring the Negro the recognition for which he was looking."[34]

Garvey put these sentiments into practice. Literature was valued for propaganda, not aesthetic reasons. As a result, Renaissance writers quickly disassociated themselves from *Negro World* and found other outlets for their work. Even Eric Walrond, who rejected Garvey's efforts to subordinate art to politics, left the paper in 1923 and took a job with the rival publication, *Opportunity*. *Negro World* continued to publish literature, but primarily the work of its own stable of writers who were thoroughly committed to the program of the UNIA and who possessed mediocre talent. Garvey's literary contests even more clearly reflected his determination to promote his political cause (and his leadership of that cause). While the guidelines of the competition had always been restrictive, requiring the subject matter of entries to relate to some aspect of the political agenda of the UNIA, the 1926 contest went even farther. That year all contest entries had to be essays that addressed the subject, "Why I Am a Garveyite." Obviously such a blatant attempt to channel black literature into self-serving propaganda did not win the endorsement of the participants in the Harlem Renaissance.[35]

Not surprisingly, Garvey also strongly criticized ghetto realism. Like Du Bois and the other conservative critics of the Renaissance, he demanded that black literature portray the race in a positive light, reflecting the "true ideals and aspirations of the Negro," and he was sharply critical of the misrepresentations and distortions he perceived in a work like Claude McKay's *Home to Harlem*. He accused McKay and his ilk of being "literary prostitutes" and called upon all blacks to boycott their work. The flaw in the Harlem Renaissance, according to Garvey, was that it pandered to the demands of white publishers and white readers, and betrayed all blacks by exposing their worst elements to a critical white audience. Such criticism was not unique—Du Bois and others generally agreed with this assessment of much of the Renaissance. However, Garvey also levied this charge against mainstream and conservative black writers like James Weldon Johnson, Walter White, and even Du Bois.[36]

As always, most of the writers and poets of the Harlem Renaissance resented these efforts by critics to restrict their literary freedom and dictate appropriate subject matter and themes for their literature. However, their criticisms of Garvey were surprisingly focused and vicious, they were voiced by almost every participant in the Renaissance (including those who generally agreed with conservative criticisms of ghetto realism), and they were echoed by other critics of the Renaissance. Virtually every Renaissance writer, from conservatives like Countee Cullen to devotees of ghetto realism like Rudolph Fisher, satirized Garvey and the UNIA in their work. While some of this satire was relatively benign, much of it was quite brutal, focusing on Garvey's physical appearance as well as his policies and occasionally tending toward racial slurs with a its focus on his dark complexion or West Indian origin. George Schuyler, for example, described his fictional version of Garvey as "250 pounds, five-feet-six inches of black blubber," while Du Bois characterized him as "a little, fat black man, ugly but with intelligent eyes" and labeled him "without a doubt, the most dangerous enemy of the Negro race in America and in the world. He is either a lunatic or a traitor." Some attempted to diminish the Jamaican by characterizing him as a clown or a fool because of his addiction to pomp, elaborate costumes, and haughty titles; others worried that these affectations would bring ridicule to all blacks; still others were frightened by the control he exercised over the black masses and viewed him as a dangerous demagogue.[37]

The effect of this intense animosity between Garvey and the Renaissance was that, despite the fact that Garvey had considerable influence among the black masses, the fact that he did contribute to black literature in the early 1920s, and the fact that he clearly anticipated much of the racial pride that characterized black literature in the late 1920s, he did not exert a significant influence on the movement. There were several reasons for this. First, Garveyism was rapidly declining in influence by the time that the Renaissance emerged in the mid-1920s. Charges of mismanagement and fraud led to investigations of the UNIA and Garvey's leadership that resulted in his indictment, trial, and conviction in 1922 and 1923, his imprisonment in 1925 at the federal penitentury in Atlanta, and his deportation in 1927. As Garvey's empire unraveled, he became increasingly defensive and intolerant of criticism, and he intensified his attempts to focus black literary activity on subjects and themes that would further his political agenda. He also became increasingly isolated from the mainstream of the black intelligentsia. Few black leaders rallied to his defense or viewed his legal problems as unjust or racially motivated. Indeed, most black writers, even those like McKay and Walrond who flirted with the UNIA in the early 1920s, went to great lengths to distance themselves from Garvey in the mid-1920s, while Du Bois, by now his most adamant critic, applauded his conviction and imprisonment. "No Negro in America," he wrote, "ever had a fairer and more patient trial than Marcus Garvey. He convicted himself by his own admissions, his swaggering monkey-shines in the court room. . . . this open ally of the Ku Klux Klan should be locked up or sent home."[38]

There were also subtler reasons for the split between Garvey and the Renaissance. Though articulate and possessed of a native intelligence, Garvey was uneducated and unpolished; his movement focused on the black masses. In contrast, the participants in the Renaissance, despite the bohemian or working-class affectations of some, were middle class and well educated. Even though several embraced bohemianism and would turn on a supporter of their cause like Alain Locke in an effort to deny their bourgeois roots, they also were offended and embarrassed by the vulgarity of Garvey and the excessive pageantry with which he draped himself and his movement. There was also an undertone of prejudice against West Indians in the anti-Garveyism of several Renaissance writers. It is certainly no coincidence that the Renaissance figures most closely involved with Garvey in the early years, writers Eric Walrond and Claude McKay (as well as Casper Holstein, who contributed several articles to *Negro World* and financially supported the UNIA, and Arthur

Schomburg, who helped organize the Garveyite literary activities at the Harlem branch of the public library) were also West Indian. Nor is it a coincidence that many Harlem blacks were openly hostile to the Harlem's growing West Indian population. As a character in one of Rudolph Fisher's short stories observed, Garvey should take all of the "monkey-chasers" from the West Indies back to Africa. While black intellectuals expressed no such prejudice openly, their frequent reference to Garvey's Jamaican origins (as in "West Indian charlatan" or "black, pig-eyed, corpulent West Indian from Jamaica") made the same point.[39]

Finally, the antagonism of Renaissance writers toward Garveyism undoubtedly was related to Garvey's demands that literature function as political propaganda. In this area, at least, their rejection of Garvey's leadership corresponded to their rejection of similar demands by Du Bois and other conservative critics of the Renaissance.

Marcus Garvey was not the only critic of the Renaissance who evoked a reaction from black writers. Consistently, a number of black writers resented and resisted efforts of some black intellectuals to define or control the nature of black literature; others, however, agreed with much of the criticism levied against the movement. Jessie Fauset and especially Countee Cullen agreed with many of the misgivings that Brawley and Du Bois voiced about the movement. Fauset never attempted to impose her standards on others, but her own work reflected the middle-class ethic that the conservative critics were looking for. As a writer, Cullen was sensitive to the need for literary freedom, but he was willing to place limits on this freedom because of the precarious position of blacks in America. In his *Opportunity* column he advised black writers that to "let art portray things as they are, no matter what the consequences, no matter who is hurt is a blind bit of philosophy. . . . Every phase of Negro life should not be the white man's concern. The parlor should be large enough for his entertainment and instruction." This statement was quite revealing. Cullen not only justified placing limits on the selection of appropriate subject matter for black art, but he also asserted that a function of black art was to instruct (or propagandize) the white reading public.[39]

Most black writers during the Harlem Renaissance disagreed with Cullen's advice and with the efforts of black critics to define what subjects were suitable for black literature. Wallace Thurman was especially critical of the "prejudiced, myopic" public, but especially the black public "that resent[s] any novel, no matter how meritorious, that does not deal with what they call 'the better class of Negroes.' " Claude McKay, whose poem "If We Must Die" was one of the strongest political protest pieces to come out of the Renaissance, strenuously objected to any effort to restrict artistic freedom, even for the sake of political or social reform. "I believe in organized political propaganda," he proclaimed, "I don't in organized propaganda art." In the 1920s it was Langston Hughes who was the most articulate defender of the right of black writers to select their subject matter, theme, and literary style without bending to outside pressures, whether from supporters or critics. In his essay "The Negro Artist and the Racial Mountain," he spoke for most of his colleagues when he proclaimed:

> We younger Negro artists who create now intend to express our dark-skinned selves without fear or shame. If white people are pleased we are glad. If they are not, it doesn't matter. We know that we are beautiful. And ugly too. The tom-tom cries and the tom-tom laughs. If colored people are pleased we are glad. If they are not their displeasure doesn't matter either. We build our temples for tomorrow, as strong as we know how, and we stand on top of the mountain, free within ourselves. [40]

It is obvious that the black intelligentsia made an important contribution to the Harlem Renaissance. Both the promoters and the critics struggled to understand the movement, assess its impact on black America, and, if possible, direct it along paths they felt desirable. While black writers might chafe at this unwelcome interference and even rebel at some of the criticism, they depended on the assistance and the nurturing of a literary community that went with it.

8 Black Writers and White Promoters

While the black intelligentsia played a major role in the Harlem Renaissance, their efforts alone were not enough to create a major literary movement. Black America in the 1920s did not possess the resources to develop a full-fledged literary movement. Blacks did not control the publishing houses, they could not mobilize a large enough body of book buyers, and they lacked the capital and contacts in their own community to sustain a major literary movement. Consequently, while the Harlem Renaissance was a black literary movement, it had significant and indispensable links to the white literary community.

White involvement in the Renaissance took several forms. First, a number of white publishers centered in New York and led by firms like Alfred Knopf played a major role in identifying and promoting black literary talent. White publishers worked through their contacts with black writers and the black intelligentsia, or through white writers and literary promoters who had such contacts. The link between black writers and white publishers is itself an interesting aspect of the black literary movement. A second group of whites involved in the movement were those who provided financial support to black writers and black literary activity. They included patrons who established individual associations with specific black writers as well as those whose funding activities affected larger numbers of Renaissance participants. The relationship between white patrons and their black protégés, while often cordial, sometimes resulted in misunderstandings and problems. The third category of whites involved in the movement was the handful who found that the Renaissance overlapped their own literary or political activities. Theirs was generally a brief but occasionally intense involvement. Obviously these categories are not mutually exclusive. Some white supporters of the Renaissance could be placed in two categories; Carl Van Vechten fell into all three. Whatever its nature and however well intentioned, white involvement in the Renaissance always generated a certain amount of suspicion and resentment, some of which was warranted, some of which was not.

Of all the whites involved in the Renaissance the most necessary were the publishers. In the early twentieth century blacks were almost totally dependent on white-owned publishing houses for the publication and distribution of their literature. Except for black-owned newspapers and periodicals and a few small publishing ventures usually affiliated with black newspapers or churches, this industry was exclusively white. While black poets could see their verses in black newspapers and magazines and while black short story writers could occasionally place a piece with *Opportunity* or *Crisis*, true literary success, measured by the production of a book, required working with white publishers.

The dependence of black literature on white publishers is easily documented by examining the experiences of pre-Renaissance black writers. Relatively successful writers like Chesnutt and Dunbar established close contacts with white publishers, while those who were less successful, like James Edwin Campbell and Raymond Dandridge, failed to convince the major white publishing houses of the quality of their work. Throughout the period preceding the Renaissance, black writers struggled to get their work published. Chesnutt, for example, negotiated with Houghton Mifflin for five years before it agreed to publish his first book of poetry. Then, after the commercial failure of his first two novels, he shifted to Doubleday for his last novel. Dunbar, on the other hand, privately printed his first two volumes of poetry and attracted the attention of a major commercial publisher, Dodd, Mead, only after William Dean Howells had identified him as a major poetic talent.

James Weldon Johnson had a similar experience. Even though he had enjoyed some success as a songwriter, he had great difficulty placing and marketing his first literary works. *The Autobiography of An Ex-Colored Man* was issued by a small, virtually unknown Boston publishing house, Sherman, French, but received no real promotion and consequently did not sell well until it was reissued by Knopf during the Renaissance. Johnson had even more trouble with his first book of poetry, *Fifty Years and Other Poems*. His mentor, William Stanley Braithwaite, finally arranged for the volume to be published by Cornhill Publishers, a Boston firm of which he was part owner. Again, the marginal resources of the

Table 7
Black Writers and Their Publishers: 1895–1935

1895–1919

WRITER	PUBLISHER
William S. Braithwaite	H.B. Turner
	J.W. Luce
James E. Campbell	Donohue & Henneberry
Waverley Turner Carmichael	Cornhill
Charles W. Chesnutt	Houghton Mifflin
	Doubleday, Page
Joseph S. Cotter	Bradley, Gilbert
	Cosmopolitan Press
	Cornhill
Raymond G. Danbridge	self-published
Daniel Webster Davis	Helman-Tatlor
W.E.B. Du Bois	A.C. McClurg
Paul Laurence Dunbar	self-published
	Dodd, Mead
John W. Holloway	Neal Publishing
James Weldon Johnson	Sherman, French
	Cornhill
Claude McKay	Watts (London)
	Aston Gardner (Jamaica)

1920–1935

WRITER	PUBLISHER
Arna Bontemps	Harcourt Brace
Sterling Brown	Harcourt Brace
Countee Cullen	Harper
W.E.B. Du Bois	Harcourt Brace
Jessie Fauset	Boni & Liveright
	Frederick A. Stokes
Rudolph Fisher	Alfred A. Knopf
Langston Hughes	Alfred A. Knopf
Zora Neale Hurston	J.B. Lippincott
James Weldon Johnson	Harcourt Brace
	Alfred A. Knopf
	Viking

Table 7
Continued

1920–1935

WRITER	PUBLISHER
Nella Larsen	Alfred A. Knopf
Claude McKay	Harcourt, Brace
	Harper
Wallace Thurman	Macaulay
Jean Toomer	Boni & Liveright
Carl Van Vechten	Alfred A. Knopf
Eric Walrond	Boni & Liveright
Walter White	Alfred A. Knopf

publishing house prevented the book from being adequately promoted and achieving any popular success. In both instances Johnson had to become financially involved in the publication process. He helped pay promotional costs for his novel, and he had to subsidize the cost of printing his first book of poetry. [1]

The growing public fascination with blackness that was reflected in the Harlem vogue and the higher quality of literature produced by young black writers in the mid-1920s helped open the doors of the major publishing houses to black literature. No longer were black writers forced to raise money to publish their material; no longer did they have to rely on the disorganized and inadequate resources of the black community to promote and market their work.

The degree to which white publishers opened their doors to black writers before and during the Renaissance is clear from the publishing experiences of individual black writers. Except for Dunbar and Chesnutt, before 1920 black writers had to rely on small, unknown, local presses or else publish their own works. If there was a center for the publication of black literature, it was Boston, where Braithwaite's Cornhill Company and several other small presses published the work of four of the nine black writers who were unable to attract the attention of the major companies. Marketed primarily by the authors themselves, these books suffered from poor distribution and consequently had no real impact on black literature. After 1920, however, major publishing houses, most of which were located in New York, were much more accessible to black writers. Each of the Renaissance writers listed after 1920 published with a major press; all but Zora Neale Hurston published with a New York City publishing house. Of the seven publishers involved in the movement, two (Alfred A. Knopf, which published six Renaissance authors, and Harcourt Brace, which published five) dominated but did not monopolize the publication of black literature.

Although the door to the major white publishing houses was open to black writers during the Harlem Renaissance, they rarely gained entrance on their own. As in the case of Chesnutt and Dunbar, the dynamics of the process through which a black author obtained a contract with a major publishing house still required someone to run interference—to introduce the unknown black writer to the white publisher, vouch for the literary merit of his or her work, and generally serve as liaison between writer and publisher. During the Renaissance this position was almost always filled by a white.

Examples of this process abound. Although Alain Locke arranged for the publication of two of Jean Toomer's poems in *Crisis* in the Spring of 1922, and Claude McKay accepted three of his pieces for *Liberator* late that summer, it was Waldo Frank who wrote the foreword for *Cane*, took the manuscript to Horace Liveright in December of 1922, and then telegraphed Toomer on January 2, 1923, with the information that Boni & Liveright had agreed to publish the book. A year earlier, in the fall of 1921, Joel Spingarn, chairman of the board of the NAACP and associated with the new publishing firm of Harcourt, Brace, arranged for that company to publish *Harlem Shadows*, Claude McKay's first American book of poetry. This was not the first time that Spingarn had promoted McKay's career. Five years earlier he had introduced him to Waldo Frank, who eventually accepted several of his poems for *The Seven Arts*. Max Eastman wrote the introduction for *Harlem Shadows*.[2]

Alfred and Blanche Knopf would be the most active publishers of the works of the Harlem Renaissance. They not only published more of the writers associated with the movement than did any other publisher, but also, more than the others, they were active promoters of the Renaissance. The Knopfs were close friends with the Van Vechtens and with the James Weldon Johnsons. Indeed, the friendship of the multiethnic threesome—Carl Van Vechten (the WASP), Alfred Knopf (the Jew), and James Weldon Johnson (the black)—reached an intimacy of great depth that encompassed far more than their common literary interests and endured far longer than the Harlem Renaissance. This friendship and the professional association that went with it placed the Knopfs and their firm in a position from which they could greatly influence the development of black literature. Not only did Van Vechten publish his novels with Knopf (including the blockbuster *Nigger Heaven*), but he served as talent scout, critic, photographer, and at times almost a partner for the firm, especially in developing black literature. James Weldon Johnson provided the link between Knopf and the black intellectual establishment.

Harcourt, Brace also had close ties with the black community. Joel E. Spingarn, one of the founders of that publishing company, provided a strong link between the white publishing world and Harlem. The descendant of a wealthy German Jewish family and a former professor of literature at Columbia University, Spingarn was best known as a civil rights activist. He was a founding member of the NAACP, and he served that organization through the 1920s alternately as treasurer, president, and board chairman. He had also headed a drive at the outset of World War I to recruit black officers for the army. He provided the funding for the initial *Crisis* literary prize in 1925 and, along with Alfred Knopf, published and promoted the work of talented black writers. Together, the two firms published the majority of Renaissance writers.[3]

Despite the new opportunity that firms like Knopf and Harcourt, Brace offered it was still not always easy for black writers to get their work published, especially in the early and mid-1920s, before the Renaissance had established the popularity and marketability of black books, and especially during this early period if the subject matter was controversial. Walter White's early efforts to get his work published clearly illustrates this situation.

By the early 1920s Walter White had achieved a degree of prominence as an officer of the NAACP, and he would be remembered by Langston Hughes for his fine apartment overlooking the Hudson and for the hospitality he showed to the "hungry literati." In 1922, largely at the urging of H.L. Mencken, White began writing a novel that chronicled the experiences of a college-educated black in the South and concluded with an exposé of the brutality of southern prejudice. Initially things went well for White—he wrote the book in one marathon twelve-day stint and, with the assistance of John Farrar, editor of *The Bookman*, he received the promise of a publishing contract from Doran. For a time it looked as if White would publish the second book of the emerging Renaissance.[4]

Unfortunately, Doran began having second thoughts about the book. Although associate editor Eugene Saxton liked it, as did John Farrar, George Doran worried about the impact the book might have on the South and, more importantly, on the business his company did there. In a meeting that included Saxton and Farrar, Doran asked White to make revisions, because the "Negro characters . . . are not what the readers expect." White did make a few revisions and even moderated the racist views of one of the southern characters, but this was not enough. Doran sought the opinion of Kentucky humorist Irvin S. Cobb, who warned that the publication of such an outspoken novel would trigger race riots in the South and make it impossible for Doran to sell any more books there. Saxton, who still liked the book and acknowledged the accuracy of its description of the racial situation in the South, wrote White in August 1923 that Doran was withdrawing from the project. Although "disheartened and disillusioned," White tried to change Doran's mind. At Saxton's suggestion he collected affidavits from prominent civil rights leaders attesting to the validity of *The Fire in the Flint*'s descriptions of racial violence and assuring the publishing house that there was no basis for libel or court action against the novel. These efforts fell flat. In October Saxton passed on the news that George Doran still refused to publish the novel.[5]

White's experiences indicate that as late as mid-1923 at least some major publishing houses still were reluctant to print a book by a black author that they considered racially inflammatory, even though it had the support of industry figures like John Farrar and Eugene Saxton. Southern criticism, whether real or imagined, intimidated Doran—the warnings of a Kentucky humorist carried more weight than the recommendations of one of his senior editors or the publisher of a prominent literary magazine. The publication of Jean Toomer's *Cane* a few months earlier had not yet broken the ice. Despite the fact that it was clearly a book which addressed the realities confronting black Americans, *Cane* still veiled much of its social criticism with extensive and occasionally obscure symbolism; it was more avant-garde than incendiary. White, always more of a reporter than an artist, openly confronted southern racism with realism rather than symbolism, to a degree that no one had since Chesnutt. Doran lacked the will or the courage to pioneer with such a book.[6]

After the rejection from Doran, White sent his manuscript to H.L. Mencken, who urged him to send it to his own publisher, Alfred Knopf. Mencken advised White that "I have already told Knopf that I think it would be good business to publish the novel." Knopf issued White a contract in December 1923, and *The Fire in the Flint* appeared in September 1924. While the book created something of a stir, it was generally well received. White and Knopf were able to mobilize considerable support in their efforts to promote the book. Lawrence Stallings, critic for the *New York World* and a native of Georgia, praised the book, affirming the accuracy of its setting, characters, and plot; Sinclair Lewis, Carl Van Vechten, and Carl Van Doren joined Mencken in acclaiming the book in reviews and publicity statements prepared for Knopf. The ever irascible Mencken devised the strategy of sending review copies to the most "Negrophobe" southern newspapers; the ensuing controversy boosted sales in the South, while the strong endorsements by northern writers and critics generated curiosity and sales in that region of the country. The result, as White noted, was that the book became "a modest best seller far beyond its literary merits," and, consequently, "Knopf and I will be able to pay our bills for some time." The novel and the surrounding publicity also made White something of a minor celebrity in both Harlem and Manhattan and enabled him to establish contacts with men like Alfred Knopf and Carl Van Vechten that would later blossom into valuable and useful friendships.[7]

The Fire in the Flint appeared about six months after Boni & Liveright brought out Jessie Fauset's *There Is Confusion*. Along with Claude McKay's *Harlem Shadows* (Harcourt, Brace, 1922) and Toomer's *Cane* (Lippincott, 1923). These books opened the doors to the white publishing houses. While none became best sellers, their sales were respectable, as were the reviews. Similar success greeted Countee Cullen's first volume of poetry, which Harper brought out in 1925. However, the real flood of black books followed the appearance of Carl Van Vechten's *Nigger Heaven* in 1926. That novel and the rancor that surrounded its publication opened the gates. *Nigger Heaven* launched the "Negro vogue" and established the popularity of books about Harlem. It also suggested that no theme or subject matter was too controversial to be included in black literature—indeed many concluded that controversy and exposé were necessary ingredients for popular success. In the six years that followed, as table 8 indicates, thirty-one books, representing the major works of the Harlem Renaissance, appeared.

Publishing houses like Knopf, Harper, and Harcourt Brace not only provided a new level of opportunity for black writers to publish their work but also promoted black literature, and in some cases actually attempted to influence the output of their writers. For this the publishers relied on their contacts with interested white literary figures like Carl Van Vechten and with black writers and intellectuals like James Weldon Johnson and

Figure 3

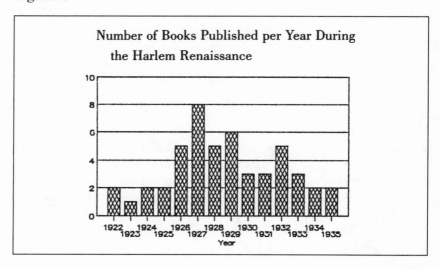

Walter White. To say that white publishers controlled the literary output of the Harlem Renaissance is not accurate; black writers were dependent on white publishers, but white publishers like Knopf were sincerely interested in black literature, and they worked closely with black writers and intellectuals to achieve a viable literary movement. Of course, they were also interested in making money.

Examples of the efforts of publishers to promote black literature are numerous. Alfred Knopf was particularly sensitive to the need to promote black literature. His organization worked closely with its authors to place review copies of their books in appropriate hands and to solicit promotional endorsements and friendly reviews from other writers and well-known critics. For example, when Knopf reissued James Weldon Johnson's *The Autobiography of an Ex-Colored Man* in 1927 the company closely coordinated promotional efforts with the author; Knopf agents set up appearances for Johnson to read selections from his novel on three New York radio stations, arranged for an autograph session at Gimbels department store, synchronized publicity and appearances in Chicago bookstores to take advantage of a Johnson lecture tour there, and solicited from Johnson a portrait photograph by Carl Van Vechten and a quote from a congratulatory note from Clarence Darrow to use in their promotion. Johnson was an active participant in these efforts. He suggested linking his speaking tour with a promotional campaign in Chicago, urged Knopf to send publicity material to bookstores in towns where newspapers had featured reviews or articles about the book (and to Great Barrington, Massachusetts, where he was well known and had a part-time residence), and supplied Knopf with the names of appropriate reviewers for his books.[8]

Alfred Knopf was not the only publishing firm to promote its black writers energetically. Countee Cullen, who was much younger and less sophisticated about the business of marketing books when he published his first collection of poems with Harper in 1925, also benefited from the strong promotional support provided by his publisher. In the fall of 1925, when the Jordan Marsh department store in Boston asked Harper to provide one or two writers for their book week celebration, Frederick Lewis Allen, chief editor at Harper, asked Cullen, who had just published *Color* and was attending classes at Harvard, to represent the publishing company. Harper also promoted Cullen's first collection of poetry by arranging for Walter White to review the book in *Saturday Review* and Mark Van Doren to review it in the New York *Herald Tribune*. In addition the firm's publicity department worked closely with Walter White in "the exploitation" of the book. In December 1925, obviously pleased with both the early sales and the critical response to *Color*, Allen informed Cullen that Harper was entering his book in the Pulitzer Prize competition. Alluding to Cullen's recent receipt of the Witter Bynner undergraduate poetry prize, Allen quipped that the Pulitzer "would be the next logical step in your prize-winning career."[9]

Harper paid close attention to the interests of their young poet. During 1925 and 1926 they supplied him with regular and encouraging reports of the book's sales. When they decided to print a second edition in late 1925, Allen pointed out to Cullen that his was the only second edition for a volume of poetry in recent years, except for "Miss Millay's." Such praise certainly must have been pleasing to the young writer. Harper also assisted Cullen in other ways. When Cullen was having difficulty getting into Professor Copeland's popular course at Harvard, Allen intervened on his young client's behalf. In early 1926, when Cullen was approached by a musician who wanted to obtain exclusive rights to set several of the poems from *Color* to music, Harper's editorial staff, while willing to accede to any arrangements that Cullen might want to make, cautioned him that by granting exclusive rights he might be giving away too much, and eventually they entered directly into the negotiations (which dragged

Table 8

Year-By-Year Publication of Major Works of the Harlem Renaissance, 1922–1935

Year	Author	Book
1922	James Weldon Johnson (ed.)	*The Book of American Negro Poetry*
	Claude McKay	*Harlem Shadows*
1923	Jean Toomer	*Cane*
1924	Jessie Fauset	*There Is Confusion*
	Walter White	*The Fire in the Flint*
1925	Countee Cullen	*Color*
	Alain Locke (ed.)	*The New Negro*
1926	Langston Hughes	*The Weary Blues*
	Eric Walrond	*Tropic Death*
	Walter White	*Flight*
	Carl Van Vechten	*Nigger Heaven*
	James Weldon Johnson (ed.)	*The Book of American Negro Spirituals*
1927	Countee Cullen	*Copper Sun*
	Countee Cullen	*Ballad of the Brown Girl*
	Countee Cullen (ed.)	*Caroling Dusk*
	Langston Hughes	*Fine Clothes to the Jew*
	James Weldon Johnson	*The Autobiography of an Ex-Colored Man*
	James Weldon Johnson	*God's Trombones*
	James Weldon Johnson (ed.)	*The Second Book of American Negro Spirituals*
	Charles S. Johnson (ed.)	*Ebony and Topaz*
1928	W.E.B. Du Bois	*Dark Princess*
	Rudolph Fisher	*The Walls of Jericho*
	James Weldon Johnson	*Fifty Years, and Other Poems*
	Nella Larsen	*Quicksand*
	Claude McKay	*Home to Harlem*
1929	Countee Cullen	*The Black Christ, and Other Poems*
	Jessie Fauset	*Plum Bun*
	Walter White	*Rope and Faggot*
	Nella Larsen	*Passing*
	Claude McKay	*Banjo*
	Wallace Thurman	*The Blacker the Berry*

Table 8
Continued

Year	Author	Book
1930	Langston Hughes	*Not Without Laughter*
	James Weldon Johnson	*Black Manhattan*
	James Weldon Johnson	*St. Peter Relates an Incident of the Resurrection Day*
1931	Arna Bontemps	*God Sends Sunday*
	Jessie Fauset	*The Chinaberry Tree*
	James Weldon Johnson (ed.)	*The Book of American Negro Poetry* (revised edition)
1932	Sterling Brown	*Southern Road*
	Langston Hughes	*The Dream Keeper and Other Poems*
	Claude McKay	*Gingertown*
	Countee Cullen	*One Way to Heaven*
	Wallace Thurman	*Infants of the Spring*
1933	Jessie Fauset	*Comedy: American Style*
	James Weldon Johnson	*Along This Way*
	Claude McKay	*Banana Bottom*
1934	Langston Hughes	*The Ways of White Folks*
	Zora Neale Hurston	*Jonah's Gourd Vine*
1935	Countee Cullen	*The Medea and Some Poems*
	Zora Neale Hurston	*Mules and Men*

out for almost a year) in an effort to guarantee that the poet shared in any profits that might be made from his creations. Harper also helped promote Cullen's financial well-being by helping arrange a lecture tour, under the management of Lee Keedrick, which the publishers felt "should bring in a substantial income."[10]

Meanwhile, Harper continued to encourage Cullen's writing efforts. A few months after it published *Color*, Allen began soliciting poems for *Harper's* magazine. In 1927 Allen wrote to Cullen that the magazine staff had "broken a record" accepting one of his poems after only ten minutes of deliberation. Indeed, the success of his first book relieved Cullen of most of the difficulties that previous black writers experienced with their publishers. In 1926, for example, when Cullen proposed editing an anthology of black poetry, Harper responded promptly, "we are all enthusiastic about your suggestion for the Anthology. . . . Let me thank you for thinking first of Harper's." The anthology, *Caroling Dusk*, appeared in 1927, as did Cullens's second and third volumes of poetry, *Copper Sun* and *The Ballad of the Brown Girl*, making that year a banner one for the young poet and illustrating Harper's commitment both to Cullen and to black poetry.[11]

Success also brought queries from other publishers. Back in 1925 when the popularity of *Color* was at its peak, Carl Van Vechten wrote Cullen congratulating him and soliciting future work for Knopf: "I shall never cease to regret that we [Knopf] did not publish Color, but that was not my fault, if you recall. However, if you would send your next book to Knopf, I think they will only be too delighted to welcome it." Such a solicitation undoubtedly flattered the young poet. The experience of having rival publishers compete for yet unwritten manuscripts was at this time unique among black writers, and it was not common for poets of any hue. While Cullen did not switch publishers, he did maintain cordial relations with Van Vechten, even though he disapproved of *Nigger Heaven*, and with the Knopfs, and he helped that firm promote Langston Hughes's first book of poetry by preparing a prepublication review for *Opportunity*. Van Vechten, in turn, also helped Cullen find a management firm that could arrange lecture tours for him.[12]

While there was nothing unusual or extraordinary in these promotional efforts, they do contrast greatly with the experiences of black writers a decade or two earlier. These differences are perhaps most vividly evident in the problems that James Weldon Johnson had faced with his novel *The Autobiography of an Ex-Colored Man* in 1912. The original publisher, Sherman, French of Boston, lacked either the resources, the skill, or the will to promote the book effectively. Johnson blamed the sluggish sales on the failure of what he termed an "ultra-conservative publishing house" to market the book effectively. Arna Bontemps caught the essence of the situation when he observed that "one could almost say it was published in secret." When he returned to New York in 1914, Johnson took on the promotional duties himself. In late 1914 he openly acknowledged his authorship of the novel and suggested strategies to his publisher for selling the remaining copies of the book; in 1915 he personally paid for the printing and distribution of Brander Matthews's favorable review of the book. Through these efforts Johnson did sell off the remaining stock of the novel, but the *Autobiography* was hardly a success until it was revived in 1927 by Knopf. This time, effectively marketed by a major publishing house and enjoying the popularity of black literature generated by the Renaissance, it sold respectably, and it has remained in print for more than fifty years. Johnson seemed almost relieved that his only novel was finally in the hands of a publisher that appreciated it. [13]

In addition to the major publishing houses, a number of relatively small literary magazines joined in the campaign to promote black literature during the 1920s. Generally this took the form of actively soliciting materials from black writers. For example, Ralph Cheney, editor of *Contemporary Verse*, asked Countee Cullen to submit any poems that he might have—and apologized in advance for being unable to pay anything. Harriet Monroe, on the other hand, not only sought material from Cullen—"your work interests us," she wrote—but also awarded him the John Reed Memorial Prize of $100 for the "general promise and quality of your work" that had been published in her magazine, *Poetry: A Magazine of Verse*, in May 1925. [14]

The little magazine that had the greatest impact on the Harlem Renaissance was Idella Purnell's *Palms: A Magazine of Poetry*. Purnell was born in Guadalajara but educated in Baltimore and Los Angeles. After she graduated from the University of California at Berkeley, where she studied under poet and critic Witter Bynner, she returned to Mexico and began publishing her magazine. With some support from her mentor at Berkeley, who became associate editor and undoubtedly contributed the resource of his extensive literary contacts, Purnell made *Palms* a rather influential magazine in the field of avant-garde American poetry. [15]

Countee Cullen was the first Renaissance poet to appear in *Palms*. Cullen, who had placed second in the Witter Bynner undergraduate poetry contests in both 1923 and 1924, was directed to *Palms* by the Berkeley critic. In its early summer issue of 1924 *Palms* published Cullen's "Ballad of the Brown Girl," a seven-page poem—the longest in the magazine. Cullen placed three more poems in the magazine that fall, and several more the following year. Furthermore, Cullen received twenty dollars from the magazine when his contributions were selected as the second most popular poems by a poll of *Palms* readers in both 1924 and 1925, and another $150 as winner of the Witter Bynner Undergraduate Poetry Prize which, beginning in 1925, was administered jointly by the Poetry Society of America and *Palms*. [16]

In its January 1926 issue *Palms* made a major commitment to the Harlem Renaissance. First, it published two poems by Langston Hughes, who now joined Cullen as one of the magazine's up-and-coming young black poets. Second, *Palms*, which rarely reviewed books of poetry, published a lengthy and very favorable review of Countee Cullen's *Color*. The reviewer, John M. Weatherwax, celebrated Cullen as "one of the greatest of the younger American poets," noted that "there are enough *good* poems in this 'little collection' for five ordinary books of verse," and concluded with the terse proclamation, "Countee Cullen. Twenty-two. Watch him." Finally, the magazine announced that it intended to devote an entire issue to black poetry. The review of *Color* was followed by the notice: "PALMS takes great pleasure in announcing that Countee Cullen has consented to act as Editor for a Negro Poets' Number of the magazine."[17]

Idella Purnell's announcement in January 1926 of her plan to publish a black poetry issue of *Palms* was well timed to relate to the Harlem Renaissance at a critical time when the black literary movement was just gathering momentum. During the preceding eighteen months Cullen had published his first volume of poetry and Fauset and White had published their first novels; Langston Hughes's first book of poetry would appear early in 1926. The *Opportunity* literary contests were under way, and Locke had edited the "Harlem: Mecca of the New Negro" issue of *The Survey Graphic* and his own anthology, *The New Negro*. In the fall of 1926, while Du Bois was wrapping up his *Crisis* symposium on the role of blacks in art and literature, and only a few weeks after the publication of Van Vechten's *Nigger Heaven*, which did so much to launch the "Negro Vogue" and popularize black literature, Purnell and Cullen released their "Negro Poets" issue.

The black poetry issue of *Palms* appeared in October 1926. Purnell described it as containing work by "every negro [sic] poet of note in the U.S." and observed that it "came like a dark constellation, shining in the American world of letters with a new light." While much of this "new light" had been preempted by *The Survey Graphic*, Cullen did take special care to include work from a broad spectrum of black poets, ranging from the most conservative "old school" poets like Braithwaite and Du Bois, to newcomers like Arna Bontemps and Helene Johnson. As an introduction, Cullen arranged for Walter White to write an essay on the Negro Renaissance, and the issue contained Carl Van Vechten's review of *The Weary Blues*. It also announced that Langston Hughes had won $150 for first place in the Witter Bynner American Undergraduate Poetry Prize, making this the second consecutive year that a black poet had won this prestigious award. [18]

The black poetry issue of *Palms* was well received in almost all quarters. Cullen reported from New York that the issue was the talk of all Harlem, and he sent Purnell a list of black and white periodicals that should receive review copies. The best indication of success, though, was the fact that the issue entirely sold out in only a month and that over a hundred requests for copies could not be met. Purnell admitted that it had never occurred to her that the issue could be so extraordinary, but "it seems that most people find the idea breathtaking—and when they recover from their surprise, like it." In November 1926 Cullen wrote Purnell that popularity of the project had convinced him to prepare an anthology of black poetry based largely on the *Palms* issue, and he announced that Harper had already agreed to publish it. [19]

As soon as the success of the Negro Poets' issue of *Palms* became apparent, both Purnell and Cullen indicated their interest in repeating the project. They continued to discuss this for more than two years and even began making concrete plans in 1928, but the issue never appeared. Purnell continued to publish black poetry and even began listing Cullen as an assistant editor of the magazine in 1927, but following her marriage in August 1927, the magazine seemed to lose its focus. *Palms* went though several changes in its editorial direction as it moved from Guadalajara to Washington state, to New York, and then back to Mexico, and as her husband, John M. Weatherwax, assumed a more active role as the magazine's publisher. Purnell continued her interest in black poets, and especially helped Sterling Brown by publishing some of his first verses in 1930, but by that time, neither Idella Purnell nor her magazine wielded the influence that they once had in the literary world. *Palms* ceased publication in 1930.

In the early 1930s, as the Harlem Renaissance was beginning to decline, another literary magazine, *Contempo*, attempted to attract black writers from the Harlem Renaissance to its pages and to develop a relationship with Harlem writers similar to that of *Palms*. *Contempo* was a somewhat daring southern literary magazine published in Chapel Hill, North Carolina, initially under the leadership of Anthony J. Buttitta. Buttitta and his staff were determined to involve black writers in his magazine in order to make the publication "more representative." They implored black writers to submit poems, essays, and short stories to them, and they reviewed most books written by blacks. Countee Cullen, Langston Hughes, James Weldon Johnson, Walter White, and Wallace Thurman were among the Renaissance writers who either submitted material to *Contempo* or were requested to. Langston Hughes visited the *Contempo* offices on his tour through the South in November 1931, and he stayed with Buttitta during his three days in Chapel Hill. That trip cemented a relationship between the two that would soon be reflected in the magazine. The December issue of *Contempo* listed Hughes as one of its six contributing editors, and the April 1932 issue announced that Hughes would edit a special forthcoming "Negro Arts Edition" of the magazine. Throughout the summer of 1932 *Contempo* carried an advertisement for *Scottsboro Limited*, which it described as "4 poems and a play in verse by Langston Hughes. . . . for the benefit of the Scottsboro Boys."[20]

Unfortunately *Contempo*'s efforts to become a southern outlet for the literature of the Harlem Renaissance did not succeed. Symbolic of its failure was the fact that its "Negro Arts Edition," conceived as the major expression of its commitment to black literature, never materialized. A variety of circumstances combined to prevent this and to weaken the relationship of the magazine with the Harlem Renaissance and, indeed, to undermine the magazine itself. First, the editors of *Contempo* simply did not possess the gift of timing that Idella Purnell and *Palms* did. By 1932 the appearance of another anthology of black literature in a regional literary magazine (even a southern one) would do little to help the Renaissance. A decade earlier such an event would have been significant, but the "Negro Arts" issue of *Vanity Fair*, the Negro issue of *Palms*, Alain Locke's *New Negro*, Charles S. Johnson's *Ebony and Topaz*, and anthologies by Countee Cullen and James Weldon Johnson had effectively saturated the market as well as filled the need for such an edition. The announcement of the *Contempo* number was met, therefore, with a real lack of enthusiasm. Walter White, for example, credited *Contempo* for bringing a "new note into the South which is sorely needed," but then said that he had no material ready to contribute and that, because of his demanding work schedule, "I have had to abandon all thought of writing for the present." Countee Cullen echoed these sentiments almost verbatim: "I am glad that you are going to do a Negro number of Contempo. . . . Unfortunately, I have not been writing lately, and have nothing at the moment which I can send you." If this lack of excitement among black writers undermined the project, internal dissension at *Con-*

tempo finished it off. By mid-October Buttitta was no longer associated with the magazine. Three months later the new editors warned their readers that any paper that Buttitta might publish, whether called *Contempo* or not, would not be the "original and authentic" *Contempo*. The magazine did not survive this schism. In early 1934 it ceased publication.[21]

In addition to publishing and marketing black literature during the Renaissance, white publishing houses and the editors of literary magazines also served as literary advisers and critics for black writers. Ideally this relationship was one between equals or colleagues in the literary world, and neither race nor the distinction between writer and editor and publisher intruded; occasionally the positions in the relationship were reversed, and the black writers assisted their white colleagues. Sometimes, however, the relationship was strained or even shattered by economic or racial differences.

Usually the literary advice that white editors offered black writers focused on details related to the style or content of their work. For example, when Cullen submitted the poem "Spirit Birth" to the *American Mercury*, H.L. Mencken accepted it but suggested that the title be changed to "Shroud of Color" or "The Black Man Speaks"; similarly, John Farrar accepted one of the young poet's pieces on the condition that he improve the rhyme in one of its lines. Idella Purnell urged Sterling Brown to send examples of his work to Witter Bynner for assessment, and she suggested that he work on the "diffuseness" which marred much of his poetry. This kind of criticism was widespread and a common aspect of the editor-writer relationship.[22]

On several occasions, however, editors attempted to become much more involved in the literature of their writers. In the fall of 1927, shortly after Knopf reissued *The Autobiography of an Ex-Colored Man*, Blanche Knopf suggested that James Weldon Johnson write a new novel for the firm. Flattered by the suggestion, Johnson agreed to meet with Mrs. Knopf to talk about the idea. However, Johnson was preoccupied, first with speaking engagements, and then with his study of blacks in New York, and on several occasions postponed the meeting to discuss the novel. Blanche Knopf remained persistent. In December 1927 she suggested a topic—a fictionalized account of the life of boxer Jack Johnson. Although James Weldon Johnson seemed interested in the idea, he remained engrossed in his own projects. Eventually, in 1928 Blanche Knopf got Walter White to go to work on the "prize-fighter novel," but she still attempted to convince Johnson to do a novel for Knopf. In August 1930, after Johnson had finished *Black Manhattan*, his study of New York, she even sent him a contract for the still undefined novel. In spite of these efforts, Johnson did not write the novel. Johnson politely declined the contract and concentrated his literary energies on a revision of his earlier anthology of black poetry and on his autobiography.[23]

In January 1930 Eugene F. Saxton, now editor for Harper, made an even more detailed proposal for a book to Countee Cullen. Saxton wanted Cullen to write a long, book-length poem which would chronicle the history of blacks in America, beginning with "the pageant of the Negro's arrival from Africa, his period of slavery, and his eventual emergence into the highways of the New World." The project was to be elaborate—Harper would commission original wood blocks to illustrate the poem; Saxton envisioned a book similar to "Steve Benet's 'John Brown's Body.'" Cullen indicated his interest in the project but never really began work on it. Instead, like Johnson, he became side-tracked by a project of his own, his novel *One Way to Heaven*.[24]

The determination of black writers to pick their own subject matter (a right they also demanded from their black critics) was a sign of the growing maturity of black literature. It certainly contrasted with Dunbar's need to continually produce the dialect poetry demanded by his editors. It also indicated that at least in some ways black writers achieved a parity with their editors and with the white literary world in the late 1920s. While it is important not to read too much into this, the popularity of black writers during the hey-day of the Renaissance gave them a freedom and, at least in literary areas, an equality which has rarely been seen in any area of American life.

One sign of this equality was an interesting parity in the relationship of many black writers with their editors, especially those connected with the small literary magazines. While blacks certainly depended on these magazines to publish their work, the magazines and their editors also needed the black writers, and often solicited their services. Idella Purnell, for example, not only utilized Countee Cullen's talents and his contacts in the black literary community to create the most popular issue in *Palms* history, but she also asked for his help in raising money, selling subscriptions, and finding patrons for *Palms* in the black community. Anthony J. Buttitta not only published black writers in an effort to broaden the appeal of *Contempo* (and establish its credentials as an avant-garde literary magazine in the South), but he also asked both James Weldon Johnson and Langston Hughes to help promote *his* literary career by critically evaluating the manuscript of his novel. And, Norman W. Macleod, the editor of *Palo Verde Southwestern Poetry Magazine*, asked Countee Cullen to serve as the sole judge for selecting the best poem in their magazine.[25]

There were of course limits to this equality. The relationship between writer and publisher is not always a relationship of equals; likewise, racial prejudice did not vanish in the twenties. Indeed, to one degree or another it colored all relationships. Sometimes racial considerations, real or imagined, created a rift between black writers and their publishers. The conflict between Walter White and George Doran over the publication of *The Fire in the Flint* was only one example of this friction. Ironically Alfred Knopf, who ultimately came to White's rescue and published his controversial novel, did not always get along with his black writers. Claude McKay, in particular, was extremely bitter about what he viewed as Knopf's biased handling of the manuscript of "Color Scheme," which he sent to Knopf in 1925. "Color Scheme" was McKay's first attempt to write a novel. He wrote the manuscript in 1924 and 1925 while in France, drawing largely on his experiences in Harlem. Walter White and Louise Bryant, McKay's most reliable patron during the mid-1920s, contributed to the Jamaican's support while he was writing, while White and James Weldon Johnson convinced the Garland Fund to provide him with a monthly stipend during 1924. White also arranged for Sinclair Lewis to provide critical advice, and Lewis persuaded the Garland Fund to extend McKay's grant through the summer of 1925. When McKay finished the manuscript, he sent it to Arthur Schomburg and instructed him to send it on to Alfred Knopf. In August Knopf rejected the manuscript because its literary quality was "uneven" and because the firm was concerned that its explicit sexual references would be found obscene by the courts.[26]

McKay did not accept the stated reasons for the rejection. McKay wrote to H.L. Mencken for assistance in getting the manuscript published. McKay admitted that the novel was flawed but felt that its realistic portrayal of Harlem life and the fact that it was a first novel compensated for its unevenness. Mencken provided no help. In his frustration McKay saw himself the victim of a conspiracy. Knopf, he believed, had held his novel for six months to guarantee that Van Vechten's novel of Harlem life was published first; Walter White, "an unreliable mulatto," was loyal to

Van Vechten, and consequently McKay had been deprived of the fame and wealth that he should have received as the author of the first novel of Harlem local color.[27]

This was not McKay's first or last encounter with Knopf, nor was it the only time that he felt betrayed by the firm. In 1919 he thought that Knopf had agreed to publish his first American volume of poetry. A year later he wrote Braithwaite that Knopf had "failed me at the last moment." Knopf failed him again in 1933 when McKay was down on his luck in Tangier and trying without any success to find a publisher for his new novel, "Savage Love." Few liked the novel. Even his friend and benefactor Max Eastman was critical, as was Eugene Saxton of Harper, who had published McKay's first four novels but now advised the Jamaican that he was an "expired fad." Knopf for a time considered publishing the manuscript, but finally rejected it because it was poorly constructed, dated, and likely to "lose a good deal of money."[28]

Claude McKay, who was frequently penniless, often in ill health, and almost always in the midst of some sort of life crisis over his work, his philosophy, or his friends, often saw a conspiracy behind his misfortune, and consequently he could be a very difficult person to work with. A more accurate picture of the difficulties that sometimes arose between black writers and their publishers, and how these difficulties affected the writer-publisher relationship, can be seen in the conflict that developed between Langston Hughes and Alfred Knopf over a collection of poems that Hughes wrote in the early 1930s.

Between 1931 and 1933 Hughes was out of the country on an around-the-world jaunt that began when he accepted an invitation to join a film company attempting to make a movie in the Soviet Union. While he was abroad, Hughes was especially dependent on his publisher, Alfred Knopf, to handle his business affairs. For two years the Knopfs served as Hughes's primary link with the Renaissance. They received and forwarded mail, received and stored the manuscripts that he sent back to the United States, served temporarily as his literary agent, placed one of his short stories with H.L. Mencken and the *Mercury*, and finally found him a fulltime literary agent.[29]

Hughes, of course, was grateful for this assistance. However, his experiences abroad, especially in the Soviet Union, strengthened Hughes's leftist tendencies and his perception of himself as a "proletariat" or "social poet." For example, while he expressly deferred to Blanche Knopf's judgment in the selection of a literary agent, he wrote that a friend in Moscow suggested that he attach himself to Liberman, a New York agent who was in touch with "the liberal and left-wing publications who are most likely to print my stuff," and observed that *Scribners* had recently rejected one of his stories because "it would shock our good middle class audience to death." Wisely, Blanche Knopf ignored the advice that Hughes received in Moscow and placed him with a mainstream New York literary agent. However, Hughes's leftward shift would create a more difficult problem for his publishers.[30]

Among the material that Langston Hughes sent the Knopfs from Moscow was the manuscript for a book of political poems. Blanche Knopf immediately sent the book to Carl Van Vechten for his opinion. Van Vechten, who was not at all pleased with Hughes's flirtation with communism, described the manuscript as a very weak collection of poems whose revolutionary pieces were "more hysterical than lyrical" and predicted that if this were published, it would hurt Hughes's reputation. When Blanche Knopf forwarded Van Vechten's evaluation to Hughes, along with her suggestion that he try to revise the manuscript, the poet was not pleased. He responded that he would be happy to undertake revisions if Knopf was really interested in eventually publishing the collection, but he could not base his revisions on Van Vechten's critique: "Carlo, as you know, did not like the book at all except for a few lyrics, so I could hardly revise it on the basis of his letter. There wouldn't be anything left in it afterwards." Hughes sent the Knopfs "two Moscow opinions on the book," and, implying that most of Van Vechten's comments were politically biased, he added, "I trust you have given it to some left-wing critics for a reading."[31]

Both the Knopfs and Van Vechten were very concerned about the reaction and the feelings of their young poet. Alfred Knopf suggested that they send the manuscript to another reader, and even expressed regret for having sent it to Van Vechten in the first place. Blanche attempted to distract Hughes away from the poetry book with another project. She suggested that he continue working on his "black and white" series of short stories but provide them with enough continuity so that they could easily be combined into a book; she even proposed a title for the collection, *The Ways of White Folks*. Hughes agreed to the plan and sent in fifteen stories, "most written from the Negro point of view concerning situations derived from conditions of inter-racial contact." Van Vechten, who also reviewed this manuscript for the Knopfs, seemed almost relieved when he read it: "I am delighted to be able to report at once that I find

myself tremendously enthusiastic about Langston's book. . . . I am glad
to feel that way after my reaction to that communist poetry book." Van
Vechten went on to call the book Hughes's "best work to date," and
concluded his report with the observation that "I have long believed that
Ethel Waters and Langston Hughes had more genius than any others of
their race in this country. . . . This boy grows under your eye." When
The Ways of White Folks neared publication, Blanche Knopf worked
closely with Hughes to guarantee that the book did not interfere with the
sale of several of the stories to magazines—she even delayed the publication date several months so that he could sell stories to *Esquire* and
Scribners.[32]

The publication of Hughes's collection of short stories did not resolve
the issue of his poetry collection. In February 1934 he sent a revised
manuscript to Knopf with a note stating he had received favorable comments on the poems from Lincoln Steffens and several other leftist literary
figures in California and that he believed there was a market for the book.
Van Vechten still disagreed. He argued that the book was not nearly so
good as Hughes's other volumes of poetry, and he asserted that in his
opinion Hughes had gone as far as he could go as a poet—that he should
be advised "to leave the Muse alone henceforth." Van Vechten urged
Knopf to reason with Hughes, to point out that it would be difficult to sell a
book of these poems because "communists do not buy books and few
others will want to hang a book in which the communist sentiment is
stronger than the art." However, Van Vechten advised that if Hughes still
wanted the book published, Knopf should publish it.[33]

The same day that she received Van Vechten's recommendation,
Blanche Knopf communicated her decision to Hughes. Knopf would
publish the collection of poetry if Hughes insisted, but she strongly and
frankly advised against it:

> I have given the question of your book of poetry a good deal of
> thought and have come to the following conclusion, which I write you
> because I think we know each other well enough to be completely
> frank and have no pretense as a barrier.
>
> I don't think that this is the moment for you to publish a book of
> poems—I think that you have become much more important than
> this poetry is and that the publication of such a book now would tend
> to hurt your name rather than help it. This in my very humble
> opinion, is not as good a book of poetry as your earlier ones.

Defiantly I think the place for these poems is between magazines and not book covers, now. By this I don't mean that ultimately at some future time the poetry should not or cannot be published; but I don't believe that a propaganda book in verse is wise for you nor do I think that the communists would back you up and buy it. From a publishing point of view I would much rather not do your poems now and do your next prose book when it comes along if we both agree on that.

Now that I have written my worst I want to add that if you still feel defiantly that you want us to publish the book of poetry, we are your publishers and I would not want to let you go elsewhere, so if you insist on the publication, of course we will do it. I am merely giving my best advice and my opinion and I hope you will take it in the way that I mean, which is in deepest friendship.

Hughes did not insist that Knopf publish the poems. Instead he decided to arrange for a radical press to bring out an inexpensive edition and distribute it through workers' book shops and union halls. Van Vechten concurred with this decision. [34]

Significantly, the dispute over Hughes's radical poetry did not affect his relationship with either the Knopfs or Van Vechten. The Knopfs remained Hughes's primary publisher, and Hughes, Van Vechten, and the Knopfs continued to work closely together throughout the 1930s and the 1940s. Van Vechten provided the promotional material for *The Ways of White Folks*, and Hughes suggested the use of Van Vechten's photographs to publicize his autobiography which Knopf published at the end of the decade. [35]

While white editors and publishers played an obvious and visible role in the Harlem Renaissance, they were not the only whites involved in the movement and not the only ones to have a significant impact on it. Nor were they the only whites to assist and befriend black writers or to endure a sometimes stormy relationship with them. White patrons of black literature, both individuals and institutions, also were involved in the Renaissance and with individual black writers.

White patronage of the black arts took several forms, but generally it consisted of providing money for prizes, grants, scholarships, and the support of individual writers. Occasionally this could take the form of an anonymous contribution to a young artist. In December 1923, for example, Countee Cullen was surprised to receive a five-dollar check from an unknown benefactor who identified himself as Jedediah Tingle. Tingle, the pseudonym for an unidentified person who sent contributions to individuals for something they said, did, or wrote, mailed Cullen the check because he was impressed with a poem and story about the young poet he had read in the *New York Times*. Most patrons of the Harlem Renaissance were more organized or more specifically involved in the promotion of black literature than was the mysterious Mr. Tingle.[36]

Many of the awards and contests that helped launch the Harlem Renaissance were funded by white contributors. White liberals associated with the Urban League, for example, were largely responsible for convincing *The Survey Graphic* to let Alain Locke produce the Harlem issue in 1925. Joel Spingarn funded the Spingarn medal, which was awarded annually to the black who had done the most to promote the cause of his or her race, and he funded the initial *Crisis* literary competition. Other literary prizes funded by white patrons included the Van Vechten award of $200 for the best poem, short story, or essay appearing each year in *Opportunity*, and the $1000 W.E.B. Du Bois literary prize. The most prestigious awards presented to black writers during this period were the prizes bestowed annually for five years beginning in 1926 by the William E. Harmon Foundation for "distinguished achievement among Negroes in creative endeavors." Each year the foundation offered a $400 gold prize and a $100 bronze prize in each of eight fields, including the fine arts and literature. Countee Cullen, Claude McKay, James Weldon Johnson, and Nella Larsen were among the black writers who received Harmon prizes during the Renaissance. In 1926 the publishing house of Boni & Liveright announced a $1000 prize for the best novel on "Negro life" written by a black author.[37]

The various literary contests and prizes were designed to stimulate the development of black literature by holding out the promise of public recognition and financial windfall. In addition, philanthropic agencies like the Guggenheim Foundation, the Julius Rosenwald Fund, and the Garland Fund provided fellowships that several black writers used either to finance their education or to support themselves while writing. Virtually every writer associated with the Harlem Renaissance benefited in some way from these contests, prizes, grants, and fellowships. Langston Hughes, for example, received the following awards during his long career:

> First *Opportunity* poetry prize
> Witter Bynner undergraduate poetry award

Harmon Gold Medal for literature
Guggenheim fellowship
Rosenwald Fund fellowship
American Academy of Arts and Letters grant

This institutional patronage provided Renaissance writers with a source of economic support that pre-Renaissance blacks never saw. Furthermore, except for the unsuccessful efforts of Du Bois and Braithwaite to manipulate the prizes in their efforts to divert black literature away from ghetto realism, black writers received these benefits while surrendering little of their artistic freedom.[38]

This was not always the case, however, with the more direct and personal patronage that was also widespread during the Harlem Renaissance. In some instances the gifts or support that patrons provided had few strings attached. Claude McKay, for example, received financial assistance from Louise Bryant off and on from 1924 to 1928. Bryant, the widow of revolutionary John Reed and later the wife of a wealthy Philadelphian, not only assisted McKay financially, but also helped market the essays and short stories he wrote during his years in France, and provided him with emotional support and guidance during a difficult and frustrating time in the Jamaican writer's life. Despite his tendency to quarrel with his friends and benefactors, McKay and Bryant remained friends throughout this period.[39]

Zora Neale Hurston also benefited from the support of several benefactors, especially that of her patron and friend Fannie Hurst, who maintained contact with her long after the Renaissance ended. Hurston arrived in New York from Howard University in January 1925 with only $1.50 in her pocket. She headed straight for the offices of *Opportunity*, which had already published two of her short stories. Charles S. Johnson took her under his wing, and Hurston achieved rapid success, largely because of the intervention of two white patrons. Annie Nathan Meyers arranged for her to attend Barnard College and funded her education; Fannie Hurst hired her to be her live-in secretary, driver, and traveling companion. The arrangement between Hurston and Hurst was mutually advantageous. Hurston received room and board and a place to live and write while acquiring a first-rate education as an anthropologist and folklorist; Hurst, on the other hand, gained a crash course in black life and culture from the mercurial Hurston, who became the inspiration for and the model for her later best-selling novel of black life, *Imitation of Life*. Both Meyer and

Hurst maintained interest in and involvement in Hurston's career long after she left Barnard, and the relationship between Hurst and Hurston evolved into a deep friendship. In addition to providing references for Hurston when she applied for Guggenheim fellowships in 1934 and 1935 and in other ways promoting her career, Hurst exchanged frequent chatty letters with Hurston throughout the 1930s and early 1940s, and in the summer of 1940 Hurston offered to come to New York to take care of Hurst during an illness.[40]

Hurston also benefited from the patronage of Charlotte Osgood Mason, an aged, very wealthy, somewhat mysterious white woman, who held court in her Park Avenue apartment as the self-styled "godmother" of the Renaissance and provided generous support for her favorites. Mason's fascination with the "primitive" nature of blacks attracted her to Hurston, who by virtue of her studies with Franz Boas had become an accomplished folklorist. Hurston delighted Mason with her animated stories of rural black folk; Mason responded by providing her with a grant of $200 per month for two years to collect black folk material. Hurston's relationship with Mason was very close. In her autobiography Hurston wrote that "there was and is a psychic bond between us." Hurston credited her with forcing her to be intellectually honest—to Mason the most serious crime was insincerity, no matter how cleverly it might be disguised—and impressing her with the significance and beauty of primitive cultures.[41]

The relationship between black writer and white patron was not always so idyllic. While black writers undoubtedly reaped considerable financial and professional benefit from the attention that whites showered on them during the Renaissance, they also occasionally faced the risk of becoming snared by their benefactors. Although a patron might provide a writer with the economic freedom to pursue his or her profession, this same patron might, at the same time, either consciously or unconsciously, limit the artistic freedom that his or her protégé required to produce really first-rate work.

The most widely publicized conflict between patron and writer over these issues occurred between Langston Hughes and his patron, the same Charlotte Osgood Mason, whom Zora Neale Hurston praised so unequivocally. Hughes met Mason through Alain Locke during one of his trips to New York City while he was in his third year at Lincoln University. When Mason learned that Hughes was working on a novel, she offered to support him during the summer so that he could focus entirely on his writing. After he graduated from Lincoln, she provided him with a monthly

allowance sufficient to allow him to spend a year free from economic
worry. Like most other writers who knew her, Hughes was quite taken with
this woman. Years after he had broken with her he still remembered her
with a mixture of awe and affection:

> My patron (a word neither of us liked) was a beautiful woman, with
> snow-white hair and a face that was wise and very kind. She had
> been a power in her day in many of the movements adding freedom
> and splendor to life in America. She had great sums of money, and
> had used much of it in great and generous ways. She had been a
> friend of presidents and bankers, distinguished scientists, famous
> singers, and writers of world renown. Imposing institutions and
> important new trends in thought and in art had been created and
> supported by her money and her genius at helping others. Now she
> was very old and not well and able to do little outside her own home.
> But there she was like a queen. Her power filled the rooms. Famous
> people came to see her and letters poured in from all over the
> world. . . .
> She was an amazing, brilliant, and powerful personality. I was
> fascinated by her, and I loved her. No one else had ever been so
> thoughtful of me, or so interested in the things I wanted to do, or so
> kind and generous toward me.

Although she was quite elderly, Mason remained up-to-date in her ideas
and outlook. In the twenties she added an interest in the New Negro to her
long-standing commitment to racial justice. Like many other patrons of
the Renaissance, she was not only concerned about the well-being of
blacks in America, but she possessed certain well-defined attitudes
concerning the nature of blacks and their potential contribution to American civilization. Like Zora Neale Hurston, Hughes discovered Mason's
fascination with the primitive:

> Concerning Negroes, she felt that they were America's greatest link
> with the primitive, and that they had something very precious to give
> to the Western World. She felt that there was mystery and mysticism
> and spontaneous harmony in their souls, but many of them had let
> the white world pollute and contaminate that mystery and harmony,
> and make something of it cheap and ugly, commercial and, as she
> said, "white." She felt that we had a deep well of the spirit within us
> and that we should keep it pure and deep.[42]

The characteristics that Hughes so admired in his patron—wealth, a strong will, and a belief in the primitive nature of black Americans— were also the source of their estrangement. Unlike Zora Neale Hurston, Hughes became uncomfortable with the economic gulf that separated him (and the blacks among whom he lived) from Mason, and he became increasingly troubled by her focus on the primitive. The differences between the two intensified as Hughes became more and more political in the late 1920s and early 1930s. Although he appreciated the economic freedom that Mason's generosity provided him, he grew increasingly uncomfortable with the disparity between the poverty of Harlem and the luxury of Park Avenue, especially in the months following the stock market crash, and he became frustrated with his patron's insistence that he focus his art on the primitive element in black life. As the economic situation worsened, Hughes became particularly sensitive to the plight of the unemployed. As he recalled, "it was impossible for me to travel from hungry Harlem to the lovely homes on Park Avenue without feeling in my soul the great gulf between the very poor and the very rich in our society."[43]

Hughes expressed his growing alienation indirectly, through two political poems. The first, "Advertisement for the Waldorf-Astoria," was a fairly long poem satirizing an advertisement announcing the opening of New York's finest and most luxurious hotel. Hughes considered the Waldorf an obscene flaunting of wealth at a time when thousands of homeless slept in doorways and had little to eat, and he was further incensed by the fact that the hotel neither employed blacks nor admitted them as guests. The second poem, "Park Bench," was a short, incisive indictment of Park Avenue wealth with clear revolutionary implications, and a thinly veiled attack on Mason herself:

> I live on a park bench.
> You, Park Avenue.
> Hell of a distance
> Between us two.
>
> I beg a dime for dinner—
> You got a butler and a maid.
> But I'm wakin' up!
> Say, ain't you afraid.
>
> That I might just maybe,
> In a year or two,

> Move on over
> To Park Avenue?

Years later Hughes recalled clearly that Mason was not pleased by "Advertisement for the Waldorf-Astoria." "It's not you," she complained, "It's a powerful poem! But it's not you." However, it was Hughes, at least at this stage in his career. Poet and patron never reconciled their differences, and in December 1930 they severed their relationship. As Hughes simply stated, "in a little while I did not have a patron anymore."[44]

Hughes felt that Mason objected to his political poems, not merely because of their political content, but because they focused on politics instead of the primitive nature of black life. Nowhere did these verses express the soul of Africa or the jungle rhythms that she looked for in black poetry; nor did they give voice to the "mystery and mysticism and spontaneous harmony" that she had come to expect. The problem was that Mason was looking for something in Hughes that did not really exist:

> She wanted me to be primitive and know and feel the intuitions of the primitive. But, unfortunately, I did not feel the rhythms of the primitive surging through me, and so I could not live and write as though I did. I was only an American Negro—who had loved the surface of Africa and the rhythms of Africa—but I was not Africa. I was Chicago and Kansas City and Broadway and Harlem. And I was not what she wanted me to be.[45]

Primitivism was a complex issue for participants in the Renaissance. Many whites expected to find it in black writing. Zora Neale Hurston felt very comfortable dealing with it, and some of her peers did develop primitive African themes in their literature (including Langston Hughes in "A Negro Speaks of Rivers"). Others were simply amused or shared Hughes's discomfort or were even hostile to those who seemed to be confining blacks to a stereotype of primitiveness and sensuality. Mary Love expressed these feelings in Carl Van Vechten's *Nigger Heaven*; so did Harold Jackman, who admitted, half seriously and half in jest, that he did not get the same thrill from jazz that blacks were reputed to experience, and he questioned the validity of the new racial stereotypes that many whites had imposed on blacks during the Renaissance. Writing to Claude McKay, he asked:

> Tell me, frankly, do you think colored people feel as primitive as many writers describe them as feeling when they hear jazz? So many

writers, Negro and white, assert this. I know that we are a rhythmic people. It doesn't take much observation to see that, but this business of feeling the music so deeply that we almost become intoxicated is beyond me. . . . I always wish I could enjoy such an experience. There is so much hokum and myth about the Negro these days (since the Negro Renaissance, as it is called) that if a thinking person doesn't watch himself, he is liable to believe it.[46]

When the relationship between black writers and white patrons (or editors and publishers) was based on such stereotypes, there was always the danger that black writers would pay too high a price for the financial support that they received, and consequently that the quality of black literature would suffer.

Another potential source of conflict between black writers and their white patrons, publishers, and supporters was the question of money. The major publishing houses had few problems in this area because their financial relationship with the black writers was handled on a purely contractual basis, and most publishers were careful to protect the economic interests of all of their authors. But for the editors of small literary magazines and anthologies, who generally had limited economic resources, and for some patrons economic questions and misunderstandings about economic arrangements were a source of potential conflict with black writers.

Usually misunderstandings were avoided. Most literary magazines announced up front that they could not afford to pay for the poetry they published, and few black writers seemed surprised by this information. Early in his career Cullen expressed his understanding of the situation philosophically when he wrote Idella Purnell at *Palms*, "Mr. Bynner explained to me that Palms does not pay for contributors, but what poet is ever concerned about money?" Several free copies of the magazine containing one's poems was the usual payment that novice poets received from small magazines. However, despite Cullen's comments to Purnell, no Renaissance writer was uninterested in money; indeed, all of them hoped to make a living from their craft. Several years later Cullen demonstrated more concern about the earning potential of his writing when he instructed his publishers not to allow any of his poems to be reprinted in anthologies without remuneration, noting that this was the situation he faced when he collected material for *Caroling Dusk*. In the mid-1930s he again demonstrated his sophistication about the publishing business when he negotiated with Harper to reprint *Copper Sun* by agreeing to reduce his royalty to make the project economically feasible.[47]

The best-documented misunderstanding over money occurred between heiress Nancy Cunard and Claude McKay in the early 1930s. Cunard, whose interest in the Renaissance grew out of both her personal life (her well-publicized love affair with a black American musician) and her revolutionary politics (which involved her in the crusade to liberate the nonwhite peoples from European imperialism), devoted considerable energy in the early 1930s to the collection of material for a new anthology of black art and literature. In pursuing this goal, Cunard came in contact with a number of black writers. Sterling Brown, who was just beginning his writing career, was particularly infatuated by her, while Langston Hughes, who initially agreed to send her a couple of his poems and help her identify other potential contributors to the anthology, especially among lesser-known black writers, discovered that she was a kindred soul, at least in terms of her revolutionary politics, and the relationship between the two blossomed into a friendship that lasted into the 1960s.[48]

Initially the relationship between Cunard and McKay was equally close. The two began corresponding in 1931 while Cunard was soliciting contributions for her anthology and McKay was living in North Africa. They exchanged a rather extensive correspondence of lengthy letters in which McKay discussed in detail his political views and his frustrations over the criticism of his work and his politics in Harlem, the commercial failure of most of his books, and his failing health. Cunard, in turn, recounted the unpleasant reception that she and her lover received in Harlem. The two also assisted each other. McKay arranged for his brother U'Theo to be her host when she visited Jamaica, and Cunard helped McKay cash checks and get funds transferred to Tangier; she also tried to arrange for the publication of *Banana Bottom* in London.[49]

This increasingly intimate relationship was shattered when McKay finally sent his manuscript to Cunard and asked when he might anticipate payment. Cunard responded that she had expected the contributors to write without compensation, out of a shared commitment to the project's goal, "to throw light on the appalling way the entire color question is handled." McKay, who had written Cunard only two months earlier of his poor health and poverty, was taken aback. As he explained, "I told you once in a letter that I was 'romantic' about artists and creative work, but my romanticism is different from those nice people who ask and expect artists to write, sing, act, and perform in other ways freely and charitably for a cause while they would not dream of asking the carpenter and caterer, others who do the manual tasks, to work for nothing." When Cunard reiterated that she was unable to pay contributors, McKay angrily demanded the return of his manuscript:

> Writing is my means of livelihood. I wrote the article "Up To Date" for payment. You are not paying for articles, you say. Well, the very obvious way out is to *leave my article altogether out of your Anthology*. . . . I have not the slightest wish now to appear in your anthology, and I hope you will respect that wish.

That was the end of the friendship. McKay's article did not appear in Cunard's anthology, *Negro*.[50]

McKay was not the only Renaissance writer who refused to contribute to *Negro* without payment. Eric Walrond also boycotted the project, while Cunard pressured Cullen to release the poems without his customary charge, with the threat that otherwise she would be forced to leave him out of the book. Jean Toomer refused to contribute anything on the grounds, "I am not a Negro." On the whole, however, Cunard's project was supported by most black writers and poets, and the volume was very favorably received when it appeared in 1934, despite the fact that it contained Cunard's rather critical article on Du Bois and the NAACP, "A Reactionary Negro Organization." Alain Locke sent his congratulations and promised to promote the book among his acquaintances, while Arthur Schomburg promised that his review of the book would appear in three hundred black newspapers and offered his services as an agent for the book among black Americans. He also castigated Walrond, and especially McKay, for refusing to participate in the project without pay.[51]

Misunderstandings like that between McKay and Cunard had the potential of sowing discord between black writers and their white supporters, especially in the early 1930s as the Harlem vogue began to dissipate and the onset of the Great Depression intensified the economic pressures that black writers faced. Sometimes blacks could joke about their dependence on white capital, but these jokes were often bittersweet. For example, the black journal, *The Messenger*, which relied heavily on white funds, had earned the dubious reputation among blacks of vacillating between a radical or socialist paper and a black society sheet, depending on who was paying the bills at the moment. While black writers could laugh about *The Messenger*, they lost their sense of humor when they faced the loss of their own patronage. As the Renaissance began to lose its popularity in the mid-1930s and white interest and white funds began to dry up, several black writers became bitter about the turn of events. To many it seemed that they had only been a fad, and now that the moment had passed, no one had much interest in their writing or their careers.[52]

In spite of the occasional problems associated with it, patronage was a vital and necessary element in the development of the Harlem Renaissance. While some patrons inhibited the freedom of their protégés, most placed few strings on their financial support. Amy and Joel Spingarn, for example, generously supported black art and literature without restricting the creativity of the artists and writers. Almost every participant in the Renaissance acknowledged that not only was Carl Van Vechten the most important white contributor to the movement, but that his association was more that of a friend and colleague than a patronizing banker. The sincerity of Van Vechten's support can easily be demonstrated by the fact that his interest in black literature transcended the Renaissance. He first became involved with black writers in the early 1920s before there was a literary movement, he was one of the handful of whites who deserve credit for helping to establish the movement, and he continued his interest and his help long after the "fad" had run its course.[53]

Van Vechten's contributions to the movement took several forms. The public side of his involvement was well known. It ranged from providing financial support to one of the *Opportunity* literary prizes and serving as one of the patrons of *Fire!!*, to almost singlehandedly generating the Negro vogue with *Nigger Heaven* and then perpetuating it with the infamous "tours" of Harlem night spots that he conducted, always with a crowd of white celebrities in tow. He was equally famous for the parties that became so important to the Harlem literary scene and "so Negro" that they were reported "as a matter of course in the colored society columns, just as though they occurred in Harlem" instead of at the West 55th Street apartment that he shared with his wife, actress Fania Marinoff. In addition Van Vechten was always ready to assist black writers in any way he could. In 1925, for example, he helped Langston Hughes publish his first book of poetry and quickly gained the reputation among black writers as a friend they could turn to if they had difficulty finding a publisher for their work. When Zora Neale Hurston had her first novel accepted in 1933, she asked him to write an advance review and help promote the book. Van Vechten also worked behind the scenes with Blanche Knopf as an unofficial but de facto editor at Knopf for black literature. The Knopfs regularly sent manuscripts from known and unknown black writers to him for his critical evaluation, and they almost always followed his recommendations.[54]

What truly distinguished Van Vechten's involvement in the Harlem Renaissance and set him apart from other white editors and patrons was the fact that, more than any other white man, he developed close, personal friendships with a number of Renaissance figures. His correspondence with black writers and intellectuals reflected not only a concern for their professional careers but also a genuine interest in their personal lives and personal problems. Novelist Nella Larsen and her husband felt close enough to confide in Van Vechten when they were having marital problems. Zora Neale Hurston valued Van Vechten's friendship more than his patronage and even expressed concern that he might mistake her friendship for favor-seeking. Van Vechten's personal relationships with blacks were so close and so well known that a number of his friends joked that he was more black than white. In Van Vechten's favorite caricature of himself, artist Covarrubias gave substance to the jest by portraying him with distinctly Negroid features.[55]

Van Vechten was especially close to James Weldon Johnson, Walter White, and Langston Hughes. Historian David Lewis graphically described these friendships: "James Weldon Johnson, as dear to him as his own father and possessing greater 'tact and discretion'; Walter White, with whom he got on like 'a house afire' and who was soon to bestow Van Vechten's name on his son; and Langston Hughes, who was like a son and a colleague." James Weldon Johnson and Van Vechten formed a personal understanding that whoever lived longer would assume control over the papers and literary material of the other. When Johnson died in 1938, Van Vechten honored the arrangement by establishing the James Weldon Johnson Collection of Negro Arts and Letters at Yale University. Despite their political differences, Hughes and Van Vechten remained close long after the end of the Renaissance. Hughes, perhaps, best captured the depth and simplicity of Van Vechten's racial views and his relationship with his black friends in his description of a birthday celebration:

> For several pleasant years, he [Van Vechten] gave an annual birthday party for James Weldon Johnson, Young Alfred A. Knopf, Jr., and himself, for their birthdays fall on the same day. At the last of these parties, the year before Mr. Johnson died, on the Van

Vechten table were three cakes, one red, one white, and one blue—
the colors of our flag. They honored a Gentile, a Negro, and a Jew—
friends and fellow Americans. But the differences of race did not
occur to me until days later, when I thought back about the three
colors and the three men.

Carl Van Vechten is like that party. He never talks grandilo-
quently about democracy or Americanism. Nor makes a fetish of
those qualities. But he lives them with sincerity—and humor.[56]

Carl Van Vechten represented white support of black literature at its
best—sincere and with unselfish intentions. However, even unselfishness
and sincerity could not always prevent misunderstandings between black
writers and white patrons, nor could it prevent white support from imposing restrictions, as unintentional as they might be, on black literature.
There were always elements that strained the relationship between blacks
and whites—political disagreements, disparate views about the purpose
and appropriate nature of black literature, economic misunderstandings,
and ultimately the racial differences that underlie almost every aspect of
American life. Even a person as totally dedicated to helping the development of black literature as Van Vechten, and one who did as much as
anyone to popularize and aid the Renaissance, did conflict with Hughes
over politics and also unwittingly helped establish the stereotypes about
ghetto life and the primitive nature of blacks which ensnared some black
writers. Indeed, Van Vechten, *Nigger Heaven*, and the whole Negro vogue
reflected the major dilemma of the Harlem Renaissance: no matter how
committed to giving expression to the black experience, the Renaissance
was, in the final analysis, dependent on white audiences, white magazines, white publishers, and white money. What is amazing is that on the
whole the black-white literary partnership worked fairly well and fairly
equitably.

9   Literature

and Politics

The Harlem Renaissance emerged during turbulent political times for the world, for the United States, and for black Americans. World War I and the Bolshevik Revolution had left the world in turmoil and provided stimulus for the anticolonial movements that would take root throughout the third world. In the United States two decades of progressive reform had ended in the often vicious reaction of 1919—the red scare, the race riots, and the isolationism—which led to the political retrenchment of the twenties under generally conservative Republican administrations. Frustrated by a general lack of racial progress under the progressives, stunned by racial violence during and following the war, but armed with new civil rights organizations, blacks confronted the decade with new determination. The twenties would witness the beginning of a long, legal struggle against political disenfranchisement in the South, and a reevaluation of traditional black political alignments in the North. At the same time feminists, flush with victory in their long struggle for suffrage, faced more subtle and less dramatic obstacles to their quest for equality. Finally, the ghettoization of American cities, the persistence of poverty in the midst of prosperity, and the disproportionate involvement of blacks in both of these processes challenged perceptions about the effectiveness of the American system. While the Harlem Renaissance was not a political movement, its participants were affected by the political world around them and reacted in varying ways to their political environment.

The most obvious way that black writers addressed political issues was through political and protest writings. Claude McKay, for example, expressed his anger toward the race riots of 1919 in his sonnet, "If We Must Die," and urged blacks to meet violence with violence, defying the odds and gaining dignity in their struggle: "Like men we'll face the murderous, cowardly pack, / Pressed to the wall, dying, but fighting back!" James Weldon Johnson, in poems like "Fifty Years," Langston Hughes, especially in his radical poetry of the early 1930s, and Arna Bontemps in "A

Black Man Talks of Reaping" are only a few examples of writers protesting in their literature. However, such writing was only a small and, on the whole, minor aspect of the Renaissance. While virtually every writer involved in the movement produced one or two protest pieces, only two, Claude McKay and Langston Hughes, made protest a significant element in their work, and even for them protest was never the exclusive or even the major characteristic of their writing. Fortunately, for the breadth and quality of black writing during the Renaissance, the early efforts of people like James Weldon Johnson to focus the talents of the young writers on protest poetry never really bore fruit.

If protest poetry was eschewed as a major literary form during the Renaissance, this did not mean that black writers were blind to the political environment in which they operated. It did mean, though, that most chose to address their political concerns in a more subtle, less direct manner. Race-consciousness was a constant theme, and the bold expression of racial pride was nearly universal in the black writing of this period.

In addition, a number of individuals associated with the Renaissance assumed that black literature could be an important weapon in the struggle for civil rights. As we have seen, James Weldon Johnson was convinced that a successful literary movement would undermine prejudice, win respect for black intellectual and artistic achievements, and consequently promote the cause of equal rights. Other black intellectuals shared his view; some, like W.E.B. Du Bois, used these arguments as a justification for their efforts to censor literary expression, deflect black writers away from ghetto realism, and create instead a literature of propaganda that would focus on the life and achievements of the black middle class. Du Bois's failure to win over most black writers to his point of view illustrates that most Renaissance writers gave priority to their art and to their artistic freedom—but it does not mean that all of them ignored the political potential of their literature or that they had no commitment to the civil rights efforts of black organizations. Likewise, the refusal of most black writers to subvert their art to a political cause does not mean that the movement itself was totally apolitical or that all black writers were equally uninterested in politics and political literature.

One link between the Harlem Renaissance and politics can be found in the response of major civil rights organizations like the NAACP and the Urban League to the political issues of the 1920s and early 1930s. Interestingly, both organizations were very cautious politically, and maintained an essentially non-partisan position during this period.

Opportunity and its sponsor, the Urban League, certainly made no effort to align themselves with any political party and remained carefully neutral in national political campaigns. In fact, during the 1920s the magazine devoted very little space to such campaigns. In 1924, for example, it first mentioned the political campaign in the November issue; it endorsed no candidate, but in a major article it did observe that all three candidates in the presidential race (Coolidge, Dawes, and LaFollette) were openly bidding, to an unprecedented degree, for the black vote and that blacks were defecting from the Republican party in record numbers. Four years later it still made no political endorsements, but it expanded its coverage significantly. In the June 1928 issue *Opportunity* analyzed the potential of electing a black to Congress from a Chicago district, and it discussed political disenfranchisement in its August, September, and November issues. The November issue also contained a series of one-page guest editorials, one endorsing the candidate of each party—Republican, Democratic, and Socialist. In 1932 the magazine expanded its coverage even further. It conducted a series of polls on the political preferences of blacks in the spring of the year; it again presented guest editorials in the November issue, this time adding one for the Communist candidate. Again the magazine made no endorsement but praised the growing inafluence of the black vote, which was no longer tied to one party.[1]

Like its rival, *Crisis* avoided political endorsements. However, reflecting the more openly political orientation of the NAACP, it devoted more attention and space to political coverage than did the Urban League and *Opportunity*. In 1924 it began its coverage of the presidential elections in August with an editorial lambasting LaFollette for not openly condemning the Ku Klux Klan and an article arguing that blacks could no longer vote a straight party ticket because both major parties "catered" to the Klan. A month later it published a lengthy article reiterating the NAACP's policy not to endorse any candidate but warning its members not to vote Republican from past gratitude, to remember that the Democrats in the South had a miserable record on racial issues, and to look closely at third-party candidates. An editorial in the October issue summarized the issues and the options facing black voters, while the November issue contained a symposium of short letters from prominent blacks urging readers of *Crisis* to vote for one candidate or another. Although the magazine made no official endorsement of any candidate, its editor, W.E.B. Du Bois, announced in his contribution to the symposium, "I shall vote for LaFollette."[2]

In the late 1920s and early 1930s *Crisis* shifted to the left in its political coverage. While the magazine itself continued the policy of endorsing no candidates, coverage of socialists and communists increased, and Du Bois's Marxist leanings became increasingly pronounced. In an article on the 1928 presidential election, Du Bois criticized both major parties for their poor record on racial issues, and he advised his readers to cast their ballots for one of the third parties. In its election issue *Crisis*, like *Opportunity*, printed a brief guest essay outlining the merits of each candidate; while the magazine remained neutral, Du Bois wrote the essay that endorsed Norman Thomas. He urged his readers to vote for the Socialist candidate because of his willingness to speak out on unpopular issues and because his party endorsed black suffrage. In November 1930 *Crisis* featured an article by socialist journalist Heywood Broun urging blacks to break their ties with the Republicans and vote Socialist. In the months before the 1932 election *Crisis* featured articles exploring the relationship between blacks and the Communist party and, as the election drew near, printed articles outlining the platforms and the efforts of both the Socialist party and the Communist party to win the black vote. However, the magazine focused its preelection coverage on Hoover and Roosevelt. Du Bois did not endorse any candidate, but he did write a lengthy editorial in the November 1932 issue detailing his opposition to Hoover.[3]

In addition to the positions that they took during presidential campaigns, both *Crisis* and *Opportunity* spoke out on political issues. *Opportunity*, for example, carefully chronicled the struggle against black disenfranchisement in the South, especially the legal battle against the white primary in Texas, and it closely reported the efforts of blacks to win national office. *Crisis* outlined a five-issue political agenda in early 1928, which included continuing the struggle against residential segregation in southern cities and against the white primary in Texas, combating school segregation in the North and the segregation of government workers in the nation's capital, improving the image of blacks by countering false reports of black violence and rioting, eliminating legal barriers against interracial marriage, and taking the struggle for equal rights into the South itself. The major difference between the political stance of the two journals was that *Opportunity* remained more committed to mainstream American politics and focused primarily on the shifting political alignment of blacks within the two-party system, while *Crisis*, influenced by its editor's shift to the left, encouraged its readers to consider placing their political allegiance outside of the two major parties.[4]

There was nothing particularly radical about the political position taken by *Opportunity*, and even *Crisis* did nothing more radical than suggest that its readers should consider voting for third party or Socialist candidates. Certainly the issues that both magazines championed were well within the American political mainstream and were based on nothing more than the exercise of political rights granted by the Reconstruction era Constitutional amendments. Their political coverage was exceptional only in that it provided a forum for Socialist and Communist candidates as well as those of the Republicans and Democrats. Far more dramatic than the rather cautious political stance of *Opportunity*, or even the suggestion in *Crisis* that socialism and communism represented possible electoral choices for black Americans, was the flirtation with revolutionary communism by several Renaissance writers.

The 1917 Bolshevik Revolution excited the imagination of many black Americans, who applauded the emergence of a revolutionary regime pledged (at least on paper) to racial and ethnic equality and the brotherhood of the working class. In the early 1920s the Communist party of the United States made a major commitment to racial equality in its efforts to build a power base among black Americans. The party dedicated itself to social and political equality for blacks and instructed its members to "encourage social interaction and intermarriage as movement policy." In the second half of the decade the party intensified its efforts to recruit blacks. In 1925 the "Bolshevization" of the party consolidated political control under centralized leadership. Three years later the Sixth World Congress of the Communist International passed a resolution defining the "Afro-American" as an oppressed nation with the right of national self-determination in those areas of the deep South where they constituted a majority of the population. The organizational reforms of 1925 gave the upper echelon of party leadership the authority to mobilize local units to recruit black members and engage in the campaign for black liberation outlined in the 1928 resolution. The party's black initiative involved it in a well-organized and well-publicized crusade against discrimination and racial violence that achieved its greatest success in the highly visible role that the party played in the 1931 Scottsboro case. However, in spite of its efforts the party failed to attract significant support among black Americans; while its activities championing the cause of equality obviously pleased many blacks, communism was never able to sustain itself as a major issue in the political or intellectual life of black America.[5]

Reflecting its failure to establish a power base among black Americans, the Communist party did not enjoy the support of most of the black writers and intellectuals associated with the Harlem Renaissance, nor did it play a major role in the literary movement. However, two major writers, frustrated by racial problems in America and already strongly committed to the black working classes, became deeply interested in the Bolshevik experiment in the Soviet Union, and for a time became involved in radical politics. Both Langston Hughes and Claude McKay were clearly attracted to communism as a potential solution to the racial and economic problems that confronted black America. Both men were prominent in the Harlem Renaissance; both defined themselves as radicals, associated with socialists and communists, visited the Soviet Union, and expressed sympathy with the goals of the Bolshevik Revolution. More than anyone else associated with the Renaissance, they flirted with communism. But neither ever joined the party, and both eventually denounced the movement.

Claude McKay was the first Renaissance writer to become involved with the Communist party. McKay had initially been introduced to socialism while a student at Kansas State University. When he first arrived in New York in the years before the Renaissance had taken root in Harlem, McKay's literary contacts were not with the emerging Harlem literary community but with Max and Crystal Eastman and other Greenwich Village radicals. During 1919 and 1920 McKay spent several months in London, where, at the International Socialist Club, his political education continued and he first was introduced to the writings of Marx. As McKay recalled in his autobiography, the International Socialist Club, a venerable institution founded in 1849 and located in the East End, served in the heady years following the Bolshevik Revolution as the hang-out for a wide assortment of prominent radicals from all over Europe, and it was the scene of endless political discussions and debates: "for the first time I found myself in an atmosphere of doctrinaire and dogmatic ideas in which people devoted themselves to the discussion and analysis of events from a radical and Marxian point of view. . . . The contact stimulated and broadened my social outlook and plunged me into the reading of Karl Marx." Surprised to find that Marx was more of a scholar than a revolutionary, McKay quickly became a convert, if not to Soviet communism, at least to Marxism, and marveled "that any modern system of social education could ignore the man who stood like a great fixed monument in the way of the world."[6]

As McKay's commitment to revolutionary Marxism crystallized, he aligned himself with Sylvia Pankhurst's Workers' Socialist Federation, one of several factions in Britain's confused jumble of leftist political groups that proclaimed wholehearted support for the Bolshevik Revolution and international communism. McKay took a job on the editorial staff of Pankhurst's magazine, the *Workers' Dreadnought*, and during the five months that he worked there, he published twenty-four political articles, poems, and reviews, which represent his revolutionary thoughts at their most radical. Never comfortable with the intellectual discipline that the revolutionary left imposed on its cadres, however, McKay had occasional disagreements with Pankhurst over the political content of his work. When, in the turmoil surrounding the arrest of Pankhurst and a general move to suppress Bolshevism in England, McKay learned that he was suspected by some of his comrades of being a police spy, he decided it was time to return to the United States.[7]

McKay arrived back in New York in the winter of 1921. Continuing to follow the radical path he had entered in London, he went to work as associate editor of *The Liberator*, a leftist journal edited by his close friend Max Eastman and committed to the cause of the proletariat, Lenin, Trotsky, and the Bolshevik Revolution. When Eastman left the magazine, McKay and Herbert Gold shared control as co-editors until they quarreled in a policy dispute in 1922 and McKay resigned. With financial support from his friends McKay then journeyed to the Soviet Union. Years later McKay emphasized that he had toured the Soviet Union and attended the Fourth Party Congress in Moscow, not as a member of the United States delegation to the Congress or even as a party member, but as a writer, who, though sympathetic with the Russian Revolution, "went into Russia as a free spirit and . . . left the same." McKay insisted that rumors that he was a Soviet agent were false; he pointed out that he had paid his own way to the country by working on a ship and borrowing from friends, and "although the bolsheviks tried to *make* me represent the Negro race, I let them know I was a free spirit, although politically my sympathies were Communist." Whatever the exact circumstances surrounding McKay's trip to the Soviet Union, it was the high point of his involvement in radical politics.[8]

During this period McKay's poetry reflected his politics. However, his best-known poetry—published in America, focusing on the black experience, and signed with his name—was not overtly Marxist even though much of it examined the life of the black working class. Its themes were race, not class; when he turned to political subjects, as in his most powerful protest poem, "If We Must Die," it was to protest racial oppression, not the plight of the proletariat. Typical of his work during the period was his study of a Harlem prostitute in "Harlem Shadows." McKay neither moralized against prostitution nor romanticized it. Instead he concentrated on the dreariness of the whore's life, describing her weariness in the same terms he might use for a charwoman:

Through the long night until the silver break
    Of day the little gray feet know no rest;
Through the lone night until the last snow-flake
    Has dropped from heaven upon the earth's white breast,
The dusky, half-clad girls of tired feet
Are trudging, thinly shod, from street to street.

When he wrote about his experiences in the Soviet Union, as in "Moscow," his sympathies with communism shone through, but in no sense could the work be labeled politically doctrinaire:

And often now my nerves throb with the thrill
When, in that gilded place, I felt and saw
The simple voice and presence of Lenin!

McKay's major body of work may have had a strong radical element, and much of it did examine the life of the black proletariat, but it cannot be classified as Marxist.[9]

However, there was also a less well-known body of McKay poetry, mostly written in England while he worked on the *Workers' Dreadnought* and much of it written under pseudonyms. In these poems and in a series of political essays McKay proclaimed his allegiance to international communism. The Jamaican linked his new political commitments to his continuing concern with racial injustice by arguing that socialism and the international communist movement was the most appropriate way to "bridge the gulf that has been created between the white and coloured workers by Capitalism and its servant, Christianity." In "Travail," which appeared in *Workers' Dreadnought* in January 1920, he claimed that international communism represented "the grandest purpose, noblest path of life," while in April, in "Song of the New Soldier and Worker," he followed his description of "the hungry, hideous huge machine" of capitalism with a call to the barricades:

> O pull the thing to pieces! O, wreck it all
>   and smash
> With the power and the will that only holy hate
>   can give;
> Even though our broken bodies may be caught in
>   the crash—
> Even so—that children yet unborn may live.

Great poetry this was not, but it represented McKay's politics at the height of his commitment to communism.

McKay's ardor for communism apparently was cooled by his visit to the Soviet Union. He had some difficulty with the official American delegation to the Communist party's Third International Congress—especially with the lone "mulatto" who was the official communist spokesperson for black Americans. But, his real concern with communism was the party's effort to impose intellectual and artistic discipline on its members. He had a small taste of that in England on the *Workers' Dreadnought* and a larger dose in Moscow. As he later explained to Cunard, although he essentially agreed with the social and economic programs of the communists, he objected to their attitude toward art and artists. McKay detailed these concerns: "I think the communist theory of proletarian art is wrong. It means really propaganda art and while I believe in organized political propaganda I don't in organized propaganda art. About art I am romantic." This romanticism about art made dogmatic politics ultimately unappealing to McKay and left him a "free spirit."[11]

After McKay left the Soviet Union, he spent the next twelve years in Europe (Berlin, Paris, and then Marseilles) and North Africa. This was a period of change for him. First, he began writing novels instead of poetry. His first novel and greatest commercial success, *Home to Harlem*, was essentially an apolitical celebration of the freedom, spontaneity, and sensuality of the black lower classes. When he published the novel he still considered himself a leftist, and in response to criticism from the American left, he described the book as a "proletarian novel":

> I consider the book a real proletarian novel, but I don't expect nice
> radicals to see that it is, because they know very little about pro-

letarian life and what they want of proletarian art is not proletarian
life, truthfully, realistically, and artistically portrayed, but their own
false, soft-headed and wine-watered notions of the proletarian.

Most Marxists would reject this description, because there was nothing
political or doctrinaire in the theme of *Home to Harlem*, but it was
consistent both with the themes McKay developed in his Harlem poetry
and with his attitude toward propaganda art. For McKay a realistic
portrayal of the working classes was the feature that defined his work as
proletarian, not the dictates of a commissar of culture. [12]

McKay's politics also underwent change during the late 1920s and
early 1930s. While his later novels continued to focus on the black lower
classes, by the early 1930s his leftist political activities ceased. In 1931
he wrote from Tangier that he was seriously thinking about converting to
Islam. In a letter to Johnson he explained his new religious interests in
racial and artistic but not political terms: "I am seriously contemplating
becoming a Moslem. The social side of the life that is blind to racial and
color prejudices appeals to me greatly and as the religion is mostly great
poetry, I can conscientiously subscribe to it, as a poet." By 1933 he had
given up on Islam and was trying to return to the United States. McKay
was convinced that the difficulty he encountered from immigration officials before he was finally readmitted to the United States was based on
his earlier radical activities, especially his trip to the Soviet Union, and
the rumor that he was a communist. [13]

McKay spent much of the rest of his life attempting to convince the
public that he was not a radical and that he had never been a communist.
After he returned to the United States, he believed for several years that
his career was being sabotaged by liberals and radicals, who, believing he
had betrayed the left, were highly critical of his work and blocked his
efforts to find a job. During this period, McKay became increasingly
anticommunist. He criticized the party's call for the creation of a black
homeland in the southern United States and continued to condemn the
efforts of the party to suppress independent thinking and opposing opinion. In the late 1930s McKay attempted to thwart the party's efforts to
expand its influence in the black community. First, he proposed to create
an organization of black writers and journalists that would be concerned
about the social and cultural problems of blacks but which would bar from
membership anyone who did not "believe in Democracy or who pledge
allegiance to any form of Dictatorship." When this organization failed to

take root, McKay made anticommunism the focus of his last book. Although *Harlem: Negro Metropolis* was essentially an examination of life in the black city, the last third was devoted to a lengthy and detailed critique of communist activity in the black community.[14]

McKay had come full circle. While he had initially supported radical causes and sympathized with the Bolshevik Revolution, during the last years of his life he became an outspoken critic of communism. However, in spite of this rather dramatic shift in his political beliefs, there was also a thread of consistency in McKay's behavior. Throughout his career the Jamaican poet was strongly attracted to order and structure. His poetry certainly reflected this proclivity, being stylistically very traditional and not at all experimental. In fact, many of his more radical poems, including "If We Must Die" and "Moscow," utilized the highly disciplined and structured form of the sonnet. Also, McKay was initially attracted to a Marx who was not a "torch-burning prophet of social revolution" but a scholar who developed a highly structured system of social and political analysis and who had studied the "history and philosophy and science of the world, so that he might outline a new social system for the world." Then, when his commitment to Marxism faded, McKay turned to religion. First, in North Africa he flirted with Islam, then after returning to the United States he embraced Catholicism. The revolutionary enthusiasm of his youth had given way to a quest for structure and order.[15]

If McKay was a poet seeking order, his colleague, Langston Hughes, remained unstructured and experimental. Despite the obvious differences in their literary styles and backgrounds, the two men had much in common. Both wrote extensively about the black lower classes and both were attracted to radical political movements. While McKay referred to himself as a proletarian poet, his counterpart from Kansas called himself a "social poet." Both men traveled to the Soviet Union and published a number of their poems and essays in left-wing magazines. Hughes moved farther to the left than McKay, but, like the Jamaican poet, he too disavowed communism late in his career. Despite their similarities, the two poets had little contact with each other during the heyday of the Harlem Renaissance. Their paths may have crossed briefly in late 1921 and 1922 while McKay was working on *Liberator* and Hughes had first arrived in Harlem. McKay, though, spent the next twelve years out of the country, and by the time he returned to Harlem in early 1934, Langston Hughes had been gone for two years. The lack of personal contact did not prevent McKay in 1932 from labeling Hughes one of the few real talents of the Renaissance.[16]

Like his Jamaican colleague, Langston Hughes focused much of his work on describing the life and experiences of the black masses. As he explained, his background made it difficult for him to do otherwise:

> Beauty and lyricism are really related to another world, to ivory towers, to your head in the clouds, feet floating off the earth. Unfortunately, having been born poor—and also colored—in Missouri, I was stuck in the mud from the beginning. Try as I might to float off into the clouds, poverty and Jim Crow would grab me by the heels and right back to the earth I would land.

Like McKay's, Hughes's best poetry described the day-to-day life of the black masses, which provided the best material for his art: "they furnish a wealth of colorful, distinctive material for any artist because they hold their own individuality in the face of American standardizations."[17]

Typical of the poetry that Hughes wrote during this period of his career was the poignant image of the poverty and deprivation of black life that he developed in "Mother to Son":

> Well, son, I'll tell you:
> Life for me ain't been no crystal stair.
> It's had tacks in it,
> And splinters,
> And boards torn up,
> And places with no carpet on the floor—
> Bare.

Throughout most of the 1920s Hughes focused on the experiences of the black lower class; few of his poems, though, contained any overt political message. Hughes also borrowed his poetic style from the black working class. In particular, he utilized black music to set the tempo and the rhythm of many of his poems. The blues, black work songs, and especially jazz enabled him to capture the tedium of menial labor and the bustling rhythms of ghetto life.[18]

Hughes's poetry began to sound more political in the early 1930s. In the early months of the Depression Hughes, troubled by the contrasts between rich and poor (and perhaps feeling guilty about the comfortable life that he enjoyed through the generosity of his Park Avenue patron), produced an extremely bitter poem satirizing the opening of the Waldorf-Astoria. In the poem Hughes revealed for the first time the extent of his political radicalism. Hughes's satire failed to veil his outrage; the poem concluded with a call for revolution:

> Hail Mary, Mother of God!
>> the new Christ child of the Revolution's about to be
>> born.
> (Kick hard, red baby, in the bitter womb of the mob.)
> Somebody put an ad in *Vanity Fair* quick!
> Call Oscar at the Waldorf—for Christ's sake!
>> It's almost Christmas, and that little girl—turned whore
>> because her belly was too hungry to stand it anymore—
>> wants a nice clean bed for the Immaculate Conception.
> Listen, Mary, Mother of God, wrap your new born babe in
>> the red flag of Revolution: the Waldorf-Astoria's the
>> best manger we've got. For reservations: Telephone EL
>> 5-3000.

This poem launched Hughes's career as a leftist poet. Already it was as radical as anything that McKay wrote during his days at *Workers' Dreadnought*.[19]

In 1932, after ending his relationship with his patron, Hughes left New York and went to the Soviet Union along with twenty-seven young black writers and students to participate in a motion picture project. The movie was never made, but Hughes took the opportunity to see the world. For fifteen months he traveled throughout the Soviet Union, Japan, Korea, and China. In Russia he visited cotton collectives in Uzbekistan, crossed the central Asian desert with Arthur Koestler, and met Boris Pasternak. Unlike McKay, Hughes had no reservations about what he saw in the Soviet Union. He returned to the United States in 1933, a more committed revolutionary than when he left (but not a party member).[20]

Although he returned to the United States in 1933, except for brief visits Hughes did not return to Harlem until 1942. Isolated from the Harlem Renaissance by the intensity of his political commitments, Hughes spent most of the 1930s in California and the West. During this period he wrote his most radical poetry. *A New Song*, the volume of poetry that so upset Carl Van Vechten and that the Knopfs were only reluctantly willing to publish, was ultimately brought out in 1938 by the International

Workers Order. It contained most of the radical pieces that Hughes wrote during the 1930s.

During this period Hughes consistently interpreted the country's social and racial problems on the basis of class conflict, and he advocated the unification of the working classes under the banner of Marx and the Bolsheviks. Racial prejudice, for example, was only a manifestation of capitalism:

> You're the smart guy, White Man!
> You got everything!
> But now,
> I hear your name ain't really White Man.
> I hear it's something
> Marx wrote down
> Fifty years ago—
> That rich people don't like to read.
> Is that true, White Man?
> Is your name in a book
> Called the Communist Manifesto?
> Is your name spelled
> C-A-P-I-T-A-L-I-S-T?

Based on this analysis of the social situation, Hughes called for all workers to rally behind the red banner of revolution:

> Better that my blood makes one with the blood
> Of all the struggling workers of the world—
> .   .   .   .
> Until the Red Armies of the International Proletariat
> Their faces, black, white, olive, yellow, brown,
> Unite to raise the blood-red flag that
> Never will come down!

Hughes also wrote in very positive terms about his impressions of life in the Soviet Union. Writing from Moscow in 1933, he acknowledged that life was hard and that the Russians experienced shortages of many products Americans took for granted. However, he also claimed that he witnessed no trace of racial prejudice or segregation, and he observed that he and other writers earned far more than they would in the United States.[21]

Unlike McKay, Hughes was willing to admit the need for some political discipline among writers and the necessity at times to subordinate literary freedom to the revolutionary cause. Consequently he was much less critical of restrictions placed on writers and artists by the Soviet government and by the American left. The Renaissance writer who, in the mid-1920s, had been the most articulate defender of the right of black writers to render the truth without concern for whom it might offend or what implications might be read into it, had, by the mid-1930s, become much more concerned with the political impact of literature. Hughes now reminded writers that they had social responsibilities and warned his colleagues that "words have been used too much to make people doubt and fear. Words must now be used to make people *believe and do*. Writers who have the power to use words in terms of belief and action are responsible to that power *not* to make people believe in the wrong things." Hughes stopped short of attempting to dictate subject matter or even specific values to other writers, but he was no longer willing to defend artistic freedom without also insisting that writers be aware of the social and political realities of the world in which they live and the effect that their literature has on that world. [22]

Hughes continued to defend the Soviet Union and communism through the 1940s, long after McKay had abandoned the left. Hughes's politics did not begin to change until the early 1950s, when the intensification of the cold war and the rise of McCarthyism brought tremendous pressure to bear on him to define his political views. In March 1953 he testified before McCarthy's subcommittee on investigations that, although he had been sympathetic with Soviet ideology in the 1930s and early 1940s, he had never joined the Communist party and had begun to become disillusioned with communism at the time of the Nazi-Soviet Pact. He further maintained that he had ultimately rejected communism because of the absence of literary freedom that he observed during his visits to the Soviet Union and because of the great strides that the United States had made in solving its racial problems. Following his testimony Hughes expended considerable energy to publicize his disillusionment with communism and to verify his loyalty to the United States. [23]

The attraction communism held for writers like McKay and Hughes is not difficult to understand. The Bolshevik Revolution and its promise of a new social order was appealing to those who believed that they and their people had been betrayed by the old social order. The Communist party in the United States consciously targeted blacks and in a highly visible manner championed the cause of equal rights at a time when mainstream American political parties ignored racial injustice. The involvement of McKay, Hughes, and other black writers (such as Richard Wright and Ralph Ellison) in the late 1930s and 1940s in leftist political movements reflected both their frustration with the refusal of most American institutions to confront this issue and the leadership that the party took in protesting events like the Scottsboro case, in which nine young black men (one of whom was only thirteen years old) were sentenced to death for allegedly raping a white woman. Ultimately, though, the writers of the Harlem Renaissance disassociated themselves from communism, although they continued their deep commitment to racial equality. Political realities in the United States without doubt contributed to their rejection of the revolutionary left. McKay's desire to be readmitted to the United States and Langston Hughes's confrontation with the repression of McCarthyism forced political choices on each man. However, certainly in the case of McKay and to some degree in the case of Hughes, the ardor for communism had faded long before they renounced the ideology. The truth was that the Communist party failed to maintain its hold over McKay and Hughes because it did not address adequately the realities that they, and indeed most black Americans, confronted. It did not offer a viable solution to the social and racial problems of the United States, and it could not maintain the image that the Soviet Union had developed a free society which had eliminated racism, anti-Semitism, and economic equality, and had promoted the intellectual and artistic freedom of its citizens.

Communism was not the only political ideology that had an impact on some writers of the Harlem Renaissance. The feminist movement, which had actively pursued the goal of equal rights for women during the Progressive era and had achieved its goal of women's suffrage in 1920, exerted a real, although often subtle influence on a number of participants in the Renaissance.

Women were involved in black literature at all levels—they were writers, patrons, promoters, and publishers. Despite the extent of their involvement, the Harlem Renaissance remained in many ways a male-dominated movement, just as American society remained a male-dominated society despite the efforts of feminist activists and the enactment of the Nineteenth Amendment. Women writers had a more difficult time getting published, receiving grants and patronage, and having their work seriously considered on its literary merits. This situation was somewhat ironic given the role that female patrons like A'lelia Walker and Charlotte

Osgood Mason and female editors like Idella Purnell, Jessie Fauset, and Blanche Knopf played in the movement. However, as Gloria Hull argues in her recent study of the period, despite their visible presence in the Renaissance, there were "broad social factors and patterns of exclusion" that resulted in women writers being "penalized for their gender."[24]

Black women writers suffered in two ways. First, they had less access than men to patronage and support. Hull cited Alain Locke as one of the key obstacles that blocked women writers from sources of patronage. Locke was notoriously anti-woman. Stories of the way he dismissed women students were legendary at Howard University, as was his clear preference for young men. The result was that except for Zora Neale Hurston, who somehow, for a time, gained Locke's favor, support, and a very valuable introduction to Charlotte Mason, Locke did nothing to promote or even encourage the careers of women writers. Hull also contrasted the financial support that James Weldon Johnson, Walter White, and Louise Bryant arranged from the Garland Fund for Claude McKay while the Jamaican was struggling with his career in France, with the lack of support or even real concern for the needs of equally talented women poets like Alice Dunbar-Nelson and Georgia Douglas Johnson.[25]

The second problem that black women writers faced was difficulty in getting their work published, especially by major imprints. The fact that Jessie Fauset published her work with Boni & Liveright and Frederick Stokes, while Hurston published with J. B. Lippincott and Nella Larsen published with Knopf disguises the difficulty that lesser-known black women faced in finding suitable publishers. Except for Alice Dunbar-Nelson's first book, which was accepted in 1899 by Dodd, Mead, the publisher of her well-known husband's poetry, none of the women listed in table 9 succeeded in placing their work with a major publishing house. Johnson and Grimk were forced to subsidize the printing of their work. The question that their experience raises is whether their difficulties reflected the quality of their work, the time that the work was published, or the fact that they were women.

Gloria Hull asserted that these women were at least as competent as the secondary Renaissance poets like Arna Bontemps, and she suggested that Georgia Douglas Johnson was a poet as accomplished as Langston Hughes or Countee Cullen. A more plausible explanation is that these women published most of their work before 1921, and before the Negro vogue had opened the doors of publishing houses to black writers; conse-

Table 9

Selected Black Women Writers and Their Publishers

1899–1928

AUTHOR	PUBLISHER
Alice Dunbar-Nelson	Dodd, Mead
	Douglas Publishing
	J.L. Nichols
Angelina Grimké	Cornhill
Georgia Douglas Johnson	Cornhill
	B.J. Brimmer
	Harold Vinal

Source: Gloria T. Hull, *Color, Sex, and Poetry: Three Women Writers of the Harlem Renaissance* (Bloomington, IN: Indiana University Press, 1987), 221–31.

quently, their difficulties were no greater than those of James Weldon Johnson and numerous other less-famous black writers during the first two decades of the twentieth century. However, this does not explain why in 1928, at the peak of the Renaissance, Georgia Douglas Johnson could not find a major press to publish her third and best volume of poetry, *An Autumn Love Cycle*, or why it had taken seven years to find any publisher at all. Neither the intervention of William Stanley Braithwaite, who began circulating the manuscript among publishing houses in 1921, nor that of Countee Cullen, who sent the manuscript along with a strong letter of support to Harper in the late spring of 1927, enabled Johnson to sign with a major commercial publisher.[27]

Despite these difficulties women not only made a major contribution to the literature of the Harlem Renaissance but also introduced, often quite discreetly, themes that explored the role of women in black America. Unlike their male counterparts who became actively involved in leftist politics, the women did not join feminist movements or embrace any activist feminist cause. They had played no visible role in the suffrage movement, nor were they associated with the women's political network of the 1930s that Susan Ware identified. They confined their politics to their writing, but even there one finds no overt commitment to feminism. Instead, through literary themes, character development, and subtle images, these writers raised serious issues as they confronted the fact that black women not only faced the prejudices of racial bigotry but also had to deal with the sexual prejudices of black men.[28]

Three novelists—Jessie Fauset, Nella Larsen, and Zora Neale Hurston—were the women who made the most significant contribution to black literature during the Harlem Renaissance. Together they wrote eight of the twenty-three novels published by blacks during the Renaissance; indeed, no black writer of the period published more novels than did Jessie Fauset. Though not sharing a common vision of the appropriate role of black women in American society, each struggled with the issues in her own way and presented well-defined images of fictional women who addressed the problems that black women faced in the 1920s and 1930s.

Of the three the work of Jessie Fauset is the most deceptive. On the one hand it is tempting to dismiss her as a novelist whose very traditional literary style and tone, as well as her subject matter, bring to mind the work of Edith Wharton. Fauset focused on describing the lives of the black middle class, and she was more conservative in style and tone than most other Renaissance writers. Her work has also failed to achieve much critical acclaim. While acknowledging that she was one of the most productive black writers of the period, producing four novels between 1924 and 1933, critics such as Robert Bone argued that her efforts to convey a flattering image of respectable black society led to novels that were "uniformly sophomoric, trivial, and dull."[29]

In many ways Fauset was a paradox. Although she was ten to fifteen years older than most of the other black writers of the period and described as both conservative and rather prim, this "elder sister" of the movement was universally respected, even by the bohemian element. It was to honor her and the publication of her first novel, *There Is Confusion*, that the famous Civic Club dinner of 1924 was initially planned. Fauset, as we have seen in chapter 6, was also one of the major promoters of black literature, especially during the years that she served as literary editor of *Crisis*. Finally, Fauset's novels are somewhat more complex than they appear at first glance. Fauset not only portrayed the life of the black middle class, but she also attempted to define the choices that women faced, especially in their relationships with men. While her efforts were not totally successful, they do elevate her otherwise flawed novels above the level of triviality.

Fauset's exploration of the options confronting black middle-class women are best seen in her second novel, *Plum Bun* (1928). This novel traced the unsuccessful attempts of a young woman, Angela, to find happiness by rejecting her black heritage, turning her back on her darker-skinned sister, and passing for white. At the novel's conclusion, however, Angela publicly asserted her blackness (at some personal cost), was reunited with her sister, Virginia, and, through a series of rather far-fetched coincidences, won the man of her dreams. What was noteworthy about *Plum Bun* obviously was not its melodramatic plot, or even its concern with passing and racial identity, but Fauset's exploration of the roles of women in black middle-class society. One role that Fauset explored was that of the supportive and submissive wife, personified by Angela's mother, Mattie. Mattie devoted her life to her husband so completely that when he died suddenly she lost her will to live. As Mattie prophesied early in the novel, "when her husband died, she would die too, she was sure of it; and if death came to her first it would be only a little while before Junius [her husband] would be there stretching out his hand guiding her through all the rough, strange places," just as he had guided her through life. The relationship between the two strains credibility: "Mattie her husband considered a perfect woman, sweet, industrious, affectionate, and illogical. But to her he was God." While romantically idealized, this relationship was not a truly viable option for women.[30]

Angela and Virginia were somewhat better prepared for life than their mother. Junius wanted his daughters to be independent and insisted that they receive a "good, plain education" that would enable them to earn a living. Their mother, perhaps recognizing the vulnerability of her existence, concurred: "My girls shall never [experience poverty] . . . they were both to be school-teachers and independent."[31]

Mere independence, however, was not enough for Angela. Following her parents' deaths, her quest for happiness and meaning took her to New York and across the color line. There she encountered a second role model: the "modern" woman who embraced feminism. Paulette, whom Angela met in Greenwich Village, epitomized a new approach to life for women. While not "unfeminine" in appearance, Paulette acknowledged:

There is a great deal of the man about me. I've learned that a woman is a fool who lets her femininity stand in the way of what she wants. I've made a philosophy of it. I see what I want; I use my wiles as a woman to get it, and I employ the qualities of men, tenacity and ruthlessness, to keep it. And when I'm through with it, I throw it away just as they do. Consequently I have no regrets and no encumbrances.

In addition to this image of ruthlessness, there was also a very attractive side to Paulette's life:

She had met with every conceivable experience, had visited France, Germany, and Sweden; she was now contemplating a trip to Italy and might go to Russia. . . . all experience meant life to her in various manifestations. She had been on a newspaper, one of the New York dailies; she had done press-agenting. At the moment she was illustrating for a fashion magazine. There was no end to her versatilities.[32]

Fauset clearly used the character of Paulette to present a portrait of a feminist that was ambiguous. Paulette was aggressive. She lived in a state of constant defiance, proclaiming, "I don't care what people think," and voicing the slogan "any woman is better than the best of men." She also ignored the conventional standards of sexual morality. And yet, Fauset did not make this image totally unappealing. It retained a certain romantic attraction, as did the image of the totally devoted wife. However, Fauset did not present either of these extremes as a truly satisfactory solution to a woman's dilemma. Fauset was not a feminist, but, as a single, professional woman, she did recognize that society restricted women. Angela's efforts to live according to her friend's philosophy led to the traditional unhappy conclusion—Angela took a lover who deserted her once his passions were sated.[33]

Rejecting the extremes represented by Mattie and Paulette, Fauset sought to define a middle ground where a woman could find both happiness and fulfillment without renouncing all traditional values and defying all conventions. The compromise that she offered in *Plum Bun* required the woman to make sacrifices for her husband, to keep house for him and nurture the children while he struggled to establish himself; at the same time, however, the wife would develop her talents (as an artist, novelist, playwright, or in a similar creative endeavor), achieve success in her own right, and bring wealth and glory to her husband. This solution might not seem very realistic, but it did reflect Fauset's efforts to redefine the role of women. If Fauset rejected the image of Mattie, a woman without any identity of her own, whose whole life was wrapped up in her husband, she also could not unequivocally embrace the feminism of Paulette. Fauset instead proposed a role where the woman was educated, somewhat independent, capable of simultaneously pursuing a rewarding career and maintaining a home and marriage, and still committed to traditional standards of sexual behavior.

Fauset only partially achieved her definition of a fulfilling life. Though she did not marry until late in life, she was financially secure through a modest inheritance. Deeply committed to literature and devoted to Du Bois (who possibly was the great unrequited love of her life), she gave up a teaching career in Washington, D.C., and moved to Harlem in 1919, where she became Du Bois's assistant at *Crisis*, set up housekeeping with her sister, and became one of the major promoters of the Renaissance. Fauset achieved meaningful career goals as a novelist, editor, and literary promoter, but she delayed becoming a wife and did not become a mother—unless nurturing the infant Harlem Renaissance and sheltering numerous young black writers and artists in her apartment count for that. Neither did she embrace the lifestyle of Paulette. She remained prim and proper, virtually untouched by Harlem's bohemian element. Her only surrender to adventure was her frequent travel to Europe, and her only surrender to the image of the sophisticated modern woman was to smoke in public.[34]

Although Jessie Fauset's characters made choices and exercised control over their lives, Nella Larsen, on the other hand, projected very negative images of women who were essentially hopeless and powerless to control their circumstances or their destinies. In the two novels that she wrote in rapid succession, *Quicksand* (1928) and *Passing* (1929), strong women characters who assume responsibility for their lives are conspicuously absent. In *Passing*, for example, the main character defined herself in terms of her family; she was concerned solely with the welfare of her children and the degree to which her husband's infidelity threatened her security. She had no professional or intellectual ambition; major decisions in her life centered around questions like what dress to wear. Her life was defined by her husband's economic, social, and professional status; she confined her efforts to control her life to manipulating her husband. To achieve happiness and security she "had only to direct and guide her man, to keep him going in the right direction." This approach, of course, failed. When a threat to her security materialized, she was virtually paralyzed, unable to assert herself or take action until the last confusing scene of the novel, when she apparently caused the death of her husband's mistress.[35]

It was in her first novel, *Quicksand*, that Larsen presented her most fully developed and most pessimistic description of the choices facing women. Larsen focused this novel on the efforts of a young middle-class black woman to find happiness and fulfillment. Early in the novel the main character, Helga, attempted unsuccessfully to define her goals: "Barring a desire for material security, gracious ways of living, a profusion of lovely clothes, and a goodly share of envious admiration, Helga Crane didn't know, couldn't tell. But there was, she knew, something else. Happiness, she supposed. Whatever that might be." The novel traced Helga Crane's periodic flights from some vague, ill-defined feeling of dissatisfaction and her never-ceasing search for happiness.[36]

Helga first looked for happiness in marriage and for financial security within the black community. After arriving in New York, she immersed herself in Harlem society and began to make vague plans for her future. "Some day," she observed, "she intended to marry one of those alluring brown or yellow men who danced attendance on her. Already financially successful, any one of them could give her the things which she had come to desire." Soon, though, she grew disenchanted with Harlem and with blacks and sought refuge with her white relatives in Copenhagen. They welcomed her, but soon it became obvious that they hoped to use her exotic allure to arrange a marriage that would elevate them socially. Helga fled again, back to Harlem, but found no easing of her dissatisfaction. She sank into what Larsen termed a "mental quagmire" and finally into mental exhaustion. Ultimately she found shelter and mental calm in a mindless religious experience. Under the influence of her intoxicating salvation, she married her preacher and returned with him to his congregation of sharecroppers in a tiny Alabama community.[37]

Helga initially confronted her new situation with enthusiasm. Although she was poor, she enjoyed relative status as the minister's wife. By the time her religious fervor dissipated and dissatisfaction again set in, it was too late. The birth of four children in quick succession sapped her strength and her health; desperate plans to escape were undermined by still another pregnancy.

The image of women that Larsen projected was a depressing one. Helga Crane, a well-educated woman, became trapped in southern poverty, not because she was black, but because she was a woman. Even the religion

that ultimately ensnared her was a manifestation of "feminine" characteristics. Faith was irrational. It required that she surrender control over
destiny to the minister, who was a symbol of masculine sexuality. As
Helga became more and more exhausted, she found that religion offered
no real salvation. Religion was the narcotic that kept her passive; its
comfort came only to those who accepted this passivity, and its relief came
from being able to divert all responsibility to someone else. When Helga
finally awakened from her opium-like haze and regained her rational
perspective, her health was ruined, she was pregnant with her fifth child,
and there was no escape.[38]

In both of Larsen's novels women lost control over their lives and
foundered in a psychological quagmire. On the surface, at least, Nella
Larsen's life was the antithesis of the characters in her novels. She
epitomized the self-confident, modern, sophisticated woman, whose
Harlem apartment "had the air of a Greenwich Village Studio with its vari-
colored pillows, paintings, books and more books, flowers, large and
small vases, and other furnishings," and who seemed the thoroughly
"modern woman, for she smokes, wears her dresses short, and does not
believe in religion, churches and the like, and believes that people of the
artistic type have a definite chance to help solve the race problem."
Unfortunately, this public image masked a less-pleasant reality. Larsen
was never able to solve her personal problems, and her literary career and
her life were almost as depressing as those of her characters. She wrote
her two novels as her marriage was falling apart; following the collapse of
her marriage, her writing career came to an end. On the basis of her first
two books she received a contract from Knopf to do two more, and she was
awarded a Guggenheim Fellowship in 1930 to travel in Europe and
prepare her third novel. Larsen never completed this book and sank into
obscurity.[39]

Zora Neale Hurston differed from Larsen and Fauset in several ways.
First, in her literature she concentrated on poor, uneducated blacks living
in the rural South rather than on middle-class northern blacks. In addition, her novels drew much from her training in anthropology and her
fascination with black folklore. Hurston also did her best writing in the
1930s, during the last years of the Renaissance. Her most important
novel, *Their Eyes Were Watching God*, was written in 1937, after the
Renaissance, by most measures, had ended. Finally, in sharp contrast to
Larsen, Hurston wrote about strong women who endured and often overcame the obstacles that life placed in their paths.

During her literary career Hurston published four novels, two books of folklore, an autobiography, poetry, and short stories. Much of her work incorporated the folk stories that she had heard as a young girl growing up in the South. Typical of this was *Their Eyes Were Watching God*. Not only did this book contain excellent descriptions of black folk life, but it also focused on the efforts of a woman to assert herself and to maintain her identity in a male-dominated environment. In the process Hurston gave us Janie, the strongest and most memorable female character to appear in any work of the Renaissance.

The novel focused on the life of Janie and her relationship with her three husbands. Janie's first marriage was arranged by her grandmother, whose only objective was to insure that her granddaughter gain a degree of security and protection. In the eyes of the old woman, the world was a cruel place for women, especially black women. As she explained:

> Honey, de white man is de ruler of everything as fur as Ah been able tuh find out. Maybe, it's some place way off in de ocean where de black man is in power, but we don't know nothin' but what we see. So de white man throw down de load and tell de nigger man tuh pick it up. He pick it up because he have to, but he don't tote it. He hand it to his womenfolks. De nigger woman is de mule uh de world so fur as Ah can see.

Janie, though, wanted love and romance; instead, she was wed to an older man whose chief attribute was that he owned sixty acres of land. Janie had the security that her grandmother sought for her, but little else. She soon realized that her husband valued her as a source of labor, not as a lover or a companion. At the first opportunity she left.[40]

Janie's second husband was not much of an improvement. He was wealthier. As the mayor and leading merchant of an all-black town, he provided her with economic security and the status that her grandmother valued so highly. Janie was not required to work hard; however, her husband exercised strict control over her personal life. He valued her as a possession to be displayed as evidence of his wealth, virility, and social position, and he had definite ideas about her role in the marriage. He did not intend for his wife to participate in the banter and gossip that was the social life of the town. "She's uh woman and her place is in de home," he insisted. Or she could help him run the store, but she was not allowed to socialize with the townspeople who regularly gathered there to gossip. The love and companionship that she longed for did not exist in this marriage either.[41]

The death of her second husband liberated Janie. For the first time in her life she felt free. She prized her freedom and ignored the courtship of dozens of suitors who sought her for her wealth and status. Instead, to the dismay of the community, she eloped with Tea Cake, a basically irresponsible younger man but one who valued Janie as an individual and not as an object. Tea Cake could not provide Janie with security or material comfort, but for the first time in her life Janie had the respect and companionship that she had sought. The wealth and social position that were so important to her grandmother proved to be worth very little without respect. As Janie explained to a friend, she no longer intended to live according to her grandmother's values:

> She was borned in slavery time when folks, dat is black folks, didn't sit down anytime dey felt lak it. So sittin' on porches lak de white madam looked lak mighty fine thing tuh her. Dat's whut she wanted for me—don't keer what it cost. Git up on uh high chair and sit dere. She didn't have time tuh think whut tuh do after you got up on de stool uh do nothin'. De object wuz tuh git dere. So Ah got up on de high stool lak she told me, but . . . Ah done nearly languished tuh death up dere. Ah felt like de world wuz cryin' extry and Ah ain't read de common news yet.[42]

For many years of her life Janie had been unhappy in a struggle to be treated as a woman and as a human, not an object. Her liberation came when she defied the conventions of her community, asserted herself, and entered into a relationship with a man who loved her for herself. As she confided after Tea Cake's death, she was happy; she was not bothered by the old women who gossiped about her escapades because she had finally participated fully in a relationship as an equal and had experienced life and love first hand.

Through the character of Janie, Hurston presented the image of a woman who possessed strength and endurance and who demanded respect. Although she lacked the culture and education of the characters in the novels of Fauset and Larsen, she came the closest of any black woman in the literature of the Harlem Renaissance to defining a viable role for women. Hurston demanded that women be partners in relationships.

Like Janie, Hurston cared little for convention or the gossip that often surrounded her. She was a character—independent, outspoken, and often outrageous, such as when she boldly stopped pedestrians in Harlem to measure their cranium size for Franz Boas. However, she did not achieve the personal satisfaction that Janie did. Instead of finding a partner with which to share her life, she experienced one disappointing relationship after another. Instead of achieving security and recognition from her career, she encountered a series of crises, disappeared from public view in the 1950s, and spent the last years of her life working as a maid in Florida.[43]

Neither Hurston, Larsen, nor Fauset was a politically active feminist. However, they explored the limits confronting black women in the 1920s and 1930s, and they attempted to expand the possibilities. The efforts of black women writers to address the problems confronting women in American society underscores the nature of the relationship between politics and literature in the Harlem Renaissance. Although poets, writers, critics, and promoters of both sexes recognized the realities of prejudice and were committed to the struggle for equality, the Harlem Renaissance was a literary movement, not a political one. Propaganda literature was generally eschewed by the black writers and poets of this period. Even McKay and Hughes ultimately rejected leftist politics. McKay, furthermore, refused to let politics intrude on his art; although Hughes lost sight of the importance of this distinction for a time in the 1930s, the vast majority of his work was nonpolitical. The women who participated in the Renaissance wove feminist themes through their work, but art, not politics, was their ultimate goal. Finally, diversity character-ized this aspect of the Renaissance as it did all others. There was no party line or political consensus in the Harlem Renaissance.

10 The Decline of the Harlem Renaissance

The Harlem Renaissance, which had begun with a burst of creativity in the mid-1920s, gradually dissipated in the early 1930s. Because a number of factors were involved in the decline of the Renaissance and because the movement itself was an abstract concept based on personal commitments and loyalties rather than on a single identifiable person or institution, it is difficult to pinpoint the moment of its death. For the individual writer the end of the Renaissance was a personal event occurring when he or she consciously disassociated from the movement. Black intellectuals also differed in their interpretation of exactly when the movement ended, with some, including historian John Hope Franklin and novelist John A. Williams, suggesting that the movement did not end but continued into the 1960s after undergoing changes in the 1930s. However, the Renaissance did not survive the 1930s. Although black literature continued to exist, it no longer focused on Harlem, and it was no longer dominated by the writers and intellectuals who had so monopolized black literature for a decade.[1]

The decline of the Harlem Renaissance was a gradual process that began about the time that the economy collapsed in the early 1930s. Rather than a mass defection of black writers from the movement, the Renaissance stopped attracting new recruits. Once vibrant and alive, the Harlem Renaissance began to stagnate in the early 1930s, in part because no new talent or new ideas were infused into the movement. As the older writers died, ceased to be productive, or faded from public view, the new generation of black writers—Richard Wright, Ralph Ellison, and James Baldwin—maintained an identity apart from the Renaissance.

While the end of the Renaissance also ended the careers of several black writers, others continued to write and continued to make a significant contribution to black literature. Langston Hughes, for example, who claimed that the Depression ended his involvement in the Renaissance, continued his active and quite diverse literary career until his death in 1967. However, as we have seen in chapter 9, he left Harlem in the early 1930s and began to take much of his literary inspiration from Marx rather than from black music. Even though he became for a time the darling of the communist literary critics, he never entirely divorced himself from Harlem and the Renaissance. He never ended his professional association or his friendship with the Knopfs and with Carl Van Vechten; also, in 1942 he returned to Harlem and to Harlem themes with *Shakespeare in Harlem*, and years after the Renaissance ended he wrote his most effective poem, "Montage of a Dream Deferred," in which he returned to the rhythms and techniques of jazz to produce a brilliant collage of Harlem life.[2]

Another black poet who remained active long after the end of the Renaissance was Sterling Brown. Brown began his career late in the Renaissance, publishing his first volume of poetry, *Southern Road*, in 1932. With this book he seemed destined to follow in the footsteps of Langston Hughes as a poet who drew his inspiration from black folk themes and black music. In the mid-1930s he even followed Hughes's shift to the left and turned to social protest poetry, although he never became quite as propagandistic or political as Hughes. However, like Hughes, Brown turned to radical magazines like *New Masses* as the major outlet for his work. Most significantly, however, Brown shifted the focus of his career from poetry to literary criticism and literary history during the mid-1930s. Along with Alain Locke and Benjamin Brawley, he became one of the three major black literary critics. After publishing his single volume of poetry, he spent the rest of his life as a professor of literature at Howard University where he published a number of articles about black literature and two books of literary criticism, and in 1941 coedited *The Negro Caravan*, an anthology of black literature. Sterling Brown survived the decline of the Harlem Renaissance by shifting his career away from the creative to the analytical side of the literary profession.

Another black writer followed Brown's example. Arna Bontemps had come to Harlem from California a few months before his friend, Wallace Thurman. During the Renaissance he was a close associate of both Thurman and Hughes and was at the center of Harlem's bohemian community. He also demonstrated considerable promise as a poet. In 1926 and 1927 he won the Alexander Pushkin award for poetry offered by *Opportunity*; also in 1927 he won first place in the *Crisis* poetry contest. In the 1930s he published three historical novels, *God Sends Sunday* (1931), *Black Thunder* (1934), and *Drums at Dusk* (1939). In the first one Bontemps examined the rise and fall of Lil Augie, a black jockey who rode in St. Louis and New Orleans at the turn of the century. Of his three novels, this one, which explored the more exotic elements in lower-class black life, was the only work that clearly reflected the literary themes of the Renaissance. In the other two novels Bontemps fictionalized the early nineteenth-century slave revolts of Gabrial Prosser in Virginia and Toussaint L'Ouverture in Haiti.

Bontemps's greatest contribution to the Renaissance was not his literature but his role after the 1930s as the movement's semi-official historian. As Bontemps himself stated, he had observed the Renaissance "from a grandstand seat." From 1943, when he began his long tenure as head librarian at Fisk University until his death in 1973, he used first-hand experiences as the basis for his study of the period. During his long and active career he wrote a number of essays covering almost every aspect of the Renaissance. In the late 1960s he became director of the Afro-American program at Yale University, where he used the material in the James Weldon Johnson Collection to institute an in-depth study of the Renaissance. At the time of his death he was working on a biography of Langston Hughes as well as his own autobiography.[3]

While Langston Hughes, Sterling Brown, and Arna Bontemps remained actively involved in black literature after the 1930s, most other Renaissance writers either died within a few years or rather quickly faded from public view. Regardless of the fate of individual writers, the Renaissance, as a viable literary movement, did not survive the decade. The reasons for its demise are fairly complex, but two factors dominate. First was the impact of the Depression, which seriously affected the market for black literature, the ability of black writers to support themselves, and the political and literary orientation of writers, promoters, and critics of black literature. Second was the sad fact that many of those involved in the Harlem Renaissance simply did not survive the decade, and many of those who did survive, like Hughes, Bontemps, and Brown, had altered their literary philosophy or their career interests to the degree that they no longer fit into the movement.

The financial collapse of 1929 and the Great Depression of the 1930s affected nearly every aspect of American life. Clearly the economic crisis quieted the roaring twenties and called home the lost generation. As economic realities impinged upon virtually everyone's consciousness, it is little wonder that American literature shifted its focus away from the individual's alienation in the modern world and stressed instead the social conflict and class struggle of a society in crisis. Not surprisingly, black literature also changed during the Depression, a change that Langston Hughes certainly epitomized. However, for most black writers the change was more gradual, and the Renaissance lingered well into the 1930s. More immediate was the economic pinch that most black writers experienced almost concurrently with the economic collapse.[4]

The first and most obvious result of the Depression was that black writers found it increasingly difficult to support themselves. However, it is not clear how well black writers had ever really been able to make a living solely through their art. Arna Bontemps claimed that only Langston Hughes supported himself through his writing, and he did not become self-sufficient until the 1930s. Countee Cullen also may have been self-sufficient for a time in the late 1920s and early 1930s. Certainly the royalties from his books and the lecture fees that he earned were enough to keep him fairly comfortable. Other black writers relied on full-time or part-time employment, the generosity of patrons, the income of their spouses, or inheritances to support their writing. Claude McKay was perpetually in debt—hardly a letter he wrote did not comment on the immediacy of his economic needs or include an appeal for funds.[5]

Whatever their source of income in the 1920s, black writers faced more difficult economic times in the 1930s. During the 1920s the largest sum Langston Hughes received was seventy-five dollars for a group of poems. Often he gave material away free to anyone who would publish it. To support himself he worked at a variety of jobs, but never made more than twenty-two dollars a week. He supplemented this income with scholarships, literary awards, and for a time with the generous allowance he received from Charlotte Mason. During the Depression these extra sources of income dried up. As Hughes recalled, "we were no longer in vogue, anyway, we Negroes. Sophisticated New Yorkers turned to Noel Coward. Colored actors began to go hungry, publishers politely rejected new manuscripts, and patrons found other uses for their money."[6]

Countee Cullen had enjoyed a fairly substantial income from his poetry and from his public lectures, supplemented by his work on the staff of *Opportunity*, scholarships, and a Guggenheim fellowship. By the end of the decade he was earning enough from his writing and speaking tours to live comfortably, if not lavishly. The Depression, however, nearly wiped out his literary income. His royalty statements from Harper vividly illustrated the reversal of his fortunes. During the first six months of 1932 Cullen received $706.97 in royalties from Harper for six books, including his new novel, *One Way to Heaven*, that had just been published. During that same six-month period two years later, Cullen's royalty income had declined to $53.28; in 1938 his total income from royalties was $147.17. In June 1935, in order to enable Harper to justify economically a new printing of *Copper Sun*, Cullen agreed to reduce his royalty from 15 percent to 10 percent. In December 1934 he became a teacher at Frederick Douglass Junior High School in Harlem.[7]

The loss of support from their patrons was especially difficult for some writers. Since nearly every Renaissance writer received support from a patron during at least some point in their career, the absence of these funds represented an economic hardship that some deeply resented. In 1935 Claude McKay remarked that several Renaissance writers were "very bitter against the 'patrons' of Negro Art, who took them up for a brief period and dropped them." However, not all black writers shared this bitterness. In 1929 Nella Larsen had recognized that the fascination with black literature and the Negro vogue was only a fad, "but an awfully good fad," and that the fad would inevitably pass, but black writers would benefit by the attention showered on them and by the opportunities to lay "the foundations for our . . . contributions to American culture." Also, black writers were not completely deserted during the Depression, so their situation was not as bleak as it might seem from McKay's viewpoint. A number of black writers benefitted from New Deal programs. McKay himself, along with Sterling Brown and Arna Bontemps and a number of younger writers who had never been a part of the Renaissance, participated in the Federal Writers Project, where they received not only government employment but also encouragement to publish the work that they produced on their own time.[8]

Black writers, especially unknown ones, did find that it was more difficult to find a publisher for their work in the 1930s than it had been during the heyday of the Renaissance. Poets found it particularly difficult. In 1937 Alfred Knopf pointed out that it had become a poor bet to publish poetry unless the author was well known. Other publishers apparently agreed, because only one black poet, Frank Marshall Davis, succeeded in getting a book published during the Depression after Sterling Brown's *Southern Road* appeared in 1932. On the other hand, publishers did not close their doors completely to black writers. They just became more selective and more concerned about the cost and potential income of a manuscript. In fact, an informal survey indicates that, while the output of poetry declined, black writers published as many novels during the Depression as they did prior to 1929.[9]

Perhaps the most important change the Depression brought was a shift in the focus of black writing away from the themes of the 1920s. In the 1930s a preoccupation with economic matters replaced the preoccupation with defining the meaning of the black experience. While black writers did not ignore their roots, there was a clear tendency, as illustrated by Langston Hughes's radical poetry, to concentrate on class or social issues in addition to racial ones. Alain Locke, in his 1932 review of black literature, complained that black writing had moved away from the blithe creative writing of the Renaissance as black writers became more serious and socially conscious. Reflecting this new orientation, *Opportunity* shifted its editorial focus. Following Charles S. Johnson's departure, the magazine deemphasized black arts, discontinued its literary prizes, and announced instead that the Julius Rosenwald Fund would underwrite an annual award of $1000 for "notable true stories of the efforts of individual Negroes in the economic field." In other words, one of the leading promoters of the Renaissance ended its support of black literature and instead encouraged blacks to describe their efforts to make a living. This, more than anything else, symbolized the real effect of the Depression had on black literature. It was not that black writers could no longer support themselves or find publishers. These problems existed but were not insurmountable. The more serious problem was that blacks and black institutions, including those which had once been the most avid support-ers of the Renaissance, now had a new set of priorities and no longer had as much time or resources to channel into the arts.[10]

An even more crippling blow to the Harlem Renaissance was a growing awareness among black writers and critics that the movement was dying from within. To a large degree the Renaissance declined in the 1930s because black writers and critics either became disillusioned with the movement or else became convinced that the movement was a sinking ship, and they abandoned it. Since the Renaissance had been born out of a conviction among a number of black intellectuals and young black writers that something exciting was happening in black literature, and since the movement never found any common ideology to bind together its adherents other than their shared participation in this magic moment in black literature, it is not surprising that when the magic faded and the conviction gave way to doubts that the movement collapsed.

In the 1930s a number of black writers began to doubt the continued vitality of the Renaissance as a literary movement. Langston Hughes, recently emancipated from his patron and convinced that the Depression signaled the end of the Renaissance, left Harlem in the spring of 1931 and, except for a few brief visits, did not return for a decade. Wallace Thurman, discouraged with the literary shortcomings of both the Renaissance and his own writing, turned his back on black literature following the publication of his third novel, *Infants of the Spring*, in 1932. Charles S. Johnson, perhaps realizing earlier than most that the Renaissance had peaked, left *Opportunity*, Harlem, and the Renaissance in the late fall of 1928 for a career as a sociology professor at Fisk University. Alain Locke, only slightly prematurely, wrote an obituary celebrating the passing of the movement in early 1931. He voiced doubts about the cultural and aesthetic validity of the movement that he had done so much to define:

> The much exploited Negro renaissance was after all a product of the expansive period we are now willing to call the period of inflation and overproduction; perhaps there was much in it that was unsound, and perhaps our aesthetic gods are turning their backs only a little more gracefully than the gods of the marketplace. Are we then in a period of cultural depression, verging on spiritual bankruptcy? Has the afflatus of Negro self-expression died down? Are we outliving the Negro fad? Has the Negro creative artist wandered into the ambush of the professional exploiters? By some signs and symptoms. Yes. But to anticipate my conclusion,—"Let us rejoice and be exceedingly glad." The second and truly sound phase of cultural development of the Negro in American literature and art cannot begin without a collapse of the boom, a change to more responsible and devoted leadership, a revision of basic values, and along with a penitential purgation of spirit, a wholesale expulsion of the money-changers from the temple of art.

In isolation, any one of these developments would have been insignificant. Together, though, they reflect an emerging pattern. The Renaissance had run its course.[11]

By the mid-1930s the self-doubt about the movement had created a general feeling of disillusionment among Renaissance writers. As Claude McKay wrote in 1935, "I have been seeing a few of the younger writers and artists [around New York City], notably Gwennie Bennett who was in the thick of the Harlem Renaissance and we all of us feel more or less at loose ends." As McKay went on to note, by the middle of the decade Harlem's artists and writers were foundering in an intellectual morass. Two years later McKay attempted to address this problem by organizing a "New Negroes Writers Group," a sort of Harlem Renaissance alumni association which to a greater or lesser degree involved James Weldon Johnson, Countee Cullen, Jessie Fauset, and Arthur Schomburg. Except for Countee Cullen, who genuinely encouraged McKay to proceed with his plan, there was little interest in the organization. In early 1938, following several sparsely attended meetings and an unsuccessful effort to gain control of a magazine, McKay abandoned his efforts.[12]

This intellectual stagnation and general lack of community cohesion that afflicted many of the former participants in the Renaissance was only one sign of a general affliction which rapidly thinned out the ranks of Harlem's literati. In 1931 Madam A'Lelia Walker died, and the dream of establishing a Harlem literary salon died with her. Three years later Wallace Thurman and Rudolph Fisher were also dead. Before the end of the decade James Weldon Johnson was killed in an automobile accident. Claude McKay and Countee Cullen survived into the mid-1940s, but in the last ten years of their lives they produced little of literary value. McKay published his anticommunist history of Harlem, while Cullen spent his last years writing children's stories. Other Renaissance writers suffered an even sadder fate. Nella Larsen, Jean Toomer, and Zora Neale Hurston simply faded into obscurity. Hurston's last years were particularly indicative of how far these writers had fallen from the celebrity status that they had enjoyed when Harlem was in vogue. Hurston, short of money and all but forgotten, spent the last years of her life working as a maid in Florida. In 1959 she suffered a stroke; a year later she died in a welfare home and was buried in an unmarked grave in a segregated cemetery. The Harlem Renaissance died as the people who created it ceased to exist. Some died along with the Renaissance; others vanished, forgotten entirely until an obituary appeared in a far-off newspaper. Finally, those who survived did so because they had changed along with the times, accomplishing something that the literary movement they had created could not match.[13]

If an epitaph was necessary to mark the end of the Renaissance, it came in the early spring of 1935. On March 19 a young Puerto Rican boy was caught stealing a ten-cent pocket knife from the counter of a 135th Street five-and-dime store. A minor scuffle that broke out when the police were arresting the youth sparked rumors that spread up and down the street that the police had beaten to death a black child. Within moments a large crowd gathered, loudly accusing the police of brutality and charging the white merchants in the area with practicing discrimination in their stores. Someone smashed a window, and the looting began. The riot spread into the night. By dawn three blacks were dead, two hundred stores were smashed and burned, and more than $2,000,000 worth of property damage had been done. Ironically, the boy who triggered the riot had been released the previous evening when the merchant chose not to press charges. An investigation organized by Mayor Fiorello La Guardia and conducted by an interracial committee under the direction of E. Franklin Frazier, a professor of sociology at Howard University, concluded that the riot resulted from a general frustration with racial discrimination and poverty. What the committee did not report, however, was that the riot shattered once and for all James Weldon Johnson's myth of Harlem as the black metropolis. The black metropolis, which only a few years earlier had been touted as the cultural center of black America, as the black bohemia which thrilled Renaissance writers and entertained whites looking for exotic adventure, had been exposed as a riot-torn ghetto. Burned-out store fronts might be fertile ground for political action, but not for art, literature, and culture. Harlem would see new black writers in the years to come, but it has yet to regain its position as the focal point of a literary movement.[14]

It is difficult to assess the impact of the Harlem Renaissance on American society. Different groups responded differently to the movement. Even within the black community there was no consensus on the Renaissance. However, some conclusions can be drawn. First, the Renaissance had a negligible impact on the black lower classes. As Langston Hughes observed, the literary movement and the Negro vogue did not alter significantly the day-to-day life of the black masses:

> The ordinary Negroes hadn't heard of the Negro Renaissance. And, if they had, it hadn't raised their wages any. As for all these white folks in the speakeasies and night clubs of Harlem—well, maybe a colored man could find *some* place to have a drink that the tourists hadn't yet discovered.

The failure of the Renaissance to affect the black lower classes dramatically is not surprising. Although the poor rarely buy books, especially poetry, they were not necessarily oblivious to events stirring in the black community. Their participation in large numbers in the Garvey movement that preceded the Renaissance meant that they too had looked into the black experience, examined their racial heritage, and developed a sense of racial pride. But the Renaissance could take little credit for this.[15]

The Renaissance was slightly more successful in reaching the black middle class. Even those critics who condemned the Renaissance bought and read with interest everything written during the movement. Virtually every black newspaper reviewed the work of black writers, and there was enough interest in literature among the black middle class to support lecture tours and poetry readings by a number of black authors. On the other hand, it is nearly impossible to determine exactly how much the black middle class supported the movement by buying books. There are no statistics on their book-buying habits. However, it is fairly clear that the black middle class was not wealthy enough or large enough to support a literary movement. Ultimately, as Margaret Walker observed, "whatever Negro people thought about the poetry written about Negro life did not seem to matter. In the final analysis the audience and the significant critics were white."[16]

It is also difficult to assess the impact of the Renaissance on white America. Again there are no statistics available to detail the number of books that black authors sold to the white middle class. If we assume, however, that white readers accounted for most of the sales of Renaissance books, then several conclusions are evident. First, of all the books written during the Renaissance, only Claude McKay's *Home to Harlem* made the best seller lists. Langston Hughes recalled that his first two books of poetry had gone beyond the first edition but had not become best sellers. Walter White and Countee Cullen reported that their first books sold remarkably well; however, Cullen's royalty statements for the 1930s document the fact that he did not get rich from his writing. The same can be said about the other black writers of the period. They sold well, but not spectacularly among whites.[17]

One important contribution of the Renaissance was that it opened doors for future black writers. The mere fact that during the Renaissance black writers published with major firms and that white critics took their work seriously made things easier for the next generation. Publishers and editors who had once routinely dismissed manuscripts by black authors no longer placed strict racial restrictions on what they published. Langston Hughes recalled the problems that black writers faced before the Renaissance:

When I first started writing it was said that the *Saturday Evening Post* would not accept works written by Negroes. Whether or not the *Post* actually followed such a policy, it did seem to be true of certain other magazines. . . . It can hardly be disputed that the "Renaissance" did a great deal to make possible a public willing to accept Negro problems and Negro Art.

Against this background, the solicitation of blacks' manuscripts by literary magazines and publishers during the Renaissance was revolutionary. Of course, while the situation did improve, the Renaissance did not eliminate discrimination in the literary world. Although black writers found it easier to publish, black writers, actors, and announcers were rarely employed by radio and television until the late 1960s, and few publishers and magazines hired blacks for their editorial staffs or asked blacks to review books. The result was that even following the Renaissance, unless a black was an accomplished, best-selling author, the literary world was not a good place to make a living. [18]

A more serious problem was that until very recently black writers received little recognition from white literary critics. Despite the popularity of Harlem Renaissance courses on campuses today, traditional studies of literary history, literary criticism, and cultural history have virtually ignored the Harlem Renaissance. As late as the mid-1960s Frederick J. Hoffman could survey American writing in the 1920s, mention Van Vechten's *Nigger Heaven* and the fascination with Negro primitiveness and music, but say absolutely nothing about the Harlem Renaissance or a single black author. The only notable exception to this pattern of oversight was Van Wyck Brooks, who included a chapter on Eugene O'Neill and black literature in his book, *The Confident Years*. However, Brooks concentrated on white writers like O'Neill and Van Vechten, and he failed to do more than simply mention the Renaissance writers. The Harlem Renaissance, then, made it easier for black writers to publish, but it would take the civil rights movement and the black power movement of the late 1960s to begin to bring black literature into the mainstream of literary criticism. [19]

Perhaps the most significant result of the Harlem Renaissance was its effect on a future generation of black writers. Whether they admired or rejected the direction taken by the Renaissance, they all were affected deeply by the movement. For some, the Renaissance represented the first attempt of black writers to come to terms with their racial experience.

LeRoi Jones, for example, applauded Langston Hughes and the Harlem school for describing life as they saw it and turning out a "literature about poverty, a literature about violence, a literature about the seamier side of the so-called American dream," even though they provoked the ire of many middle-class black critics. Richard Wright, during his Marxist phase, commended Renaissance writers for being the first black writers to transcend despair and race-consciousness and to focus their attention on class-consciousness. He also credited Langston Hughes with introducing a standard of realism to black literature, such as Theodore Dreiser had done for mainstream American literature.[20]

No matter how blacks interpreted the legacy of the Renaissance, they were all affected by the black literature of the 1920s. In fact, the mere existence of a black literary movement in America had a stimulating effect on potential black writers. For example, when Ralph Ellison first heard of the Harlem Renaissance, he was more interested in music than literature. Nevertheless, his first encounter with black literature left a profound impression on him. As he recalled:

> Mrs. L.C. McFarland had taught us much of Negro history in grade school and from her I'd learned of the New Negro Movement of the twenties, of Langston Hughes, Countee Cullen, Claude McKay, James Weldon Johnson and the others. They had inspired pride and had given me a closer identification with poetry . . . but with music so much on my mind it never occurred to me to try to imitate them. Still I read their work and was excited by the glamour of the Harlem which emerged from their poems and it was good to know that there were Negro writers.

Although Ellison also acknowledged the influence that T.S. Eliot, Ezra Pound, Sherwood Anderson, and other white writers of the period had on him, it was the existence of black writers that most impressed him. Ellison and many others never imagined that blacks could publish books until they came across the books of the Harlem Renaissance.[21]

The influence of the Harlem Renaissance on aspiring black writers was not confined to America. Both African and Caribbean blacks were affected to a surprising degree. Leopold Senghor, president of the Republic of Senegal and a poet and philosopher in his own right, credited the Harlem Renaissance with influencing his own literary consciousness and that of other African writers. In a speech at Howard University in 1966, he tendered "well-deserved homage to the poets whom we translated and recited and in whose steps we tried to follow: Claude McKay, Jean Toomer, Countee Cullen, James Weldon Johnson, Langston Hughes, Sterling Brown." Senghor, Aime Césaire, and other African and Caribbean writers, primarily from French-speaking areas, launched their own black renaissance in Paris in the 1920s, based to a large extent on the work of the Harlem writers. Senghor and Césaire recalled that they and other black students became friends with McKay, Toomer, Hughes, Cullen, and Locke at the home of Mademoiselle Adrée Nardol. Nardol hosted a literary salon where black artists and intellectuals from Africa, America, the Antilles, and other parts of the world met and read and discussed each other's literature. French-African students then carried the Renaissance back to their homeland where it influenced their literature.[22]

The Harlem Renaissance also reached English-speaking areas of Africa. The black South African writer Peter Abrahams recalled the impact of the Renaissance on his life. As a young boy, Abrahams encountered American black literature in the library of the Bantu Men's Social Center in Johannesburg. He first picked Du Bois's *The Souls of Black Folk* from the bookshelf. Therein he discovered a kinship between himself and American blacks that spanned thousands of miles of ocean. "Du Bois," he wrote, "might have been writing about my land and people. The mood and feeling he described were native to me. . . . [he] had given me a key to the understanding of the world. The Negro is not free." Abrahams picked up another book: "I turned the pages of *The New Negro*. These poems and stories were written by Negroes! Something burst deep inside me. The world could never again belong to white people only! Never again!" For Abrahams, other Africans, and blacks a thousand miles away in America, the Harlem Renaissance had opened doors that many had never believed existed. Literature, art, poetry, and books were not the private possessions of whites. Abrahams continued:

> In the months that followed, I spent nearly all my spare time in the library of the Bantu Men's Social Center. I read every one of the books on the shelf marked: American Negro Literature. I became a nationalist, a colour nationalist, through the writings of men and women who lived a world away from me. To them I owe a great debt for crystallizing my vague yearnings to write and for showing me the long dream was attainable.[23]

Even if only a handful of Africans read the Harlem writers, the books were available in scattered libraries where they could awaken the dreams of those who chanced upon them. This, perhaps, was the greatest contribution of the movement, not only in Africa, but for blacks everywhere.

In spite of the impact that the Renaissance had on other black writers, it is still difficult to evaluate its success as a literary movement. After all, in the opinion of a number of black writers and critics, it had failed. It is easy to accept the cynicism of Wallace Thurman. The Renaissance did not produce any great works of literature. A number of talented writers such as Toomer and Hurston never fulfilled their early promise. Others saw their careers end almost as soon as they began, cut short before they matured as writers. In fact, Langston Hughes was the only writer who truly enjoyed a lengthy career.

To many observers the Renaissance did not accomplish what it should have. Some, like writer and editor George Schuyler, denied the validity of a black literary movement in the first place. Others argued that black writers were too provincial, and too preoccupied with the peculiar problems of their racial situation to produce first-rate literature or to examine universal problems of the human experience. As one critic commented:

> The Negro writer is under tremendous pressure to write about the topical and the transient—the plight of the Negro in American society today. It may be that one or two will last because of their historical interest. It may even be that one or two will last because the writer has managed to infuse into his work some universal elements—as Dickens did, even when writing about the social conditions in the England of his day. But most Negro writers do not inject the universal element. They write only about the here and now. Thus, their novels come and go: in ten years they are forgotten.

Other critics like Benjamin Brawley were relieved by the decline of the Renaissance, hoping that now black writers would get over their preoccupation with ghetto realism. Even Alain Locke, once the optimistic midwife of the movement, interpreted its decline as a positive development. Finally, the hopes of men like James Weldon Johnson and Charles S. Johnson that black literature would be the vehicle that ended discrimination and eased the transition from the rural South to urban America were not realized. The Negro vogue, the white invasion of black nightspots, and the popularity of black literature did not cause the majority of whites to reevaluate their racial prejudice.[24]

And yet the Harlem Renaissance was a success. Individual writers, after all, were not primarily concerned with social problems. They were interested in their literature and they wanted to give expression to the black experience—to write about life as they saw it and to look deeply into the black race's existence in America. This they accomplished. The 1920s witnessed an explosion of black literature. Although no literary masterpieces were produced, more black writers wrote and published more novels, short stories, poems, and essays than at any previous time in American history. This was a victory of no small order. Furthermore, although the movement died out, black literature did not die with it. Richard Wright, Ralph Ellison, James Baldwin, Gwendolyn Brooks, and others kept black literature alive in America.

There was, finally, a uniqueness about the Harlem Renaissance. The spirit of the movement, the community of writers, each giving expression to his or her own vision, but nevertheless bound together in a shared undertaking, and the community of intellectuals, critics, patrons, and publishers pulling together to create a revolution in American literature—all of this was unique and sadly would not appear again. The excitement generated by the Harlem Renaissance has not resurfaced in black literature. The only similar experience occurred during the civil rights movement—beginning with Rosa Parks in Montgomery and culminating in the March on Washington—in which blacks again united for a magic moment in history. But this time the focus was social and political, not literary. The Harlem Renaissance was such a magic moment, when confidence and hope prevailed, when the dream that literature would free humankind seemed attainable.

In the final analysis the Harlem Renaissance must be evaluated on its own terms. It was a movement of individual writers, each approaching the problem of black literature from a personal perspective. Although most shared a middle-class background and all of them felt a deep sense of racial pride, they did not attempt to form a tightly knit movement with a well-defined political or literary ideology. None, in fact, would accept any such restrictions on their writing. Instead they were a loose coalition of writers, joined by patrons and supporters, who shared only a commitment to black literature and the feeling that they were all participating in a major literary event. Langston Hughes, perhaps better than anyone, captured the essence of the Harlem Renaissance in his essay, "The Negro Artist and the Racial Mountain":

We younger Negro artists who create now intend to express our individual dark-skinned selves without fear or shame. If white peo-

232 Black Culture and the Harlem Renaissance

ple are pleased we are glad. If they are not, it doesn't matter. We know we are beautiful. And ugly too. The tom-tom cries and the tom-tom laughs. If colored people are pleased we are glad. If they are not their displeasure doesn't matter either. We will build our temples for tomorrow, strong as we know how, and we stand on top of the mountain, free within ourselves.[25]

This was a declaration of independence to which every Renaissance writer could subscribe: this was the credo of the movement that they tried to create. They owe no apologies for their success or for their failure.

Note on Sources

At the time of James Weldon Johnson's death Carl Van Vechten and other friends of the great promoter of the Harlem Renaissance established a memorial collection at Yale University of papers and manuscripts related to the black literary movement. The intention of the founders of this collection was that it become the primary center for research in black literature and the Harlem Renaissance. Unfortunately that dream was never realized. Consequently, the most difficult problem confronting the would-be researcher of the Harlem Renaissance is the lack of a central repository for the papers of the participants in the movement. Instead, these papers are scattered in nearly a dozen major collections, and, one would guess, an even greater number of smaller collections. The principal locations of materials relating to the Renaissance include the Schomburg Center for Research in Black Culture at the New York Public Library; the Countee Cullen Memorial Collection in Special Collections at the Trevor Arnett Library of Atlanta University; the Countee Cullen Papers in the Amistad Research Center, Tulane University; the Zora Neale Hurston Collection at the University of Florida; the James Weldon Johnson Memorial Collection in the Beinecke Rare Books and Manuscript Library at Yale University; the Alain Leroy Locke Papers in the Moorland-Spingarn Research Center at Howard University; the NAACP Collection in the Library of Congress; the William Stanley Braithwaite Papers in the Houghton Library at Harvard University; the Jean Toomer Collection in Special Collections at Fisk University; the Carl Van Vechten Collection in the Manuscript Division at the New York Public Library; and the Harry Ransom Humanities Research Center at the University of Texas at Austin.

This study primarily utilized the materials in the James Weldon Johnson Memorial Collection at Yale University (which included the papers of James Weldon Johnson, Langston Hughes, Countee Cullen, Rudolph Fisher, Zora Neale Hurston, Wallace Thurman, Carl Van Vechten, Claude McKay, and Harold Jackman), the Countee Cullen Papers at the Amisted Research Center, the Jean Toomer Papers at Fisk University, and the Harry Ransom Research Center at the University of Texas. This last collection was an especially valuable find, overlooked by most previous students of the Renaissance. Not only did it include the Alfred A. Knopf, Inc. Collection, consisting of extensive correspondence with James Weldon Johnson, Langston Hughes, Carl Van Vechten, and all of the writers that the Knopfs published, as well as publicity releases and other materials related to the Renaissance, but it contained the papers of Nancy Cunard, Idella Purnell Stone, *Contempo* magazine, Fannie Hurst, and many other literary collections which included often extensive correspondence with participants in the Renaissance. The discovery of these materials suggests that similar rich lodes of Renaissance material yet may lie undiscovered in other collections.

An examination of the published Renaissance material should begin with two general studies of the period: Nathan Huggins's *Harlem Renaissance* (New York: Oxford University Press, 1971), the first scholarly study of the movement, and David Levering Lewis's *When Harlem Was in Vogue* (New York: Vintage Books, 1981), a fascinating and gossipy cultural history of the period. Classic studies of the Renaissance include the autobiograpies of Langston Hughes, *The Big Sea* (New York: Hill and Wang, 1963) and *I Wonder as I Wander* (New York: Hill and Wang, 1956); Claude McKay, *A Long Way from Home* (New York: Harcourt, Brace & World, 1970); Zora Neale Hurston, *Dust Tracks on a Road* (New York: Arno Press and The New York Times, 1969), and James Weldon Johnson, *Along This Way* (New York: Viking, 1961). Other classic studies of black literature which provide a survey of and occasionally insight into the Renaissance are Benjamin Brawley, *The Negro Genius: A New Appraisal of the Achievement of the American Negro in Literature and the Fine Arts* (New York: Dodd, Mead, 1937), Sterling Brown's two books, *Negro Poetry and Drama* and *The Negro in American Fiction*, reprinted in one volume (New York: Atheneum, 1969), and Robert Bone's *The Negro Novel in America* (New Haven: Yale University Press, 1965). Finally Arna Bontemps's edited work, *Harlem Renaissance Remembered* (New York: Dodd, Mead, 1972), contains a series of biographical essays that provide an excellent introduction to most participants in the movement.

During the last fifteen years the appearance of a number of biographies of Renaissance participants and of other significant blacks of that era has added greatly to our understanding of the movement and to black literature and culture in the early part of the century. The best of these new works are Robert E. Hemenway's *Zora Neale Hurston: A Literary Biography* (Urbana, IL: University of Illinois Press, 1977), Arnold Rampersad's first volume of his long-awaited biography of Langston Hughes, *The Life of Langston Hughes* (vol. 1) *I, Too, Sing America: 1902–1941* (New York: Oxford University Press, 1986), Wayne F. Cooper's excellent biography of Claude McKay, *Claude McKay: Rebel Sojourner in the Harlem Renaissance: A Biography* (Baton Rouge: Louisiana State University Press, 1987), and Cynthia Earl Kerman and Richard Eldridge's new study of Jean Toomer, *The Lives of Jean Toomer: A Hunger for Wholeness* (Baton Rouge: Louisiana State University Press, 1987). New studies of black women writers, like Gloria T. Hull's *Color, Sex, and Poetry: Three Women Writers of the Harlem Renaissance* (Bloomington, IN: Indiana University Press, 1987), add a needed dimension to the literature on this period, while biographies of prominent black intellectual and political leaders of the early twentieth century, such as Louis R. Harlan's *Booker T. Washington: The Making of a Black Leader, 1856–1901* (New York: Oxford University Press, 1972) and *Booker T. Washington: The Wizard of*

Tuskegee, 1901–1915 (New York: Oxford University Press, 1983), Manning Marable's study of Du Bois, *W.E.B. Du Bois: Black Radical Democrat* (Boston: Twayne Publishers, 1986), Eugene Levy's biography *James Weldon Johnson: Black Leader, Black Voice* (Chicago: University of Chicago Press, 1973), and Judith Stein's excellent new work on Garvey, *The World of Marcus Garvey: Race and Class in Modern Society* (Baton Rouge: Louisiana State University Press, 1986), round out our understanding of the period and its participants and help place the Harlem Renaissance in its historical context.

Notes

Abbreviations Used

ARC-TU The Amistad Research Center, Tulane University
HRHRC The Harry Ransom Humanities Research Center, The University of
         Texas at Austin
JTP   The Jean Toomer Papers, Fisk University Library
JWJ   James Weldon Johnson Memorial Collection of Negro Literature and
         Art, Beinecke Rare Book and Manuscript Library, Yale University

Introduction

1. The basic interpretation of the Harlem Renaissance's duration is found in works such as S.P. Fullinwider, *The Mind and Mood of Black America: Twentieth Century Thought* (Homewood, IL: Dorsey Press, 1969), and Frances Richardson Keller, "The Harlem Literary Renaissance," *The North American Review* 5 (May 1968): 29–34. See also Abraham Chapman, "The Harlem Renaissance in Literary History," *CLA Journal* 11 (September 1967): 44–45; Nathan Irvin Huggins, ed., *Voices from the Harlem Renaissance* (New York: Oxford University Press, 1976); John Hope Franklin, *From Slavery to Freedom: A History of Negro Americans*, 5th ed. (New York: Knopf, 1980), 382; Benjamin Brawley, *The Negro Genius: A New Appraisal of the American Negro in Literature and the Fine Arts* (New York: Dodd, Mead, 1937), 231–268; and Sterling Brown, *The New Negro Thirty Years Afterward* (Washington, D.C.: Howard University Press, 1955).
2. John W. Parker, "Phylon Profile, XIX: Benjamin Brawley—Teacher and Scholar," *Phylon* 10, March 1949, 22.
3. James Weldon Johnson to Claude McKay, January 26, 1928, JWJ, and James Weldon Johnson, *Black Manhattan* (New York: Atheneum, 1968), 3–4.
4. Ralph Ellison, *Shadow and Act* (New York: Random House, 1964), 17.
5. In the past decade and a half there have been numerous studies of the literature of the Harlem Renaissance and of individual writers. The best survey of this subject is Nathan Irvin Huggins, *The Harlem Renaissance* (New York: Oxford University Press, 1971).

Chapter 1

1. For a discussion of the deterioration of the racial situation following reconstruction see August Meier, *Negro Thought in America, 1880–1915: Racial Ideologies in the Age of Booker T. Washington* (Ann Arbor: University of Michigan Press, 1968), 69–82, 161–63; see also Leon F. Litwack, *Been in the Storm So Long: The Aftermath of Slavery* (New York: Vintage Books, 1979) for a discussion of the often troubled efforts of blacks and whites to adjust to the end of slavery.

2. Roger Lane, *Roots of Violence in Black Philadelphia, 1868–1900* (Cambridge, Mass.: Harvard University Press, 1986), 40–41. Lane documents the exclusion of blacks from labor unions, and hence from the better industrial jobs, in late nineteenth-century Philadelphia. Ibid., 35–41.

3. Lane, 35–41; Meier, 164–65; Henry Pringle, *Theodore Roosevelt: A Biography* (New York: Harcourt, Brace & World, Inc., 1956), 261, 322–27; Dwight W. Hoover, *The Red and the Black* (Chicago: Rand McNally College Publishing, 1976), 221.

4. It is very difficult to pinpoint accurately the number of lynchings in any given year. The figures cited here are those used by John Hope Franklin, *From Slavery to Freedom: A History of Negro Americans*, 5th ed. (New York: Knopf, 1980), 313–14, which were based on studies done between 1913 to 1933. More recent work by George C. Wright on racial violence in Kentucky suggests that these figures are very conservative. See George C. Wright *Life Behind a Veil: Blacks in Louisville, Kentucky, 1865–1930* (Baton Rouge, Louisiana State University Press, 1985), 71–76, 254–57. Wright developed his theories of lynching, including "legal lynching," even further in a paper, "Racial Violence in Kentucky: Lynching, Legal Lynching, and Mob Rule," that he delivered at Rice University, February 5, 1987.

5. Franklin, 316.

6. Ibid., 317.

7. Thomas Dixon, Jr., *The Leopard's Spots* (New York: Doubleday, Page, 1902); Thomas Dixon, Jr., *The Clansman* (New York: Doubleday, Page, 1905); Charles Carroll, *The Negro Not the Son of Ham; or Man Not a Species Divisible* (Chattanooga, TN, 1898); Charles Carroll, *The Negro, Beast or in the Image of God* (St. Louis: American Book and Bible House, 1900); Charles Carroll, *The Tempter of Eve or the Criminality of Man's Social, Political, and Religious Equality, with the Negro, and the Amalgamation to Which These Crimes Inevitably Lead* (St. Louis: Adamic Publishing, 1902); Frederick L. Hoffman, *Race Traits and Tendencies of the American Negro* (New York: Published for the American Economic Association by Macmillan, 1896). For a survey of racial thought in the United States in

the late nineteenth and early twentieth centuries see Hoover, 164–90, 218–52.

8. S. P. Fullinwider, *The Mind and Mood of Black America: 20th Century Thought* (Homewood, IL: Dorsey Press, 1969), 4.

9. Hoover, 241–53; the most notable historians who argued this position were James Ford Rhodes, John W. Burgess, and especially William A. Dunning in *Reconstruction* (New York: Harper & Brothers, 1907); see also Hoover, 211–17, 233–34; Franz Boas, "Industries of the African Negroes," *The Southern Workman*, April 1909, 217–19; and Franz Boas *The Mind of Primitive Man* (New York: Macmillan, 1911).

10. [W.E.B. Du Bois], "Close Ranks," *Crisis*, July 1918, 111; Franklin, 342; *The Works of Francis J. Grimké*, ed. Carter G. Woodson, vol. 3 (Washington, D.C.: Associated Publishers, 1942), 44, 67.

11. Franklin, 325–31; for a thorough discussion of the problems faced by black troops during World War I see Stetson Conn, ed., *The United States in World War II*, vol. 8, part 8, *The Employment of Negro Troops*, by Ulysses S. Lee (Washington, D.C.: Government Printing Office, 1966), 8–14; and Stephen E. Ambrose, "Blacks in the Army in Two World Wars," in *The Military in American Society: Essays and Readings*, ed. Stephen E. Ambrose and James A. Barber, Jr. (New York: Free Press, 1972).

12. See Robert V. Haynes, *A Night of Violence: The Houston Riot of 1917* (Baton Rouge: Louisiana State University Press, 1976) for a detailed account of the Houston riot. August Meier and Elliot M. Rudwick, *From Plantation to Ghetto* (New York: Hill and Wang, 1970), 219.

13. Franklin, 336; see also Lee, 10–11, and Ambrose, 183.

14. Franklin, 341.

15. Meier and Rudwick, 220–21.

16. Thomas J. Woofter, *Negro Migration: Changes in Rural Organization and Population of the Cotton Belt* (New York: Negro Universities Press, 1920), 170; Gilbert Osofsky, *Harlem: The Making of a Ghetto: Negro New York, 1890–1930* (New York: Harper & Row, 1966), 18. From 1870 to 1890 there was a small but steady movement of blacks northward, averaging approximately 41,000 per decade. From 1890 to 1910 this number increased to more than 100,000 per decade.

17. Emmett Scott, *Negro Migration During the War* (New York: Oxford University Press, 1920), 14; U.S. Department of Commerce, Bureau of the Census, *Negroes in the United States, 1920–1932* (Washington, D.C.: Government Printing Office, 1935), 40–43.

18. Scott, 17; Osofsky, 29; Arna Bontemps and Jack Conroy, *Anyplace but Here* (New York: Hill and Wang, 1969), 160.

19. *Negroes in the U.S., 1920–1932*, 34–36, 40–43.

20. Osofsky, 81–104; Roi Ottley and William J. Weatherby, eds., *The Negro*

in New York: An Informal Social History (Dobbs Ferry, NY: Oceana Publications, 1967), 179–83.

21. The "Tenderloin" district was an ill-defined area that included scattered pockets of black settlement stretching from Twentieth Street to Fifty-third Street on the west side of Manhattan; San Juan Hill had more precise boundaries, along Tenth and Eleventh avenues from Sixtieth to Sixty-fourth streets. See Osofsky, 12–13; *The Negro in New York*, 182–83.

22. Jeffrey S. Gurock, *When Harlem Was Jewish, 1870–1930* (New York: Columbia University Press, 1979), 146–47;

23. *Negroes in the U.S., 1920–1932*, 68; Osofsky, 123, 130.

24. Rudolph Fisher, "The City of Refuge," in *The New Negro*, ed. Alain Locke (New York: Atheneum, 1969), 57–58.

25. Ibid., 59.

26. Langston Hughes, *The Big Sea: An Autobiography* (New York: Hill and Wang, 1963), 62–64.

27. Ibid., 81–82.

28. James Weldon Johnson, *Black Manhattan* (New York: Atheneum, 1968), 3–4, 146.

29. Ibid., 284–85.

30. Osofsky, 127–49; Herman D. Bloch, "The Employment Status of the New York Negro in Retrospect," *Phylon* 20, December 1959, 327; and Thomas J. Woofter, *Races and Ethnic Groups in American Life* (New York: McGraw-Hill, 1937), 133.

31. Herbert G. Gutman, *The Black Family in Slavery and Freedom, 1750–1925* (New York: Vintage Books, 1977), 443–44, 450–55, 509–515, 643n; Osofsky, 134. Gutman defined a subfamily as either a husband and wife, two parents and their children, or a single parent and children living in the same household with another nuclear family.

32. *Negroes in the U.S., 1920–1932*, 520–26, 578; Dominic J. Capeci, Jr., *The Harlem Riot of 1943* (Philadelphia: Temple University Press, 1977), 37; Gutman, 512.

33. Capeci, 35–36, 40.

34. Ibid., 48; *Negroes in the U.S., 1920–1932*, 374–75, 452–57.

35. Carl Van Vechten, *Nigger Heaven* (New York: Harper & Row, 1971), 149.

Chapter 2

1. Alain Locke, "The New Negro," in *The New Negro*, ed. Alain Locke (New York: Atheneum, 1969), 3, 5, 11; John Hope Franklin, *From Slavery to Freedom: A History of Negro America* (New York: Knopf, 1980), 362.

2. August Meier, *Negro Thought in America, 1880–1915: Racial Ideologies*

in the Era of Booker T. Washington (Ann Arbor: University of Michigan Press, 1968), 258–59.

3. Ibid., 42–43.

4. Quoted in Meier, 44.

5. Meier, 44–45.

6. For a more detailed survey of black historiography in the late nineteenth century see Dwight W. Hoover, *The Red and the Black* (Chicago: Rand McNally, 1976), 190–99, and S.P. Fullinwider, *The Mind and Mood of Black America: Twentieth Century Thought* (Homewood, IL: Dorsey Press, 1969), 4–11.

7. Edward A. Johnson, *A School History of the Negro Race in America, from 1619 to 1890. With a Short Introduction as to the Origin of the Race; Also a Short Sketch of Liberia* (Chicago: W.B. Conkey, 1891), 9–10; George Washington Williams, *History of the Negro Race in America, from 1619 to 1880* (New York: Putnam, 1883), 22. Like Johnson, Williams refutes the thesis that Noah's curse on the sons of Ham created the black race as a separate or cursed species. For a more complete discussion of Williams's philosophy see John Hope Franklin, *George Washington Williams: A Biography* (Chicago: University of Chicago Press, 1985); William T. Alexander, *History of the Colored Race in America* (Kansas City: Palmento Publishing, 1888), 24–25.

8. Johnson, 23. One black who offered an interesting alternative to the standard argument of the decline of Africa was Martin R. Delany, who maintained that the pure African race remained the equal of the white race, while American blacks had degenerated because of miscegenation. See Hoover, 191, and Martin R. Delany, *Principles of Ethnology: The Origin of Races and Color, With an Archaeological Compendium of Ethiopian and Egyptian Civilization* (New York: Harper, 1879).

9. There was also resistance to industrial education. As a result most black colleges developed a combined liberal arts-vocational curriculum, and out of necessity provided elementary and secondary instruction as well as college-level courses. See Michael R. Heintze, *Private Black Colleges in Texas, 1865–1954* (College Station: Texas A&M University Press, 1985), 47–86, for a detailed discussion of this phenomenon; Meier, 91.

10. Whites commonly ridiculed classical education at black colleges with quips such as "Mandy, is yo' did yo' Greek yit." Heintze, 48.

11. Fullinwider, 27–28.

12. Hoover, 255.

13. Meier, 75–76; Hoover, 195.

14. Louis R. Harlan, *Booker T. Washington: The Making of a Black Leader, 1856–1901* (New York: Oxford University Press, 1972), viii.

15. Booker T. Washington, "The Standard Printed Version of the Atlanta Ex-

position Address [Atlanta, Georgia, September 18, 1895]," in *The Booker T. Washington Papers*, vol. 3, *1889–95*, ed. Louis R. Harlan (Urbana, IL: University of Illinois Press, 1975), 585–86.

16. Manning Marable, *W.E.B. Du Bois: Black Radical Democrat* (Boston: Twayne Publishers, 1986), 42.
17. Meier, 106.
18. Meier, 110–11; Marable, 41; Washington, "Atlanta Exposition Address," 583–87.
19. Harlan, 222–24.
20. Marable, 58–59; Meier, 115–116, 266.
21. *The Works of Francis J. Grimké*, ed. Carter G. Woodson, vol. 1, *Addresses, Mainly Personal and Racial* (Washington, D.C.: The Associated Publishers, 1942), 237–39.
22. Meier, 169.
23. Marable, 50–51.
24. W.E.B. Du Bois, *The Autobiography of W.E.B. Du Bois: A Soliloquy on Viewing My Life from the Last Decade of Its First Century* (New York: International Publishers, 1968), 61–65.
25. Marable, 55–58, 68–70.
26. Ibid., 43, 46–47; W.E.B. Du Bois, *The Souls of Black Folk: Essays and Sketches* (New York: Fawcett Publications, 1968), 43, 48–49; Marable, 49.
27. W.E.B. Du Bois, "The Talented Tenth," in *The Negro Problem: A Series of Articles by Representative American Negroes of Today*, eds. Booker T. Washington, and others (New York: AMS Press, 1970), 33–34, 60–62.
28. Du Bois, *The Souls of Black Folk*, 49; W.E.B. Du Bois, "Blessed Discrimination," *Crisis*, February 1913, 184–86.
29. W.E.B. Du Bois, "Marrying of Black Folk," *Independent*, October 1910, 812–13.
30. Meier, 262–63.
31. Marable, 38–40, 44.
32. For a discussion of Garvey's early life see Judith Stein, *The World of Marcus Garvey: Race and Class in Modern Society* (Baton Rouge: Louisiana State University Press, 1986), 24–37.
33. Stein, 41–64; Roi Ottley and William Weatherby, eds., *The Negro in New York: An Informal Social History* (Dobbs Ferry, NY: Oceana Publications, 1967), 209–218.

Chapter 3

1. Quoted in Chidi Ikonne, *From Du Bois to Van Vechten: The Early New Negro Literature, 1903–1926* (Westport, CT: Greenwood Press, 1981), 51.

2. William Dean Howells, "Life and Letters," *Harper's Weekly*, 27 June 1896, 630.
3. William Dean Howells, "Introduction to Paul Laurence Dunbar," *Lyrics of the Lowly Life* (New York: Dodd, Mead, 1908), xviii-xix; quoted in Benjamin Brawley, *Paul Laurence Dunbar: Poet of His People* (Chapel Hill, NC: University of North Carolina Press, 1936), 60.
4. See Virginia Cunningham, *Paul Laurence Dunbar and His Song* (New York: Dodd, Mead, 1957), 251; and Paul Laurence Dunbar, "The Poet," in *The Complete Poems of Paul Laurence Dunbar* (New York: Dodd, Mead, 1913), 191.
5. Charles L. Glicksberg, "The Alienation of Negro Literature," *Phylon* 11, March 1950, 55; see also Brawley, *Dunbar*, 76.
6. James Weldon Johnson, *Along This Way* (New York: Viking, 1961), 159. For other examples of criticism of Dunbar's dialect poetry see Glicksberg, 55; James Weldon Johnson, ed., *The Book of American Negro Poetry* (New York: Harcourt, Brace & World, 1959), 41–44; and Johnson, *Along This Way*, 158–62.
7. James Weldon Johnson, "American Negro Poets and their Poetry," unpublished manuscript of a speech given at Howard University, April 10, 1924, JWJ; Johnson, who used the medium of dialect poetry himself, was especially aware of both its strengths and its weaknesses. Other critics who praised Dunbar's dialect pieces included William Dean Howells, "Introduction" to *Lyrics*, ix.
8. Dunbar, "The Party," in *Complete Poems*, 83–86.
9. Wallace Thurman, "Negro Poets and Their Poetry," in *Black Expression: Essays By and About Black Americans in the Creative Arts*, ed. Addison Gayle, Jr. (New York: Weybright and Talley, 1969), 75.
10. Dunbar, "Ode to Ethiopia," in *Complete Poems*, 16.
11. Jervis Anderson, *This Was Harlem: A Cultural Portrait, 1900–1950* (New York: Farrar, Straus, Giroux, 1981), 32–36; and David Levering Lewis, *When Harlem Was in Vogue* (New York: Vintage Books, 1979), 29–30.
12. Paul Laurence Dunbar to Frank M. Hopkins, 25 November 1896, HRHRC.
13. Johnson, *Along This Way*, 161.
14. Charles W. Chesnutt, *The Conjure Woman* (Cambridge: Houghton Mifflin, 1899), 42.
15. William L. Andrews, *The Literary Career of Charles W. Chesnutt* (Baton Rouge: Louisiana State University Press, 1980), 126–28.
16. Charles W. Chesnutt, *The Marrow of Tradition* (Boston: Houghton Mifflin, 1901), 283–84.
17. Andrews, 17, 127–28.
18. Ibid., 25.

19. Ibid., 13–16.
20. Johnson, *American Negro Poetry*, 41–42.
21. See James Edwin Campbell, *Echoes from the Cabin and Elsewhere* (Chicago: Donohue & Henneberry, 1895), and Ikonne, 48–50.
22. Daniel Webster Davis, *'Weh Down Souf and Other Poems* (Cleveland: Helman-Taylor, 1897); John Wesley Holloway, *From the Desert* (New York: Neale Publishing, 1919); Joeseph S. Cotter, *Caleb, the Degenerate: A Play in Four Acts* (Louisville: Bradley & Gilbert, 1903); Joesph S. Cotter, *A White Song and a Black One* (Louisville: Bradley & Gilbert, 1909); Joseph S. Cotter, *Negro Tales* (New York: Cosmopolitan Press, 1912); Waverly Turner Carmichael, *From the Heart of a Folk: A Book of Songs* (Boston: Cornhill, 1918); Raymond Garfield Dandridge, *The Poet and Other Poems* (Cincinnati: Raymond G. Dandridge, 1920); see also Ikonne, 59–65.
23. Andrews, 30–34, 235.

Chapter 4

1. James Weldon Johnson, *Along This Way* (New York: Viking, 1961), 158–59.
2. For the most complete information about Johnson's early life see Eugene Levy, *James Weldon Johnson: Black Leader, Black Voice* (Chicago: University of Chicago Press, 1973), 3–73; see also Johnson, *Along This Way*, 3–156.
3. Johnson, *Along This Way*, 188–89. Eugene Levy contends that the deteriorating racial situation in Jacksonville and the declining support for black education were major factors in Johnson's decision. See Levy, 68–79.
4. Johnson, *Along This Way*, 177, 221.
5. Placing blacks in consular posts was a major problem for Anderson and Washington. President Roosevelt had difficulty identifying locations where the appointment of a black would not cause undue friction; blacks, in turn, often were reluctant to accept low-paying positions in out-of-the-way places. Given this situation Johnson became a major figure in Anderson's and Washington's efforts to keep blacks in the foreign service. See Levy, 105–108.
6. Johnson, *Along This Way*, 193, 237.
7. James Weldon Johnson to Brander Mathews, [November] 1908, JWJ; James Weldon Johnson to Carl Van Doren, December 28, 1922, JWJ.
8. For the best account of McKay's life see Wayne F. Cooper, *Claude McKay: Rebel Sojourner in the Harlem Renaissance, A Biography* (Baton Rouge: Louisiana State University Press, 1987), 1–62.
9. James Weldon Johnson, ed., *The Book of American Negro Poetry* (New York: Harcourt, Brace & World, 1959), 165–66.

10. Cooper, 64–73.
11. Ibid., 78–81, 93–95.
12. Claude McKay, "The Harlem Dancer," in *Selected Poems of Claude McKay* (New York: Bookman Associated, 1953), 61.
13. Claude McKay, *A Long Way from Home* (New York: Harcourt, Brace & World, 1970), 26.
14. Ibid., 99, 110–12, 114.
15. James Weldon Johnson, "American Negro Poets and Their Poetry," unpublished manuscript of a speech given at Howard University, April 10, 1924, JWJ.
16. For an account of Hughes's childhood see James A. Emanuel, *Langston Hughes* (New Haven: College & University Press, 1967), 18–19.
17. Langston Hughes, *The Big Sea* (New York: Hill and Wang, 1963), 16, 26.
18. Ibid., 40.
19. Ibid., 61–66.
20. Ibid., 92–94.
21. Ibid.; Johnson, "American Negro Poets."
22. Langston Hughes, "The Weary Blues," in *The Weary Blues* (New York: Knopf, 1926), 23–24.
23. Arna Bontemps, "The Negro Renaissance: Jean Toomer and the Harlem Writers of the 1920s," in *Anger and Beyond: The Negro Writer in the United States*, ed. Herbert Hill (New York: Harper & Row, 1968), 24; Countee Cullen to Jean Toomer, September 29, 1923, JTP.
24. Quoted in Arna Bontemps, "Introduction" in Jean Toomer, *Cane* (New York: Harper & Row, 1969), viii. The best biographical information on Toomer is found in Cynthia Earl Kerman and Richard Eldridge, *The Lives of Jean Toomer: A Hunger for Wholeness* (Baton Rouge: Louisiana State University Press, 1987), and in Toomer's various unpublished autobiographies, especially "Book of Parents," JTP.
25. Kerman and Eldridge, 65–75.
26. Jean Toomer, "From Exile into Being," unpublished manuscript of the second volume of Toomer's autobiography, JTP, 97–98.
27. Kerman and Eldridge, 80–81.
28. Ibid., 91–92.
29. Jean Toomer, "Exile into Being," 98–99.
30. Kerman and Eldridge, 102–103.
31. Ibid., 99–100, 108; Allen Tate to Jean Toomer, November 7, 1923, JTP.
32. Alain Locke to Jean Toomer, n.d., JTP; Alain Locke to Jean Toomer, January 4, 1923, JTP; William Stanley Braithwaite, "The Negro in American Literature," in *The New Negro*, ed. Alain Locke (New York: Atheneum, 1969), 44.

33. For a more detailed discussion of Toomer's abandonment of his literary career see Kerman and Eldridge, 100, 108–116.
34. David Levering Lewis, *When Harlem Was in Vogue* (New York: Vintage Books, 1982), 89–90; Jervis Anderson, *This Was Harlem: A Cultural Portrait, 1900–1950* (New York: Farrar, Straus, Giroux, 1981), 200–202.
35. Alain Locke, "Foreword," in *The New Negro*, xvii.
36. Alain Locke, "Negro Youth Speaks," in *The New Negro*, 47.
37. *Fire!!*, November 1926, 1.
38. Langston Hughes to Wallace Thurman, n.d., JWJ.
39. Ibid.; handwritten note by Wallace Thurman on the title page of *Fire!!*, in JWJ.
40. Countee Cullen, "From a Dark Tower," *Fire!!*, November 1926, 16; Langston Hughes, "Elevator Boy," *Fire!!*, November 1926, 20.
41. Lewis, 194.
42. Hughes, *Big Sea*, 235, 238.

Chapter 5

1. For a detailed account of the relationship between the Harlem Renaissance and the Village see Harold Cruse, *The Crisis of the Negro Intellectual* (New York: William Morrow, 1967), 22–32. See also Cynthia Earl Kerman and Richard Eldridge, *The Lives of Jean Toomer: A Hunger for Wholeness* (Baton Rouge: Louisiana State University Press, 1987), 92–93, 101–108.
2. For a detailed description of this black bohemia see S.P. Fullinwider, *The Mind and Mood of Black America: Twentieth Century Thought* (Homewood, IL: Dorsey Press, 1969), 132–33; Langston Hughes, *The Big Sea* (New York: Hill and Wang, 1963), 233–49; David Levering Lewis, *When Harlem Was in Vogue* (New York: Vintage Books, 1982), 162–239; and Jervis Anderson, *This Was Harlem: A Cultural Portrait, 1900–1950* (New York: Farrar, Straus, Giroux, 1981), 137–84. Wallace Thurman satirized the black bohemia in *Infants of the Spring* (New York: Macaulay, 1932).
3. Arna Bontemps to Harold Jackman, March 25, 1942, JWJ; Hughes, *Big Sea*, 233–34.
4. David L. Lewis, 193; Iolanthe Sidney, the owner of a Harlem employment agency, provided Thurman his room. Hughes, 234–35; Theophilus Lewis, "Wallace Thurman Is Model Harlemite," news clipping from New York *Amsterdam News*, c. February 1932, in JWJ; Anderson, 208.
5. Quoted in Hughes, *Big Sea*, 243–44; Cruse, 24–26; Roi Ottley and William J. Weatherby, eds., *The Negro in New York: An Informal Social History* (Dobbs Ferry, NY: Oceana Publications, 1967), 246–51; Lewis, 162–75.

6. Ottley and Weatherby, 249–50.
7. Ibid., 248–49; Lewis, 209–210.
8. Hughes, *Big Sea*, 153.
9. Ibid., 247–48; James Weldon Johnson, *Along This Way* (New York: Viking, 1968), 378–79.
10. Ottley and Weatherby, 247.
11. Ibid.
12. Hughes, *Big Sea*, 225–26.
13. Ibid., 249.
14. Ibid., 223–24; Johnson, *Along This Way*, 201.
15. For a good summary of Van Vechten's early life see Edward Leuders, *Carl Van Vechten* (New Haven: College & University Press, 1965), 21–22, 95.
16. Peter D. Marchent, "Carl Van Vechten, Novelist and Critic: A Study in the Metropolitan Comedy of Manners" (M.A. thesis, Columbia University, 1954), quoted in Leuders, 8.
17. Leuders, 96, 98; Cruse, 26; and George S. Schuyler, "Phylon Profile, XXII: Carl Van Vechten," *Phylon*, 11, December 1950, 363.
18. Carl Van Vechten, *Nigger Heaven* (New York: Harper & Row, 1971), 96–99.
19. Ibid., 119.
20. Ibid., 89.
21. Ibid., 89–90.
22. Schuyler, "Carl Van Vechten," 366; Carl Van Vechten, "Maonin' wid a Sword in ma Han," manuscript of an article that appeared in *Vanity Fair*, February 1926, in Carl Van Vechten Papers, Yale University Library; Leuders, 104.
23. W.E.B. Du Bois, review of *Nigger Heaven*, by Carl Van Vechten, in *Crisis*, December 1926, 81–82.
24. Richetta Randolph to James Weldon Johnson, September 1, 1925, JWJ; Benjamin Brawley, *The Negro Genius: A New Appraisal of the Achievement of the American Negro in Literature and the Fine Arts* (New York: Dodd, Mead, 1937), 235.
25. Harold Jackman to Claude McKay, June 3, 1927, JWJ.
26. Wallace Thurman, "Fire Burns," *Fire!!*, November 1926, 48; see the manuscript notes for *Nigger Heaven* in JWJ.
27. Johnson, *Along This Way*, 381; Leuders, 105–106.

Chapter 6

1. Johnson resigned from the consular service when he failed to receive a promotion from the Wilson administration. There is some question about

whether his problems with the State Department arose because he was a Republican seeking an appointment from a Democrat or because of the deteriorating racial situation within the civil service under Woodrow Wilson. See James Weldon Johnson, *Along This Way* (New York: Viking, 1961), 292; and Eugene Donald Levy, *James Weldon Johnson: Black Leader, Black Voice* (Chicago: University of Chicago Press, 1973), 116–19, 149.

2. Levy, 151–59.
3. Although Johnson was a major promoter of the Harlem literary movement, he did not approve of the use of the term "Renaissance" because it implied the rebirth of an earlier period of literary achievement after a period of inactivity; Johnson believed that the "Harlem Renaissance" was simply the public recognition of literary activity that actually had been going on for some time. Consequently, he referred to the movement as the "flowering of Negro literature." See Levy, 308.
4. By "power" Johnson meant group action to bring pressure through "every legitimate and righteous way to achieve what the individual can't achieve alone: economic emancipation, political emancipation through the ballot, and social equality." James Weldon Johnson, "A New Power for the Solution to the Race Problem," address given at the Sixteenth Annual Conference of the NAACP, Denver, Colorado, June 28, 1925, JWJ.
5. See James Weldon Johnson, "Inter-Race Relations," address given to the YMCA in Indianapolis, November 25, 1923, JWJ; James Weldon Johnson, "American Negro Poets and Their Poetry," address given at Howard University, April 10, 1924, JWJ.
6. James Weldon Johnson, ed., *The Book of American Negro Poetry* (New York: Harcourt, Brace & World, 1959), 9; W.E.B. Du Bois to James Weldon Johnson, January 11, 1916, JWJ. Years later Johnson again emphasized his belief in the effectiveness of art as a weapon against racism when he wrote to Carl Van Vechten that he was convinced that Ethel Waters singing "Summertime" did more to change the attitudes of a prejudiced person than any political essay. James Weldon Johnson to Carl Van Vechten, March 2, 1934, JWJ.
7. James Weldon Johnson, "Brothers," in *The Negro Caravan: Writing By American Negroes*, eds. Sterling Brown, Arthur P. Davis, and Ulysses Lee (New York: Arno Press and The New York Times, 1970), 327–28.
8. Johnson, "American Negro Poets."
9. Johnson, *Book of American Negro Poetry*, 5–7. These sentiments were expressed in the preface to the revised, 1931 edition of this book.
10. Johnson, *Along This Way*, 380–81.
11. James Weldon Johnson, "Negro Authors and White Publishers," *Crisis*, July 1929, 229.

12. In 1937, for example, Alfred Knopf turned down a manuscript by Robert
    Hayden when Johnson failed to endorse him. In this instance a single af-
    firmative word from Johnson would have convinced Knopf to take a chance
    on the young poet. See Alfred Knopf to James Weldon Johnson, September
    13, 1937, and September 16, 1937, JWJ; see also James Weldon Johnson
    to Arthur Spingarn, February 10, 1938, JWJ; James Weldon Johnson to
    Blanche Knopf, July 29, 1931, HRHRC; and Blanche Knopf to James
    Weldon Johnson, July 31, 1931, HRHRC.
13. For examples of this see James Weldon Johnson's correspondence with Al-
    fred Knopf, Zora Neale Hurston, or Anne Spencer, JWJ; or James Weldon
    Johnson's correspondence with Blanche Knopf, HRHRC.
14. David Levering Lewis, *When Harlem Was in Vogue* (New York: Vintage
    Books, 1982), 166.
15. Levy, 310–12; Langston Hughes, *The Big Sea* (New York: Hill and Wang,
    1963), 216; Claude McKay, *A Long Way from Home* (New York: Harcourt,
    Brace & World, 1970), xiii; and James Weldon Johnson to Claude McKay,
    September 30, 1933, JWJ. McKay's problems with immigration occurred
    because of changes in U.S. immigration laws and because he had visited
    the Soviet Union and was suspected of being a radical or even a commu-
    nist agent. Claude McKay to James Weldon Johnson, October 30, 1933,
    JWJ.
16. Fanny M. McConnell to Owen Dodson, October 20, 1933, JWJ.
17. Levy, 324–25.
18. Ibid., 318.
19. Clare Bloodgood Crane, "Alain Locke and the Negro Renaissance" (Ph.D.
    diss., University of California, San Diego, 1971), 23–33; John Hope
    Franklin, *From Slavery to Freedom: A History of Negro Americans* (New
    York: Knopf, 1980), 373; and Alain Locke, "The New Negro," in *The
    New Negro*, ed. Alain Locke (New York: Atheneum, 1969), 10–11.
20. Alain Locke, "Negro Youth Speaks," in *The New Negro*, 48, 50–51; Al-
    ain Locke, "Self-Criticism: The Third Dimension in Culture," *Phylon* 11,
    December 1950, 392.
21. Locke, "Negro Youth Speaks," 51.
22. Ibid., 51–52.
23. Cynthia Earl Kerman and Richard Elkridge, *The Lives of Jean Toomer: A
    Hunger for Wholeness* (Baton Rouge: Louisiana State University Press,
    1987), 92, 108.
24. Hughes, *Big Sea*, 93, 184–89; Blanche E. Ferguson, *Countee Cullen and
    the Negro Renaissance* (New York: Dodd, 1966), 53–54.
25. Zora Neale Hurston to James Weldon Johnson, 1937, JWJ.
26. Zora Neale Hurston, "The Chick with One Hen," copy of a letter sent to
    Opportunity, [1937], JWJ.

27. Zora Neale Hurston, *Dust Tracks on a Road* (New York: Arno Press and The New York Times, 1969), 176.

28. McKay, *Long Way from Home*, 312–13; see also Hurston, "Chick with One Hen," and Alain Locke, "Jingo, Counter-Jingo, and Us," *Opportunity*, January 1938, 10.

29. Zora Neale Hurston to James Weldon Johnson, [1937], JWJ; McKay, *A Long Way from Home*, 313–14.

30. For a detailed evaluation of Locke as a personification of the Harlem Renaissance see S.P. Fullinwider, *The Mind and Mood of Black America: Twentieth Century Thought* (Homewood, IL: Dorsey Press, 1969), 115–16.

31. Wallace Thurman, *Infants of the Spring* (New York: Macaulay, 1932), 233–40.

32. For the best biographical information on Johnson see Patrick J. Gilpin, "Charles S. Johnson: An Intellectual Biography" (Ph.D. diss., Vanderbilt University, 1973), 1–16.

33. The concept of the marginal man is usually traced to a paper by Robert E. Park, "Human Migration and the Marginal Man," *American Journal of Sociology* 33, May 1928, 881–93 and to Everett V. Stonequist, *The Marginal Man: A Study in Personality and Culture Conflict* (New York: Scribner, 1937). (Stonequist's book was originally presented as a doctoral dissertation at the University of Chicago in 1930.) The idea of the "marginal man" had been discussed among Chicago sociologists for at least a decade before Park published his paper, and it probably was developed by W. I. Thomas several years before he left the University in 1918. A version of the theory (though unnamed) appeared in 1921 in *Old World Traits Transplanted* (New York: Harper, 1921), 142–44, a book which Thomas wrote but which was published under the authorship of Park and Herbert A. Miller. Charles S. Johnson undoubtedly was introduced to the concept during his years at the University of Chicago, although he did not use this concept in his study of the Chicago riots. For the best study of the emergence of the concept of the marginal man see Stow Persons, *Ethnic Studies at Chicago, 1905–45* (Urbana, IL: University of Illinois Press, 1987), 45–46, 64–67, 98–110.

34. Fullinwider, 107, 113.

35. E.K. Jones, "'Cooperation' and 'Opportunity,'" *Opportunity*, January 1923, 5.

36. Harold Jackman to Claude McKay, June 3, 1927, JWJ.

37. Patrick J. Gilpin, "Charles S. Johnson: Entrepreneur of the Harlem Renaissance," in *The Harlem Renaissance Remembered*, ed. Arna Bontemps (New York: Dodd, Mead, 1972), 225; Jervis Anderson, *This Was Harlem: A Cultural Portrait, 1900–1950* (New York: Farrar, Straus, Giroux, 1982), 202.

38. Gilpin, "Charles S. Johnson: Entrepreneur," 226; and Charles S. Johnson, "An Opportunity for Negro Writers," *Opportunity*, September 1924, 258.

39. Charles S. Johnson, "The Contest," *Opportunity*, October 1925, 291. There was a great deal of controversy surrounding Holstein, who was a wealthy West Indian numbers banker. Many Harlemites resented the source of his wealth, even though he contributed generously to many Harlem charities and was a significant supporter of black cultural activities. See Anderson, *This Was Harlem*, 336 and Hughes, *Big Sea*, 214–16; Charles S. Johnson, "The Contest," 291–92; Charles S. Johnson, "Opportunity's Literary Record for 1925," *Opportunity*, February 1926, 38; Chidi Ikonne, *From Du Bois to Van Vechten: The Early New Negro Literature, 1903–1926* (Westport, CT: Greenwood Press, 1981), 94.

40. Charles S. Johnson, "Out of the Shadow," *Opportunity*, May 1925, 131; Charles S. Johnson, "Some Perils of the 'Renaissance,'" *Opportunity*, March 1927, 68; and Charles S. Johnson, "A Note on the New Literary Movement," *Opportunity*, March 1926, 80–81.

41. Charles S. Johnson, ed., *Ebony and Topaz: A Collectanea* (New York: National Urban League, 1927), 11–13.

42. Gilpin, "Johnson: Entrepreneur," 244.

43. Hughes, *Big Sea*, 218.

44. Lewis, *When Harlem Was in Vogue*, 129–30; Anderson, *This Was Harlem*, 336.

45. Roi Ottley and William J. Weatherby, eds., *The Negro in New York: An Informal Social History* (Dobbs Ferry, NY: Oceana Publications, 1967), 257–59; Lewis, 165–69.

46. Langston Hughes, *I Wonder as I Wander: An Autobiographical Journey* (New York: Hill & Wang, 1956), 41–63; Hughes, "My Career as a Writer" [1936], manuscript in the Nancy Cunard Papers, HRHRC; Langston Hughes to Nancy Cunard, September 30, 1931, HRHRC.

47. Lewis, 121–25.

48. Ibid.

49. Ibid., 177.

Chapter 7

1. Eugene Levy, *James Weldon Johnson: Black Leader, Black Voice* (Chicago: University of Chicago Press, 1973), 161–62, 298; William Stanley Braithwaite to James Weldon Johnson, July 17, 1915, JWJ.

2. Levy, 298; LeRoi Jones, "Philistinism and the Negro Writer," in *Anger and Beyond: The Negro Writer in the United States*, ed. Herbert Hill (New York: Harper & Row, 1968), 56.

3. Levy, 299; William Stanley Braithwaite, "The Negro in Literature," *Crisis*, September 1924, 208.

4. Wayne F. Cooper, *Claude McKay: Rebel Sojourner in the Harlem Renaissance, A Biography* (Baton Rouge: Louisiana State University Press, 1987), 78–79; Braithwaite, "Negro in Literature," 208.

5. Cooper, 225.

6. Claude McKay, *A Long Way from Home* (New York: Harcourt, Brace & World, 1970), 27; Cooper, 388. In his own literary career, Braithwaite did follow this advice. In the several volumes of lyric poetry that he published not a single verse examined radical themes or even hinted at the author's race. He was so successful at keeping his racial identity private that a number of black writers, including Claude McKay, were quite surprised when they learned that he was black. See James Weldon Johnson, ed., *The Book of American Negro Poetry* (New York: Harcourt, Brace & World, 1959), 99; and Braithwaite's two volumes of poetry, *Lyrics of Life and Love* (Boston: H.B. Turner, 1904) and *The House of Falling Leaves* (Boston: J.W. Luce, 1908).

7. William Stanley Braithwaite on *Passing*, typed releases [April 1929], Alfred Knopf, Inc. Collection, HRHRC. The somewhat restrained nature of Braithwaite's criticism of ghetto realism might have been due to the fact that Knopf published *Nigger Heaven* and nearly all of Hughes's work.

8. David Levering Lewis, *When Harlem Was in Vogue* (New York: Vintage Books, 1982), 179; Cooper, 248. Three of the four white judges voted for McKay, and he was awarded the gold medal and a $400 check in early 1929.

9. William Stanley Braithwaite to James Weldon Johnson, August 12, 1934, JWJ.

10. Benjamin Brawley, *The Negro Genius: A New Appraisal of the Achievement of the American Negro in Literature and the Fine Arts* (New York: Dodd, Mead, 1937), 1, 232.

11. Ibid., 233–34.

12. Ibid., 202–214, 221–24.

13. Ibid., 225–26.

14. Ibid., 246–248; Benjamin Brawley, "The Negro Literary Renaissance," *The Southern Workman*, April 1927, 182.

15. Benjamin Brawley to James Weldon Johnson, May 9, 1922, JWJ; Brawley, *Negro Genius*, 244–46.

16. John W. Parker, "Benjamin Brawley and the American Cultural Tradition," *Phylon* 16, June 1955, 193; Ulysses Lee, "Criticism at Mid-Century," *Phylon* 11, December 1950, 332.

17. Hughes, *Big Sea*, 266–67.

18. Elliott M. Rudwick, *W.E.B. Du Bois: Propagandist of the Negro Protest* (New York: Atheneum, 1969), 248.

19. Manning Marable, *W.E.B. Du Bois: Black Radical Democrat* (Boston: Twayne Publishers, 1986), 128–37; William H. Ferris, "Review of Darkwater" [June 1920], in *Voices of a Black Nation: Political Journalism in the Harlem Renaissance*, ed. Theodore G. Vincent (San Francisco: Ramparts Press, 1973), 342–48.

20. Robert A. Bone, *The Negro Novel in America* (New Haven: Yale University Press, 1965), 100.

21. W.E.B. Du Bois, "A Proposed Negro Journal," April 1905 in *W.E.B. Du Bois, Against Racism: Unpublished Essays, Papers, Addresses, 1887–1961*, ed. Herbert Aptheker (Amherst: University of Massachusetts Press, 1985), 78; Marable, 132.

22. *Crisis*, April 1920, 299, and September 1924, 199; Chidi Ikonne, *From Du Bois to Van Vechten: The Early New Negro Literature, 1903–1926* (Westport, CT: Greenwood Press, 1981), 98–99.

23. See *Crisis*, March and April 1926 and May through November 1926; Ikonne, 99–103.

24. Ibid., 103; Lewis, 179.

25. W.E.B. Du Bois, "Books," in *Crisis*, December 1926; W.E.B. Du Bois, "Criteria of Negro Art," *Crisis*, October 1926, in W.E.B. Du Bois, *Writings* (New York: The Library of America, 1986), 998, 1000; Ikonne, 100.

26. W.E.B. Du Bois, review of *The Walls of Jericho*, by Rudolph Fisher, in *Crisis*, November 1928, 374. Ironically Fisher had won the prize for fiction in the *Crisis* contest three years earlier; Marable, 132; W.E.B. Du-Bois, "The Browsing Reader," *Crisis*, June 1928, 202, 211.

27. W.E.B. Du Bois, review of *Plum Bun* by Jessie Fauset, in *Crisis*, April 1929, 125, 138.

28. Ikonne, 103–106.

29. "The Donor of the Du Bois Literary Prize: An Autobiography," *Crisis*, May 1931, 157; "W.E.B. Du Bois's Reply to Mrs. Mathews," *Crisis*, May 1931, 157; W.E.B. Du Bois, "The Du Bois Literary Prize," *Crisis*, April 1931, 137.

30. "Du Bois Literary Prize," *Crisis*, February 1933, 45.

31. For the most balanced discussion of Garvey and his philosophy see Judith Stein, *The World of Marcus Garvey: Race and Class in Modern Society* (Baton Rouge: Louisiana State University Press, 1986); see also Edmund David Cronin, *Black Moses: The Story of Marcus Garvey and the Universal Negro Improvement Association* (Madison: University of Wisconsin Press, 1955), 45–49; Claude McKay, *Harlem: Negro Metropolis* (New York: Dutton, 1940), 147–48.

32. Tony Martin, *Literary Garveyism: Garvey, Black Arts, and the Harlem Renaissance* (Dover, MA: Majority Press, 1983), 25–42; John Runcie, "Marcus Garvey and the Harlem Renaissance," *Afro-Americans in New York Life and History* 10, July 1986, 19–20.

33. Martin, 34–37.

34. Runcie, 7–8.

35. Ibid., 23; Martin, 39–40.

36. Runcie, 8, 22; Martin, 137.

37. George S. Schuyler, *Black No More* (New York: Collier Books, 1971), 103; W.E.B. Du Bois, "A Lunatic or a Traitor," *Crisis*, May 1924, in Du Bois, *Writings*, 990; see also Runcie, 11–18. In 1921, before Du Bois had begun his feud with Garvey and before the Jamaican had been indicted, he described Garvey as a "a sincere, hard-working idealist; he is also a stubborn, domineering leader of the mass; he has worthy industrial and commercial schemes but he is an inexperienced businessman." W.E.B. Du Bois, "Marcus Garvey," *Crisis*, December 1920, January 1921, in Du Bois, *Writings*, 979.

38. Stein, 186–208; Du Bois, "A Lunatic or a Traitor," 991–992.

39. Runcie, 9–10, 18.

40. Countee Cullen, "The Dark Tower," *Opportunity*, March 1928, 90; Wallace Thurman, "Author review of Infants of the Spring," typewritten manuscript, *Contempo* Collection, HRHRC; Claude McKay to Nancy Cunard, September 24, 1932, Nancy Cunard Papers, HRHRC; Langston Hughes, "The Negro Artist and the Racial Mountain," *The Nation*, 16 June 1926, 694.

Chapter 8

1. Eugene Levy, *James Weldon Johnson: Black Leader, Black Voice* (Chicago: University of Chicago Press, 1973), 126–28, 161–63.

2. Cynthia Earl Kerman and Richard Eldridge, *The Lives of Jean Toomer: A Hunger for Wholeness* (Baton Rouge: Louisiana State University Press, 1987), 91–92, 99–100; Claude McKay, *A Long Way from Home* (New York: Harcourt Brace & World, 1970), 147–48.

3. David Levering Lewis, *When Harlem Was in Vogue* (New York: Vintage Books, 1982), 10, 97.

4. Langston Hughes, *The Big Sea* (New York: Hill and Wang, 1963), 247–48; Walter White, *A Man Called White: The Autobiography of Walter White* (Bloomington, IN: Indiana University Press, 1970), 65–66; Lewis, 133.

5. White, 66–67; Lewis, 133–35.

6. There is another interpretation of this episode. Charles Scruggs suggests that Doran rejected the manuscript for aesthetic reasons and that White, from the moment he met Mencken in the spring of 1922 (a year before he wrote *The Fire in the Flint*), shrewdly manipulated him, first by planting the seed that prompted Mencken to suggest that White write a novel of southern life, and then deluding him about the reason Doran rejected the manuscript. In the process White triggered Mencken's antipathy toward the South by suggesting that a southern conspiracy was at work attempting to suppress the novel and recruited him as an ally in getting the manuscript published. See Charles Scruggs, *The Sage in Harlem: H.L. Mencken and the Black Writers of the 1920s* (Baltimore: Johns Hopkins University Press, 1984), 117–20. While White's recollection of the situation in his autobiography is not very detailed and undoubtedly a bit biased, it is also far-fetched to assume that a young man recently arrived from Georgia could completely bamboozle Mencken, as well as Saxton, Farrar, Knopf, and practically the entire literary establishment. Doran may have been concerned about the literary quality of White's book (White himself had been reluctant to send his unrevised twelve-day-wonder to Farrar), but he did consult with Cobb and was concerned about southern reaction to the manuscript. See White, 66; and Lewis, 133.

7. White, 68; Scruggs, 117–20; Lewis, 135–36.

8. See James Weldon Johnson to Myriam Sieve, September 8, 1927, September 11, 1927, and September 27, 1927; Myriam Sieve to James Weldon Johnson, September 21, 1927, October 1, 1927, and October 21, 1927; Myriam Sieve to Mr. Smith, October 10, 1927; Blanche Knopf to James Weldon Johnson, July 6, 1927, and December 30, 1927, Alfred Knopf, Inc. Collection, HRHRC; see also a draft of a letter from Myriam Sieve to twenty-two Chicago bookstores informing them of Johnson's itinerary in their city and offering publicity materials for the *Autobiography of an Ex-Coloured Man*, October 28, 1927, Alfred Knopf, Inc. Collection, HRHRC.

9. Frederick Lewis Allen to Countee Cullen, October 19, 1925, December 16, 1925, and Ruth Raphael to Countee Cullen, January 26, 1926, Countee Cullen Papers, ARC-TU. Unfortunately, the event at Jordan Marsh was canceled by the department store. See Frederick Lewis Allen to Countee Cullen, October 27, 1925, ARC-TU.

10. See Frederick Lewis Allen to Countee Cullen, December 9, 1925, September 30, 1925, February 11, 1926, Countee Cullen Papers, ARC-TU; Eugene F. Saxton to Countee Cullen, March 9, 1926, May 21, 1926, June 1, 1926, November 16, 1926, and May 26, 1927, Countee Cullen Papers, ARC-TU.

11. Frederick Lewis Allen to Countee Cullen, October 27, 1925, and January

11, 1927; William H. Briggs to Countee Cullen, October 27, 1926, Countee Cullen Papers, ARC-TU.

12. Carl Van Vechten to Countee Cullen, December 11, 1925, and October 13, 1925, Countee Cullen Papers, ARC-TU. For years Cullen received a substantial income presenting lectures under the management of W. Colston Leigh, the firm that Van Vechten recommended.

13. Levy, 127–28, 305; Arna Bontemps, "Introduction" in James Weldon Johnson, *Autobiography of an Ex-Coloured Man* (New York: Hill and Wang, 1960), v; James Weldon Johnson to Blanche Knopf, April 23,1926, Alfred Knopf, Inc. Collection, HRHRC. The Knopf edition made a few minor changes in the novel—the most visible was changing the spelling of "Colored" to "Coloured" in the title. See Levy, 305n.

14. Ralph Cheney to Countee Cullen, December 17, 1926, and Harriet Monroe to Countee Cullen, October 16, 1925, Countee Cullen Papers, ARC-TU.

15. Idella Purnell Stone, "Autobiographical Sketch," handwritten manuscript, Idella Purnell Stone Papers, HRHRC.

16. See *Palms* 2, Early Summer 1924; *Palms* 2, Early Fall 1924; *Palms* 3, Summer 1925; *Palms* 3, November 1925; *Palms* 3, December 1925, 93.

17. *Palms* 3, January 1926. John W. Weatherwax, who was a principal financial supporter of *Palms* and who would later marry Idella Purnell, reviewed Cullen's book.

18. Stone, "Sketch," *Palms* 4, October 1926.

19. Countee Cullen to Idella Purnell, October 5, 1926, and November 4, 1926, Idella Purnell Stone Papers, HRHRC; Idella Purnell to Countee Cullen, November 24, 1926, Countee Cullen Papers, ARC-TU.

20. See Clifton Cuthbert to Countee Cullen, August 6, 1931, and Milton Abernathy to Countee Cullen, September 21, 1931, Countee Cullen Papers, ARC-TU; Langston Hughes to Anthony J. Buttitta, November 11, 1931, and Langston Hughes to *Contempo*, April 21, 1932, *Contempo* Collection, HRHRC; Walter White to Anthony J. Buttitta, February 9, 1932, *Contempo* Collection, HRHRC; George S. Schuyler to Milton Abernathy, October 25, 1931, *Contempo* Collection, HRHRC; Countee Cullen to Anthony J. Buttitta, February 4, 1932, *Contempo* Collection, HRHRC, James Weldon Johnson to Anthony J. Buttitta, October 4 [1931], *Contempo* Collection, HRHRC. *Contempo* began listing Langston Hughes as a contributor beginning with the September 15, 1931, issue of the magazine and as one of six contributing editors beginning with the December 15, 1931, issue; they also began listing Countee Cullen as a contributor beginning with the November 1, 1931, issue. See *Contempo*, between September 15, 1931, and December 15, 1932, for an indication of its commitment to black literature.

21. White to Buttitta, February 9, 1932; Cullen to Buttitta, February 4, 1932; *Contempo* 3 (25 October 1932) and (10 January 1933). *Contempo* undoubtedly was hurt by the economic crisis of the early 1930s. In addition to the Depression's most obvious effects, it made it difficult for small magazines like *Contempo* to get review copies of books from publishers. See Blanche Knopf to Anthony J. Buttitta, March 31, 1932, *Contempo* Collection, HRHRC.

22. H. L. Mencken to Countee Cullen, August 13, [1924], and John Farrar to Countee Cullen [1923], Countee Cullen Papers, ARC-TU; Sterling Brown to Idella Purnell, March 9, 1930, Idella Purnell Stone Collection, HRHRC.

23. See Blanche Knopf to James Weldon Johnson, October 12, 1927, November 14, 1927, December 14, 1927, December 29, 1927, Alfred Knopf, Inc. Collection, HRHRC; James Weldon Johnson to Blanche Knopf, October [25], 1927, November 20, 1927, and August 24, 1930, Alfred Knopf, Inc. Collection, HRHRC; Blanche Knopf to Walter White, March 12, 1928, Alfred Knopf, Inc. Collection, HRHRC; Walter White to Blanche Knopf, March 18, 1927, Alfred Knopf, Inc. Collection, HRHRC.

24. Eugene F. Saxton to Countee Cullen, January 31, 1930, and February 27, 1930, Countee Cullen Papers, ARC-TU.

25. Idella Purnell to Countee Cullen, November 24, 1926, Countee Cullen Papers, ARC-TU; Countee Cullen to Idella Purnell, December 4, 1926, Idella Purnell Stone Papers, HRHRC; Langston Hughes to Anthony J. Buttitta, December 7, 1933, and James Weldon Johnson to Anthony J. Buttitta, October 26, 1933, and May 30, 1934, *Contempo* Collection, HRHRC; Norman W. Mcleod to Countee Cullen, June 1928, Countee Cullen Papers, ARC-TU.

26. Lewis, 140–41; Wayne F. Cooper, *Claude McKay: Rebel Sojourner in the Harlem Renaissance* (Baton Rouge: Louisiana State University Press, 1987), 216–17.

27. Cooper, 221–22; Lewis, 141–42. After Mencken failed to offer assistance, McKay burned the manuscript. However, with some financial assistance from Max and Crystal Eastman, whom he ran into in France, he began work on *Home to Harlem*.

28. Cooper, 288–89; Lewis, 296; Alfred Knopf to Carl Van Vechten, July 9, 1934, quoted in Lewis, 296; see also Claude McKay to Max Eastman, November 10, 1934, in *The Passion of Claude McKay: Selected Prose and Poetry, 1912–1948*, ed. Wayne Cooper (New York: Schocken Books, 1973), 206–208 for an example of McKay's continuing frustration with his publisher. McKay also had problems with black editors. When Alain Locke was assembling material for the Harlem issue of *Survey Graphic* in

1924, McKay submitted several short stories along with his poems. When Locke rejected one, "Mulatto," because of its extreme radical tone, McKay warned him not to publish his poems without his short stories or "you may count upon me as an intellectual enemy for life." Locke ignored the warning and published the poems anyway. McKay, of course, would become one of Locke's most outspoken critics. See Cooper, *McKay: Rebel*, 225.

29. Langston Hughes to Blanche Knopf, March 6, 1933, and April 20, 1933; Blanche Knopf to Langston Hughes, March 23, 1933, and May 2, 1933; Memo, Blanche Knopf to Alfred Knopf, May 2, 1933, Alfred Knopf, Inc. Collection, HRHRC.

30. Langston Hughes to Blanche Knopf, April 20, 1933, and June 11, 1933, Alfred Knopf, Inc. Collection, HRHRC; Blanche Knopf to Langston Hughes, May 2, 1933.

31. Blanche Knopf to Carl Van Vechten, March 24, 1933; Carl Van Vechten to Blanche Knopf, April 3, 1933; Blanche Knopf to Langston Hughes, April 6, 1933; Langston Hughes to Blanche Knopf, June 11, 1933, Alfred Knopf, Inc. Collection, HRHRC.

32. Memo, Blanche Knopf to Alfred Knopf and handwritten reply from Alfred Knopf, July 14, 1933, Alfred Knopf, Inc. Collection, HRHRC. Alfred Knopf was concerned that the political gulf was so wide between Hughes and Van Vechten that Van Vechten was biased against Hughes's political pieces, and Hughes, therefore, would pay no attention to his critical comments. Blanche Knopf to Langston Hughes, August 21, 1933, October 3, 1933, January 10, 1934, January 26, 1934, February 2, 1934; Carl Van Vechten to Blanche Knopf, December 15, 1933; Langston Hughes to Blanche Knopf, November 6, 1933, January 22, 1934, January 30, 1934, and February 21, 1934, Alfred Knopf, Inc. Collection, HRHRC.

33. Langston Hughes to Blanche Knopf, February 27, 1934, and Carl Van Vechten to Blanche Knopf, March 12, 1934, Alfred Knopf, Inc. Collection, HRHRC.

34. Blanche Knopf to Langston Hughes, March 12, 1934; Langston Hughes to Blanche Knopf [1934], Alfred Knopf, Inc. Collection, HRHRC. *New Song* was published in New York by the International Workers Order in 1938.

35. Langston Hughes to Blanche Knopf, January 30, 1934, and Memo, March 17, 1941, Alfred Knopf, Inc. Collection, HRHRC.

36. Jedediah Tingle to Countee Cullen, December 3, 1923, Countee Cullen Papers, ARC-TU. Cullen had clipped to the letter an undated item from the *New York Times* which described Tingle's exploits.

37. August Meier and Elliott M. Rudwick, *From Plantation to Ghetto: An Interpretative History of American Negroes* (New York: Hill and Wang, 1965),

207; Evelyn S. Brown, "The Harmon Awards," *Opportunity*, March 1933, 78; Lewis, 179.

38. Lewis, 100–103, 179; See the list of Langston Hughes's awards, Uncataloged Permanent Title Folders, Langston Hughes, Alfred Knopf, Inc. Collection, HRHRC.

39. Cooper, *McKay: Rebel*, 209–211, 228–29, 231, 236, 265.

40. Zora Neale Hurston, *Dust Tracks on a Road* (New York: Arno Press and the New York Times, 1969), 175–77; Lewis, 129; Annie Nathan Meyer to Zora Neale Hurston, January 13, 1935; Fannie Hurst to Henry Allen Moe, December 1, 1933, and [December 1935]; Zora Neale Hurston to Fannie Hurst, August 4, 1940, Fannie Hurst Collection, HRHRC; see other correspondence between Fannie Hurst and Annie Nathan Meyer, Zora Neale Hurston, and Carl Van Vechten in Fannie Hurst Collection, HRHRC.

41. Lewis, 151–53, Hurston, 183–85. The material Hurston collected resulted in her first two books, a collection of folk stories, *Mules and Men* (Philadelphia: Lippincott, 1935), and a novel, *Jonah's Gourd Vine* (Philadelphia: Lippincott, 1934).

42. Langston Hughes published several accounts of this relationship. The most complete were in Hughes, *Big Sea*, 312–26; and Hughes, "My Career as a Social Poet," *Phylon* 8, September 1947, 206–207. See also Nathan Irvin Huggins, *Harlem Renaissance* (New York: Oxford University Press, 1971), 315–16; and Clare Bloomgood Crane, "Alain Locke and the Negro Renaissance" (Ph.D. diss., University of California, San Diego, 1971), 174. Hughes, *Big Sea*, 314–15, 316.

43. Hughes, "Adventures as a Social Poet," 206.

44. Hughes, *Big Sea*, 320–21, 323; Hughes, "Adventures as a Social Poet," 206–207. Hughes's political poetry was also the source of his difficulties with Knopf and Van Vechten a few months later. Indeed, "Advertisement for the Waldorf-Astoria" and "Park Bench" were two of the poems in the "revolutionary" collection that so disturbed Van Vechten and created such problems for Blanche Knopf. See Carl Van Vechten to Blanche Knopf, April 3, 1933, Alfred Knopf, Inc. Collection, HRHRC.

45. Hughes, *Big Sea*, 325.

46. Harold Jackman to Claude McKay, April 22, 1928, JWJ.

47. Clifton Cuthbert to Countee Cullen, August 6, 1931; Ralph Cheney to Countee Cullen, December 17, 1926, Countee Cullen Papers, ARC-TU; Countee Cullen to Idella Purnell, May 6, 1924, Idella Purnell Stone Collection, HRHRC; Countee Cullen to Eugene F. Saxton, August 9, 1927, Countee Cullen Papers, ARC-TU; Amy Flashner to Countee Cullen, June 6, 1935, and June 10, 1935, Countee Cullen Papers, ARC-TU.

48. Cooper, 283; Lewis, 302–303; Sterling Brown to Nancy Cunard, February 7, 1932, [May 10, 1932]; Langston Hughes to Nancy Cunard, September

30, 1931, December 27, 1931, Nancy Cunard Collection, HRHRC. Hughes also sent several of his political speeches to Cunard in the late 1930s and maintained a steady correspondence with her into the 1960s.

49. Cooper, 283; McKay to Nancy Cunard, February 26, 1932, March 29, 1932, April 30, 1932, August 30, 1932, September 18, 1932, September 29, 1932, October 15, 1932, and November 28, 1932, Nancy Cunard Collection, HRHRC; Nancy Cunard to Claude McKay, September 20, 1932, JWJ.

50. Nancy Cunard to Claude McKay, January 28, [1933]; Claude McKay to Nancy Cunard, January 12, 1933, January 25, 1933, and n.d. [February 1933], Nancy Cunard Collection, HRHRC. McKay would later accuse Cunard of using her association with blacks as a club with which to beat her mother. See McKay, *Long Way from Home*, 343–45.

51. Lewis, 303; Jean Toomer to Nancy Cunard, February 8, 1932, JTP; Alain Locke to Nancy Cunard, April 14, 1934; Arthur Schomburg to Nancy Cunard, March 21, 1934, and May 8, 1934, Nancy Cunard Collection, HRHRC; Nancy Cunard to Countee Cullen, February 7, 1932, Countee Cullen Papers, ARC-TU. Ironically, although both McKay and Walrond boycotted Cunard's anthology, the two West Indian writers had long ceased to be friends. Indeed, McKay had discussed his estrangement from Walrond at length with Cunard. See Claude McKay to Nancy Cunard, September 18, 1932.

52. Hughes, *Big Sea*, 233–34; Claude McKay to James Weldon Johnson, August 8, 1935, JWJ.

53. Meier and Rudwick, 207. Of all the Renaissance writers, only Claude McKay failed to acknowledge the contribution of Van Vechten to the movement and to his own career. McKay, who was absent from Harlem during most of the Renaissance, encountered Van Vechten only once, in Paris. McKay recalled that he had expected to find Van Vechten patronizing, and instead found him friendly, but boring. McKay, *Long Way from Home*, 302. Of course, McKay might still have been bitter that *Nigger Heaven* reaped the popular and financial rewards as the first novel of Harlem life, instead of one of his pieces.

54. Lewis, 182–83; Hughes, *Big Sea*, 216, 251; Alain Locke to Carl Van Vechten, May 24, 1925; Jessie Fauset to Carl Van Vechten, October 21, 1925; and Zora Neale Hurston to Carl Van Vechten, December 4, 1933, JWJ. See Blanche Knopf to Carl Van Vechten, March 16, 1931, June 26, 1931, September 25, 1931, and November 19, 1931, Alfred Knopf, Inc. Collection, HRHRC, for examples of the relationship between Van Vechten and Knopf.

55. Elmer Imes to Carl Van Vechten, September 12, 1930; Nella Larsen Imes to Carl Van Vechten, May 22, 1930; and Zora Neale Hurston to Carl Van

Vechten, October 23, 1937, and July 24, 1945, JWJ; James Weldon
Johnson, *Along This Way* (New York: Viking, 1961), 382. Van Vechten included this sketch in his papers in the James Weldon Johnson Collection,
JWJ.
56. Lewis, 188; Edward Leuders, *Carl Van Vechten* (New Haven: College &
University Press, 1965); Johnson, *Along This Way*, 382; Hughes, *Big Sea*,
254–55.

Chapter 9

1. "The Negro Voter and the Presidential Campaign," *Opportunity*, Novem-
ber 1924, 336–39; "A Negro for Congress," *Opportunity*, June 1928, 162;
"What Negro Disenfranchisement Costs," *Opportunity*, August 1928, 228;
"Moral Issues of the Campaign," *Opportunity*, September 1928, 259; "Po-
litical Gymnastics," *Opportunity*, November 1928, 225; "The Negro and
His Ballot," *Opportunity*, November 1928, 232–33; Ira Reid, "The Op-
portunity Presidential Candidates Poll," *Opportunity*, April 1932, 115; Ira
Reid, "The Opportunity Presidential Poll," *Opportunity*, May 1932, 141;
"The National Election, 1932," *Opportunity*, November 1932, 336; "The
Candidates Speak," *Opportunity*, November 1932, 338–40.
2. *Crisis*, August 1924, 152, 154; "The NAACP and Parties," *Crisis*, Sep-
tember 1924, 199–200; *Crisis*, October 1924, 247; "How Shall We Vote,"
Crisis, November 1924, 12–14.
3. W.E.B. Du Bois, "How Shall We Vote," *Crisis*, October 1928, 346; "How
Shall We Vote: A Symposium," *Crisis*, November 1928, 368, 386;
Heywood Broun, "The Black Voter," *Crisis*, November 1930, 369; "Negro
Editors on Communism: A Symposium of the American Negro Press,"
April and May 1932, 117–19, 154–65, 170; W.E.B. Du Bois, "Colored
Editors on Communism," *Crisis*, June 1932, 190–91; "Socialists and
Communists Bid for the Negro Vote," *Crisis*, September 1932, 279–80,
300; W.E.B. Du Bois, "Herbert Hoover," *Crisis*, November 1932, 362–
63.
4. See "A Negro for Congress," *Opportunity*, June 1928, 162; "Moral Issues
of the Campaign," *Opportunity*, September 1928, 259; "The Negro in the
Democratic Primaries," *Opportunity*, July 1932, 166; "The Year's Work,"
Crisis, February 1928, 49–50, 66.
5. Mark Naison, "Historical Notes on Blacks and American Communism:
The Harlem Experience," *Science and Society* 42, Fall 1978, 324. See
also Claude McKay, *Harlem: Negro Metropolis* (New York: Dutton, 1940),
196–262; and Robert Brisbane, *The Black Vanguard: Origins of the New
Social Revolution* (Valley Forge, PA: Judson Press, 1970), 158.

6. Claude McKay, *A Long Way from Home* (New York: Harcourt Brace & World, 1970), 68–69; Wayne F. Cooper, *Claude McKay: Rebel Sojourner in the Harlem Renaissance* (Baton Rouge: Louisiana State University Press, 1987), 110–12.

7. Cooper, 114–26; McKay, *Long Way from Home*, 77–85.

8. Claude McKay to James Weldon Johnson, May 8, 1935, JWJ; Claude McKay to Nancy Cunard, September 18, 1932, Nancy Cunard Collection, HRHRC.

9. Claude McKay, "If We Must Die," *Selected Poems of Claude McKay* (New York: Harcourt, Brace & World, 1953), 36; Claude McKay, "Harlem Shadows," *Selected Poems*, 65; Claude McKay, "Moscow," in *Long Way from Home*, 158.

10. Claude McKay, "The Capitalist Way: Lettow-Vorbeck," *Workers' Dreadnought* 7 February 1920, quoted in Cooper, 116; Claude McKay, "Travail," *Workers' Dreadnought* 10 January 1920, quoted in Cooper, 116; Claude McKay, "Song of the New Soldier and Worker," *Workers' Dreadnought* 3 April 1920, quoted in Cooper, 118. For the best discussion of McKay's involvement with the *Workers' Dreadnought* and British leftist politics see Cooper, 109–133. Although many of McKay's contemporaries believed that he was a party member or even a Soviet agent, his correspondence with Nancy Cunard (herself a party member) substantiates the claims that he later made in his autobiography that he never joined the Communist party. See Claude McKay to Nancy Cunard, September 18, 1932, and October 15, 1932, Nancy Cunard Collection, HRHRC; and Nancy Cunard to Claude McKay, September 20, 1932, JWJ.

11. McKay, *Long Way from Home*, 159–60, 173, 177; Cooper, 122–23; Claude McKay to Nancy Cunard, September 24, 1932, Nancy Cunard Collection, HRHRC.

12. Claude McKay to James Weldon Johnson, April 30, 1928, JWJ.

13. Claude McKay to James Weldon Johnson, May 25, 1931, and October 30, 1933, JWJ. McKay was not an American citizen. Furthermore, the enactment of the National Origins Act in 1924, after McKay had left the United States, further complicated his readmission. When his initial efforts failed, he appealed to James Weldon Johnson for assistance. Johnson contacted an old friend from his days in the Foreign Service and was able to get McKay readmitted.

14. Claude McKay to James Weldon Johnson, May 8, 1935, May 31, 1935, April 3, 1937, July 9, 1935, and August 22, 1937, JWJ; Claude McKay, *Harlem: Metropolis*, 15; McKay, *Long Way from Home*, 69.

16. Claude McKay to Nancy Cunard, September 18, 1932, Nancy Cunard Collection, HRHRC.

17. Langston Hughes, "My Adventures as a Social Poet," *Phylon* 8, Septem-

ber 1947, 205; Langston Hughes, "The Negro Artist and the Racial Mountain," *The Nation*, 16 June 1926, 693.

18. Langston Hughes, "Mother to Son," *The Weary Blues* (New York: Knopf, 1926), 107; Hughes, "Negro Artist," 694.

19. Langston Hughes, "Advertisement for the Waldorf-Astoria," *New Masses*, December 1931, 11–12.

20. For a full discussion of Hughes's travels see Langston Hughes, *I Wonder as I Wander: An Autobiographical Journey* (New York: Hill and Wang, 1956), 69–279.

21. Langston Hughes, "White Man," *New Masses*, December 15, 1936, 34; Langston Hughes, "The Same," *The Negro Worker*, September/October, 1932. Reprinted in *Good Morning Revolution: Uncollected Social Protest Writings by Langston Hughes* (New York: Lawrence Hill, 1973), 9–10; Langston Hughes, "Moscow and Me," *International Literature*, July 1933, 61–66.

22. Hughes, "Negro Artist," 694; Langston Hughes, "Writers, Words, and the World," typewritten manuscript of a speech presented at the Paris meeting of the International Writers Association for the Defense of Culture, July 25, 1938, Nancy Cunard Collection, HRHRC.

23. U.S. Congress, Senate, Permanent Subcommittee on Investigations of the Subcommittee on Government Operations, *Hearings on State Department Information Programs-Information Centers*, 83rd Congress, 1st Session, March 3, 1953, 74–75, 79; Langston Hughes, "Langston Hughes Speaks," *Crisis*, May 1953, 279–80; Victor Navasky, *Naming Names* (New York: Viking, 1980), 191–92. Although Hughes was commended by the committee for being a model witness, he was not totally honest in his testimony about when he became disillusioned with communism. As late as 1946, in a series of articles that he wrote for the Chicago *Defender*, he still strongly defended the accomplishments of the Soviet Union in the areas of social equality and human rights against its critics. See Langston Hughes, "The Soviet Union," Chicago *Defender*, June 1, 1946.

24. Gloria T. Hull, *Color, Sex, & Poetry: Three Women Writers of the Harlem Renaissance* (Bloomington, IN: Indiana University Press, 1987), 7, 29. For a survey of the type of discrimination that black women writers faced during the Renaissance see Hull, 1–31.

25. Ibid., 7–11; David Levering Lewis, *When Harlem Was in Vogue* (New York: Knopf, 1981), 96

26. Hull, 121.

27. Ibid., 29, 175; Countee Cullen to Eugene F. Saxton, May 27, 1927, Countee Cullen Papers, ARC-TU; Eugene F. Saxton to Countee Cullen, June 1, 1927, Countee Cullen Papers, ARC-TU.

28. See Hull, 79–80, 214–15; and Susan Ware, *Beyond Suffrage: Women in*

the New Deal (Cambridge, MA: Harvard University Press, 1981) for examples of the absence of writers associated with the Harlem Renaissance and black women in general from organized feminist politics in the 1920s and 1930s.

29. Robert A. Bone, *The Negro Novel in America* (New Haven: Yale University Press, 1965), 101.

30. Jessie Redmon Fauset, *Plum Bun: A Novel Without a Moral* (New York: Frederick A. Stokes, 1929), 25, 32–33.

31. Ibid., 33.

32. Ibid., 105–106.

33. Ibid., 112, 128.

34. Lewis, 121–25; Hull, 12.

35. Nella Larsen, *Passing* (New York: Arno Press and the New York Times, 1969), 102.

36. Nella Larsen, *Quicksand* (New York: Collier Books, 1971), 37.

37. Ibid., 88.

38. Ibid., 199–200, 208.

39. See biographical sketch in *New York Amsterdam News* [April 1929], Alfred Knopf, Inc. Collection, HRHRC; Lewis, 231. Nella Larsen was the first black woman to receive a Guggenheim Fellowship. She also became involved in a plagiarism scandal earlier in the same year that she left for Europe.

40. Zora Neale Hurston, *Their Eyes Were Watching God* (Greenwich, CT: Fawcett Publications, 1969), 16.

41. Ibid., 39, 47.

42. Ibid., 96.

43. For biographical information on Hurston see Zora Neale Hurston, *Dust Tracks on a Road* (New York: Arno Press and The New York Times, 1969) and Robert E. Hemenway's *Zora Neale Hurston: A Literary Biography* (Urbana, IL: University of Illinois Press, 1977).

Chapter 10

1. John Hope Franklin, *From Slavery to Freedom: A History of Negro Americans* (New York: Knopf, 1980), 382; John A. Williams, "The Harlem Renaissance: Its Artists, Its Impact, Its Meaning," *Black World* 20, November 1970, 18.

2. Langston Hughes, *The Big Sea* (New York: Hill and Wang, 1963), 364; Langston Hughes, *Montage of a Dream Deferred* (New York: Henry Holt, 1951). Knopf continued to be Hughes's principal publisher through the 1940s.

3. Arna Bontemps was quoted in *The Negro Caravan*, ed. Sterling Brown,

Arthur P. Davis, and Ulysses Lee (New York: Arno Press and The New York Times, 1970), 254. The most significant tangible result of Bontemps's Yale project was a collection of essays written primarily by his Yale students. Arna Bontemps, ed., *The Harlem Renaissance Remembered* (New York: Dodd, Mead, 1972).

4. A clear example of this shift can be seen by comparing the work of F. Scott Fitzgerald or Ernest Hemingway from the 1920s with the novels of John Steinbeck or James T. Farrell in the 1930s.

5. Arna Bontemps, "Negro Poets Then and Now," *Phylon* 11, December 1950, 360; Wayne F. Cooper, *Claude McKay: Rebel Sojourner in the Harlem Renaissance* (Baton Rouge: Louisiana State University Press, 1987), 196–98, 200, 209–210, 229–33, 274–76.

6. Hughes, *Big Sea*, 334–35.

7. Royalty statement, January 1, 1932, to June 30, 1932, and January 1, 1934, to June 30, 1934, Countee Cullen Papers, ARC-TU; M. Brendell to Countee Cullen, March 2, 1939, Countee Cullen Papers, ARC-TU; Amy Flashner to Countee Cullen, June 6, 1935, Countee Cullen Papers, ARC-TU; Blanch E. Ferguson, *Countee Cullen and The Negro Renaissance* (New York: Dodd, Mead, 1966), 143.

8. Claude McKay to James Weldon Johnson, August 8, 1935, JWJ; manuscript of an interview with Nella Larsen and Walter White by Marion L. Starkey in the offices of Alfred A. Knopf [1929], Alfred Knopf, Inc. Collection, HRHRC.

9. Alfred A. Knopf to James Weldon Johnson, September 13, 1937, JWJ; James O. Young, *Black Writers of the Thirties* (Baton Rouge: Louisiana State University Press, 1961), 138.

10. Alain Locke, "We Turn to Prose," *Opportunity*, February 1932, 40; *Opportunity*, June 1935, 188–89.

11. See Patrick J. Gilpin, "Charles S. Johnson: Entrepreneur of the Harlem Renaissance," in *The Harlem Renaissance Remembered*, 243. Johnson left Harlem, at least in part, because he was frustrated by the decision of Eugene Kinckel Jones, the Urban League president, to cut the operating funds of *Opportunity*. Within a few issues following Johnson's departure, the magazine already was backing away from its commitment to literature and reasserting its original goal of becoming a journal of sociology and social research. Alain Locke, "This Year of Grace," *Opportunity*, February 1931, 48.

12. Claude McKay to James Weldon Johnson, August 8, 1935, JWJ; Claude McKay to Countee Cullen, September 9, 1937, and November 8, 1937, Countee Cullen Papers, ARC-TU; Cooper, 326–28. This organization also represented McKay's effort to establish a noncommunist black writers group in Harlem.

13. Robert Hemenway, "Zora Neale Hurston and the Eatonville Anthropology," in *The Harlem Renaissance Remembered*, 191. Carl Van Vechten was particularly distressed when he learned of the circumstances of Hurston's last years and of her death, and he tried to help arrange a more fitting grave and a memorial. See Carl Van Vechten to Fannie Hurst, February 5, 1960, and February 10, 1960, Fannie Hurst Collection, HRHRC.

14. Roi Ottley and William J. Weatherby, eds., *The Negro in New York: An Informal Social History* (Dobbs Ferry, NY: Oceana Publications, 1967), 275–80; Franklin, 397.

15. Hughes, *Big Sea*, 228.

16. James Weldon Johnson spoke to a number of black groups, including the Negro Sanhedrin, while Countee Cullen earned a substantial income speaking to black and white groups. In March 1932 alone Cullen gave nine lectures and earned $100 to $150 for each one. See James Weldon Johnson's speeches, JWJ, and Countee Cullen's correspondence with his agent, W. Colston Leigh, Countee Cullen Papers, ARC-TU. Langston Hughes, Zora Neale Hurston, and several other black writers gave readings and lectures to various groups all over the country. See Hughes, *Big Sea*, 285–86; and Hughes, "My Adventures as a Social Poet," *Phylon* 8, September 1947, 205–212. Margaret Walker, "New Poets," *Phylon* 11, December 1950, 345.

17. Hughes, *Big Sea*, 335; Walker, "New Poets," 346.

18. Langston Hughes and the editors of *Phylon*, "Some Practical Observations: A Colloquy," *Phylon* 11, December 1950, 308, 310.

19. Frederick J. Hoffman, *The Twenties: American Writing in the Postwar Decade* (New York: The Free Press, 1965), 306–308; Van Wyck Brooks, *The Confident Years, 1885–1950* (New York: Dutton, 1955), 544–49; Gwendolyn Brooks, "The Darker Brother," The *New York Times Book Review*, October 11, 1986, 7.

20. LeRoi Jones, "Philistinism and the Negro Writer," in *Anger and Beyond: The Negro Writer in the United States*, ed. Herbert Hill (New York: Harper & Row, 1966), 56; Richard Wright, "The Literature of the Negro in the United States," in *White Man, Listen!* (Garden City, NY: Doubleday, 1964), 141–42; Richard Wright, review of *The Big Sea* by Langston Hughes, in *The New Republic* 28 October 1940.

21. Ralph Ellison, "Hidden Name and Complex Fate," in *Shadow and Act* (New York: Random House, 1964).

22. Leopold Senghor, speech at Howard University, September 28, 1966, quoted in Mercer Cook and Stephen E. Henderson, *The Militant Black Writer in Africa and the United States* (Madison: University of Wisconsin Press, 1969), 12; Clare Bloodgood Crane, "Alain Locke and the Negro

Renaissance," (Ph.D. diss., University of California, San Diego, 1971), 210–12.

23. Peter Abrahams, *Tell Freedom: Memories of Africa* (New York: Knopf, 1954), 226, 230.

24. George S. Schuyler, "The Negro-Art Hokum," *The Nation*, 23 June 1926, 662–63; William Gardner Smith, "The Negro Writer: Pitfalls and Compensations," *Phylon* 11, December 1950, 299.

25. Langston Hughes, "The Negro Artist and the Racial Mountain," *The Nation*, 16 June 1926, 694.

Index